I0131086

Transgenerational Technology and Interactions for the 21st Century

Transgenerational Technology and Interactions for the 21st Century: Perspectives and Narratives

BY

HANNAH R. MARSTON
The Open University, UK

LINDA SHORE
Glasgow School of Art, UK

LAURA STOOPS
Age NI, UK

AND

ROBBIE S. TURNER
Spektrum-Group, Spain

emerald
PUBLISHING

United Kingdom – North America – Japan – India – Malaysia – China

Emerald Publishing Limited
Emerald Publishing, Floor 5, Northspring, 21-23 Wellington Street, Leeds LS1 4DL

First edition 2022

Copyright © 2022 Hannah R. Marston, Linda Shore, Laura Stoops, and Robbie S. Turner. Published under exclusive license by Emerald Publishing Limited.

Reprints and permissions service
Contact: www.copyright.com

No part of this book may be reproduced, stored in a retrieval system, transmitted in any form or by any means electronic, mechanical, photocopying, recording or otherwise without either the prior written permission of the publisher or a licence permitting restricted copying issued in the UK by The Copyright Licensing Agency and in the USA by The Copyright Clearance Center. Any opinions expressed in the chapters are those of the authors. Whilst Emerald makes every effort to ensure the quality and accuracy of its content, Emerald makes no representation implied or otherwise, as to the chapters' suitability and application and disclaims any warranties, express or implied, to their use.

British Library Cataloguing in Publication Data
A catalogue record for this book is available from the British Library

ISBN: 978-1-83982-639-9 (Print)
ISBN: 978-1-83982-638-2 (Online)
ISBN: 978-1-83982-640-5 (Epub)
ISBN: 978-1-83982-641-2 (Paperback)

INVESTOR IN PEOPLE

Contents

List of Figures and Tables

Figures

Tables

List of Abbreviations

AARP	American Association of Retired Persons
ADL	Activities of Daily Living
AFCC	Age-friendly Cities and Communities
AI	Artificial intelligence
AR	Augmented reality
ARPA	Advanced Research Projects Agency
AT	Assistive technology
ATAT	Adapt Tech, Accessible Technology
AWOC	Ageing without children
BA	British Academy
BBC	British Broadcasting Corporation
BMBC	Barnsley Metropolitan Borough Council
BME	Black, Minority Ethnic
CASE	Concept of Age-friendly Smart Ecologies
CCT	Controlled clinical trials
CDC	Center for Disease Control
CF	Consultative Forum
CV	Curriculum vitae
DCW	Digital Communities Wales
DD	Digital divide
DDR	Deutsche Demokratische Republik
DIAW	Digital Inclusion Alliance for Wales
DIY	Do it yourself
DNR	Do not resuscitate
DSHS	German Sport University Cologne
ECR	Early career research
ERDF	European Regional Development Fund

ESA	Entertainment Software Association
EU	European Union
GCSEs	General certification of Secondary Education
Geron	Gerontology
GEVH	Grimethorpe Electronic Village Hall
GP	General Practitioner
GT	Gerontechnology
H&W SRA	Health and Wellbeing Strategic Research Area
HCI	Human Computer Interaction
HEFCE	Higher Education Funding Council
HEI	Higher Education Institute
HGV	Heavy Goods Vehicle
ICT	Information Communication Technology
IDR	Interdisciplinary research
IoTs	Internet of Things
ISG	International Society of Gerontechnology
IUD	Intrauterine Device
IVF	in vitro fertilization
KESS	Knowledge Exchange Seminar Series
LGBTQ+	Lesbian, gay, bisexual, transgender, queer
LLTCs	life-limiting/threatening health conditions
LTC	Long-term care
mHealth apps	Mobile health applications
MIT	Massachusetts Institute of Technology
MoD	Ministry of Defence
MR	Mixed reality
NATO	North Atlantic Treaty Organization
NCB	National Coal Board
NFP	Not-for-profit
NHS	National Health Service
NI	Northern Ireland
NIA	Northern Irish Assemble
NPL	National Physical Laboratory
NUM	National Union of Mineworkers
NVQ	National vocational qualification

ONS	Office for National Statistics
PAHO	Pan American Health Organization
PC	Personal computing
PhD	Doctor of Philosophy
PHE	Public Health England
PHW	Public Health Wales
PTSD	Post-traumatic stress disorder
QoL	Quality of Life
R&D	Research and Development
RCT	Randomized control trials
RCUK	Research Councils UK
RDD&D	Research, development, design and distribution
RDG	Research development groups
SAfE	Smart Age-friendly Ecosystem
SD	Standard deviation
SES	Socio-economic status
SSAFA	Soldiers, Sailors, Airmen and Families Association
TAM	Technology Acceptance Model
TART	Transgenerational Assistive Robotic Technology
TAT	Transgenerational Assistive/Accessible Technology
TG	Transgenerational Gaming
TILL	Technology In Later Life
TLCC	Transgenerational Living Communities and Cities
TT	Transgenerational Technology
UCD	User Centred Design
UK	United Kingdom
UKRI	UK Research and Innovation
UML	Unified Modelling Language
UN	United Nations
USA	United States of America
UX	User Experience
VAs	Virtual assistants
VR	Virtual reality
WDH	Wakefield District Housing
WG	Working group

WHO	World Health Organization
WI	Women's Institute
XR	Extended reality

About the Authors

Hannah R. Marston conducts interdisciplinary research and holds a PhD from Teesside University, UK in Virtual Reality and Gerontology. Since 2010 she has worked in Canada and Germany as a researcher, prior to moving back to the UK in 2015. She has published over 40 peer-reviewed journal papers, and most recently she was part of the 'The Smart Homes and Independent Living Commission'. Her research areas include gerontechnology, UX (User eXperience) of transgenerational technologies and videogames, gender, age-friendly cities, and communities and in 2020 she led an international, multi-site COVID-19 research project focusing on technology use.

Linda Shore is a UX Designer/Researcher and currently works as part of the DHI (Digital Health & Care Innovation Centre) at Glasgow School of Art, Scotland. Her research areas include User-Centred Design (UCD) approaches that explore perceptions and adoption of emerging wearable technologies by older adults and the impact of amputation/age-related conditions on quality of life. Additional areas of research interest include service blueprint development for healthcare and transgenerational technology that adapts to users' needs. She is excited about the possibilities of technologies for the future and how these can enhance the worlds, lives, and experiences as we age.

Laura Stoops is the Impact and Evaluation Manager at Age NI, a charity that supports older people in Northern Ireland to love later life. Her professional interests are using technology-based solutions to support older people or those with a disability and assessing the impact and evaluation. She has a keen interest in using research skills to support the voluntary sector and to share this knowledge widely. She holds a PhD (2011) in Computer-Based Assessment and Diagnosis of Parkinson's Disease from the University of Ulster, Northern Ireland. As part of her PhD work, she has written and published five journal papers including a paper entitled *Assessment of Bradykinesia, Akinesia and Rigidity Using a Home-Based Assessment Tool* which was published in the International Journal of Assistive Robotics and Systems (2009).

Robbie S. Turner is a Co-founder and Senior Consultant at Spektrum-Group, a company that supports potential suppliers in penetrating government, defence, and humanitarian markets by lending them over 20 years of experience in this field. He is regarded and foremost an expert in this specialist market, and thoroughly enjoys the process of knowledge exchange and translation, knowledge that directly impacts and enhances a company's ability to participate and succeed in a perceivably exclusive environment.

Foreword

Listening to the views of older people and giving them a voice is central to Age NI's work. Through this book, we were delighted to have the opportunity to work in consultation with older people to better understand their digital technology needs, now and in the future.

Age NI has witnessed first-hand the impact that the pandemic, and its resulting social isolation, has had on older people in Northern Ireland. It has also dramatically affected the way we deliver our services, which are so heavily focused on social, face-to-face interaction.

The COVID-19 pandemic has made us all realise the power of technology. Thinking about all generations, from home-schooling through to zoom quizzes, we might wonder how we would have coped without it. For older people, with the help of digital devices, many were able to connect to friends and family – and to our services, newly delivered online.

For some, this involved adopting a new mindset, and often required offering one-to-one support to utilise the technology. For those who succeeded, the benefits of this new connectivity greatly outweighed the challenges.

However, while many have gained from digital technology, we know that there is a large section of older people missing out. Without their normal social interactions, a lack of digital connectivity has left them desperately isolated and lonely. Very sadly, we know that loneliness can be a killer, and as a nation renowned for its warm welcome, friendliness and sense of community, we believe it shouldn't have to be this way.

Although the number of older people who are digitally connected continues to rise, across the UK there are still around 5 million people over the age of 55 who are not online. And while factors such as income and levels of education play a part, age is still the biggest indicator of digital exclusion.

Through our work on this book, hearing the experiences of those older people who are embracing technology has thrown into stark relief the experiences of those who are still missing out.

Through research and innovation, we're looking at ways of supporting older people to get online, to benefit from digital communication and to do confidently and safely.

We are very grateful to the older people who have given so generously of their views and time to inform the content and narrative of this book.

The insight of this publication offers on what older people want and need, is pivotal to the current and future connectivity of older people. We believe this has a vital part to play in the mission to end loneliness.

Linda Robinson BEM Age NI CEO

Acknowledgements

We would like to express our thanks to the participants recruited through Age NI and Mencap NI for giving up their time to speak to and share their experiences and thoughts with us about their use of and responses to technology during the pandemic and for providing their future perspectives. We really appreciate the insight and guidance offered by the Age NI working group, made up of Age NI Consultative Forum members. A further thank you to Ann Murray for taking the time to review and edit the draft manuscript, your insights and comments helped make the book what it is.

Also, we would like to thank everyone who has provided critical and constructive feedback across the all the chapters throughout process. Without this depth, and insightfulness, we would not have been able to ensure the quality, discourse and narrative throughout.

Chapter 1

Introduction

> The anonymous writer referred for justification to precedents established in the United States and cited the case of an anxious mother who, convinced that her baby had the croup, called the infant's grandmother for assistance. The latter, in turn, telephone the family doctor at midnight and 'told him the terrible news'. Perhaps because of the lateness of the hour, the doctor asked to be put in telephonic communication with the anxious mamma. 'Lift the child to the telephone', he commanded, 'and let me hear it cough'. Both mother and child complied. 'That's not the croup', the doctor declared, and declines to leave his house on such small matters. He advises grandmamma also to stay in bed; and all anxiety quieted, the trio settle down happily for the night. (Aronson, 1977, p. 72)

When we talk about technology and digital practices in the twenty-first century, we seldom look back on history, and the developments, practices, and impact that inventions and innovations over the previous decades and centuries have had on our contemporary lives.

The opening quote (Aronson, 1977) details how, in November 1879, a medical professional, using the telephone, was able to ease the concerns of a mother and grandmother pertaining to the health of their child and grandchild. As the quote details, the telephone call was made late at night, and that is one reason why this method of giving a medical opinion was used. In addition, Aronson suggests this was possibly the first type of tele-healthcare assessment and prescription provided. When registering the patent for his new telephone, Alexander Graham Bell described this device as

> the method of, and apparatus for, transmitting vocal or other sounds telegraphically … by causing electrical undulations, similar in form to the vibrations of the air accompanying the said vocal or other sound. (History of Information.com, n.d.)

Transgenerational Technology and Interactions for the 21st Century:
Perspectives and Narratives, 1–12
Copyright © 2022 by Hannah R. Marston, Linda Shore, Laura Stoops, and Robbie S. Turner
Published under exclusive licence by Emerald Publishing Limited
doi:10.1108/978-1-83982-638-220221004

Aronson suggested that 'the telephone might be of considerable use to doctors to ease their practice' (Aronson, 1977, p. 72) and while this approach may have been greatly accepted by medical professionals in the United States, British doctors were more reserved to some degree. Through editorials and anonymous submissions to the Lancet over a number of years, Aronson describes various tales and narratives, noting how British medical professionals adopted this new device to suit their own needs instead of waiting for the approval of the Lancet. Even more so, doctors living and working in rural areas saw benefits in implementing the telephone in their practice as described,

> [...] country doctors saw the advantage of using it to make branch practices more manageable. Such joint medical ventures were designed, in part, to ease the patient load, to provide an occasional holiday for each doctor, and to broaden the pool of medical knowledge of the partners. Yet many of these benefits were lost because communication depended on the mails or the telegraph. (Aronson, 1977, p. 72)

A contribution to the Lancet was provided in 1888 by a Dr Alfred H. Twining, describing the experiences of adopting and using the telephone in the 'country' practice, '[...] Though five miles apart', he wrote,

> we are able to arrange our work each morning as to obviate the necessity of both going over the same ground – a distinct saving not only in horseflesh, but in time and personal fatigue. Moreover, the telephone is available for prolonged social or professional conference by day or night. (Aronson, 1977, pp. 72–73)

Dr Twining and his partner was unable to have their telephone connected via the Post Office switchboard, and instead had a private line connecting both of them (5-miles) to facilitate their communications. These descriptions and narrations illustrate how an invention of the latter part of the nineteenth century was already transforming healthcare and practice, and we will suggest that similar comments can be heard and shared in the twenty-first century society. The COVID pandemic has greatly increased the use of telehealth and telemedicine. In some countries such as Canada and Australia, taking this approach to healthcare delivery is already part of society because of the vast distances that some patients may have to travel for a 15-minute appointment. From the standpoint of the Coronavirus pandemic, the concept of using telehealth practices to access patients seems positive (Fisk, Livingstone, & Pit, 2020; Greenhalgh et al., 2021) for healthcare services and delivery.

Throughout history, innovations have facilitated not only advances in medical practice as, for example, visually narrated through the television series M.A.S.H. (Britannica, n.d.c.) but also within the homes of citizens, such as the washing machine, the television, and the radio. These products and devices situated within our homes today not only make our lives easier but also enable us to keep up with current affairs and can add to our leisure activities. For some people these products can be controlled by the Internet of Things (IoTs) and accessed or set on timers via an app on our smartphones. While Bell is known for patenting the telephone, Martin Cooper is known as the inventor and pioneer of wireless communications and the father of the handheld mobile phone (Greene, 2011; Shiels, 2003). This significant invention and innovative device were created in the 1970s. Did Cooper wonder about the impact the mobile phone would have on society?

Over the decades we have seen the mobile phone evolve in many ways, from the size of the device to the functionality, capabilities, and costs. This was specifically so when in the late 2000s the smartphone was released which in turn transformed the way people interact and use their devices, with many people upgrading from their 'old fashioned' mobile phone (which had limited functionality and capabilities) to 'all singing and dancing' devices (e.g., access to the Internet, email, downloading apps, taking photographs, accessing social media platforms, listening to music, instant communication – WhatsApp, etc.).

Yet, many of us who own and upgrade our smartphones when our contracts are coming to the end of their 24-month shelf life, also live by our smartphones, using them as a means of tracking data such as exercise (e.g., running) (Fig. 1.1), biking or even tracking altitude when undertaking exercise (Fig. 1.1). Moreover, some women and girls may choose to use apps to track their menstruation (Earle, Marston, Hadley, & Banks, 2020), or if they are planning a family to check their most fertile days, while some women who are transitioning to the perimenopause may find apps useful to track their menstrual cycles.

Nevertheless, for some people in society the use of a smartphone is not for them, and they instead choose to continue to use the simpler mobile phone or landline phone.

The term Baby Boomers is used to describe the cohort who were born between 1946 and 1964, with many people encountering different life experiences to their predecessors – the Silent Generation (Lissitsa, Zychlinski, & Kagan, 2022) born between 1925 and 1945 (Strauss & Howe, 1991). The Silent Generation are those individuals who survived the Second World War, and the Great Depression, and were parents to the forthcoming generation – the Baby Boomers. The experiences of the Silent Generation through these events led individuals in this cohort to be conservative, pragmatic and patient (Olsen, Thach And, & Nowak, 2007). Conversely, the experiences of Baby Boomers in part also experience socio, economic and political events, and opportunities including the Cold War, the Civil Rights Movement (Krauss Whitbourne & Willis, 2006), the contraceptive pill, the sexual revolution of the 1960s and the National Health Service (NHS). Furthermore, many Baby Boomers faced an enhanced standard of living to that of their parents (the Silent Generation), and the opportunity to purchase their own homes.

Like Baby Boomers, each generation of society can be defined by a set of characteristics and Generation X (1965–1980) (Fry, 2018; Vogels, 2018) is no different. In the last two decades of the twentieth century, they witnessed phenomenal political events, such as the end of the Falklands war, civil unrest pertaining to the poll tax riots, and the miners' strike), and the continuing creation and transitioning of music genres coupled with one of the major technological developments of the twentieth century – the Internet. And many citizens in the succeeding cohorts, that is, the

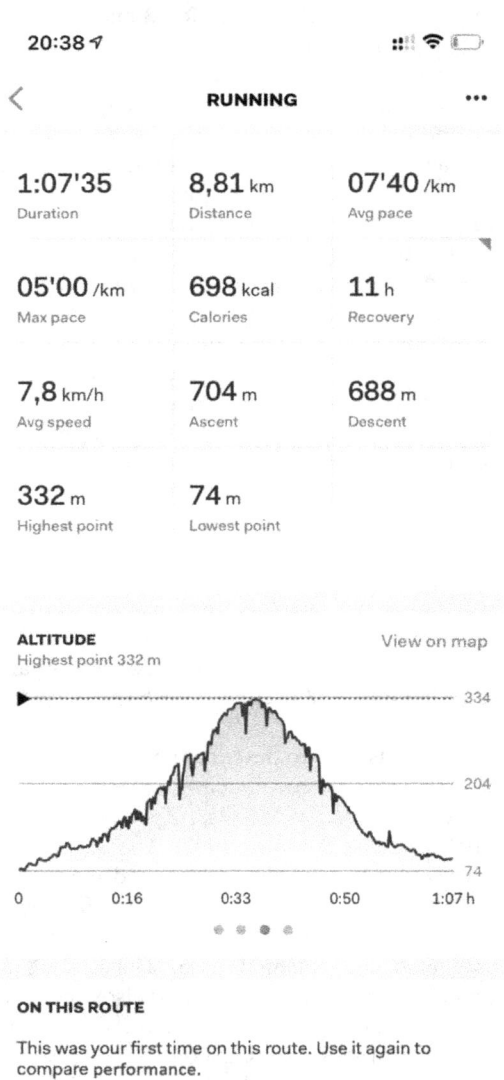

Fig. 1.1.   Overview of Running Metrics, Tracking and Analysis. *Source:* Owned by and permission granted by R. Tuner.

Millennials (1981–1996) (Fry 2018; Vogels, 2018) and Generation Z (also known as Post-Millennials and born from 1997-present) (Fry, 2018; Vogels, 2018), will also have experienced and remembered the outstanding events of their time.

One of the key transformative technological developments of the late twentieth century was the Internet which at that time had only been available for a handful of years to the public (Murphy, 2019). This new technology was for a while coupled with the possible impending doom of the new Millennium (Marston, Musselwhite, & Hadley, 2020). For many businesses and community leaders there were fears that all computers and interconnected systems would crash, resulting in chaos within the banking systems, that traffic light systems were not going to sequence and would cause accidents, and that, overall, at the stroke of midnight, on New Year's Eve 1999 the technological apocalypse would unfold (National Geographic, n.d.; Uenuma, 2019). To those who were celebrating and seeing the new Millennium in with friends and family – as Big Ben chimed, and Auld Lang Syne was sung across the UK – it became evident very quickly that we had survived into Y2K (Marston et al., 2020). There was no apocalypse, the banking systems were not affected, and all services and systems which used various computing systems continued to function. This Millennium experience is now archived into historical records which allows citizens to read, understand, and learn lessons from the past, including strategic policies which were followed through by an array of decision makers from national and regional sectors and business leaders (Marston et al., 2020).

In the proceeding section, we explore and reflect upon historical events which occurred in the latter part of the twentieth century whereby many people categorised as Baby Boomers and Generation X (or Gen X'ers) were either directly involved in or were passive players because of their age and circumstances (e.g., young children).

Historical Events of the Twentieth Century – the 1980s–1990

The twentieth century saw many medical and associated technological developments to improve the lives of people on a global scale. Drugs and vaccines, such as antibiotics (1932), and polio vaccines (1952) afforded people the opportunity to recover from illness rather than die or be severely impaired. While implantable devices such as pacemakers (1958) afforded individuals suffering with severe heart conditions the opportunity to lead healthier lives than expected, the development of in vitro fertilisation (IVF) (1959) has and continues to afford many people the opportunity to start families. We have seen during the pandemic several vaccines being created and rolled out across Western society. Throughout the twentieth century, there were many vaccines discovered including the measles (1963), and rubella vaccines (1965), the latter becoming available on the market in 1970. More recent developments can be seen in many fields including the military and medicine (Olanrewaju, Faieza, & Syakirah, 2013) enabling the use of robotics.

To provide some context specifically to 1984, the miners' strike (Adney & Lloyd, 1988) which was led by the National Union of Mineworkers (NUM) and who were opposing the decision of the then Conservative government to close the pits in various regions across the UK, including South Wales, Yorkshire, County Durham, Kent, and Scotland. South Wales mining communities witnessed 21,500 employees (99.6%) voting in favour of strike action, and 12-months later, 93% of miners voted again in favour of strike action (Pittam, 2019). While Yorkshire miners voted 97.3% in support of going on strike in November 1984 (19.11.84), this dropped to 90% by the 14th February 1985, and by the 1st of March 1985 a further reduction occurred leading to 83% (Sheffield City Council, 2009–2018). Yet, the strike was later deemed illegal (Adeney, 1988). Overall, the miners' strike lasted for 12 months and was led by Arthur Scargill who was the president of the NUM (1982–2002) (BBC News, 2010) and Ian K. MacGregor, head of the National Coal Board (NCB) (BBC Home, 1983). Because of the change in government legislation relating to the Social Security Act 1980, Clause 6 – prohibiting the dependents of strikers from receiving (Pittam, 2019; UK Government, 1980) government payments, thousands of miners, and their families, across the UK were plunged into poverty. And although there were many communities and families experiencing hardships (Bannock, 2015) there was a sense of community and brotherhood (Bannock, 2015) with many of the communities' miners' wives becoming involved in the cause (Ali, 1986; Spence, 1998); such as helping in the soup kitchens and supporting and 'standing by their men' (Ali, 1986; Spence, 1998) on the picket lines. In addition some women engaged in the political sphere and in fundraising activities (Ali, 1986; Spence, 1998). These varying forms of engagement facilitated and challenged the gender roles within the home between husband and wife, with many women seeking to upskill and, re-enter education to seek employment (Ali, 1986).

Some people may think such historical insights and events from over 30 years ago should be resigned to the history books and should not have a place in a book like this. But the events and experiences of the past for many people now in society have not changed and have been repackaged and extended into other forms of poverty, such as digital poverty. This new form of 'poverty' emerged in contemporary society and was brought to the forefront during the COVID-19 pandemic. The Digital Poverty Alliance posits,

> 70% of households earning £17.5K or less have minimum digital skills, 25% of vulnerable children do not have access to a suitable device for learning, and 82% of jobs advertised require digital skills.

Furthermore, The Good Things Foundation report 1.5 million households in the UK do not have Internet access, with a further 2 million households struggling to afford Internet services and 14.9 million people have a low level of digital engagement, with 10 million people lacking fundamental digital skills (2021).

The film 'Brassed Off' (1996) depicts many of these forgotten communities, with the plot of the film based on the struggles of the Grimethorpe community (Baker-Green, 2013) and the film soundtrack provided by the Grimethorpe Colliery Band. In 1994, the Grimethorpe area of South Yorkshire was identified by the European Union to be the poorest village in the UK (Baker-Green, 2013; McVeigh, 2015). Additionally, Baker-Green (2013) notes how the 2010 Indices of Deprivation measure shows this village (in the ward of Cudworth) to be one of the most deprived areas in England. More recent statistics published by Barnsley Metropolitan Borough Council (BMBC) shows there has been little change, whereby the Index of Multiple Deprivation 2019, displays how Barnsley is ranked the 38th most deprived area out of 317 local authorities in England (BMBC, 2019). Former mining areas as described here, coupled with ongoing levels of deprivation impact the residents across the life course and within different age cohorts. For example, young people today who have limited or no access to the Internet are unable to complete their schoolwork, while individuals in these communities who are seeking employment and who have limited or no access to the Internet, or own technology devices are disadvantaged in their abilities and opportunities to improve and upskill their digital skills engagement and improve their overall living.

From a European perspective, the 80s and early 90s witnessed the end of Communism, with the fall of the Berlin Wall in November 1989 (BBC News, 2019). The Wall had been built in 1961 (UPI.com, 1998), and the built-spatial environment being adapted segregated family members who resided in East Berlin in the DDR. With the fall of the Berlin Wall, many citizens in both East and West Berlin, in addition to those citizens who had been living in West Germany, were reunited with friends, and loved ones.

1990–2000s

People categorised as Generation X will be able to remember key conflicts such as the end of the Cold War and Communism. Whereas those living in the 1990s as adolescents and young adults witnessed the rise of several conflicts such as the 1st Gulf War (1991) (Atkinson, 1995), led by a US coalition and including 35 nations. At this point in history, many Millennials (Howe & Strauss, 2000) were being born and Generation Z was not even conceived.

The 1st Gulf War initiated live news broadcasts from the front lines (Johnson, 2015; Norman, 1991) which in turn set a precedence for future media coverage of conflicts and events in the following years and decades including the Balkans war – 1991–2001) (Prunk, 2001), and the collapse of the twin towers of the World Trade Centre (Graff, 2019; Jackson, 2021). This highly significant event of the new Millennium led to the Afghanistan War (2001–2014) (Britannica, n.d.a) and the invasion of the Iraq war (2003–2011) (Britannic, n.d.b). Moreover, and closer to home, many Baby Boomers and Generation X'ers will remember the 'Troubles' (Dorney, 2015) in Northern Ireland (1960–1998), with the Good Friday Agreement devolving power to the Northern Ireland Assembly in 1999 (UK Government, 1998). Yet, many Millennials and Generation Z's living across the UK and Ireland having grown up in the nineties with differing experiences and perspectives, with many in some instances living in a different community and society to that of their predecessors.

Conversely, one of the great inventions of the 1990s was the Internet revolution which we experience in our contemporary society and has impacted society across all aspects of daily life (e.g., business, education, day-to-day living, access to services, social connectedness, etc.). The concept of the Internet had been around since the 1960s with the creation of packet switching and the 'National Physical Laboratory' (NPL) proposed a national commercial data network in the UK (Campbell-Kelly, 1987). Various departments of the US Department of Defense were involved, including the Advanced Research Projects Agency (ARPA) which was awarded funding to develop the ARPANET recommending the adoption of packet switching (Couldry, 2012). With additional developments continuing throughout the 1980s, leading a scientist (Tim Berners-Lee) based at CERN in Switzerland to connect hypertext documents to the information system which in turn was accessible from any node on the network (1989–1990). This was the beginning of what we now know as the World Wide Web – the Internet (Couldry, 2012). It is beyond the scope of this chapter to explore the historical developments of the Internet. However, as the years passed into the 1990s and beyond, the power and impact of the Internet on a day-to-day living and business has been phenomenal.

The Internet revolution in the 1990s facilitated many Gen X'ers to access this network through universities and, businesses, and for citizens in their homes to access webpages through 'dial up'. For many people, 'dial up' was the key method of connectivity between the user and the Internet. If the Internet was going to be used, cables had to be connected via the telephone socket and this in turn resulted in other members of the household being unable to use the telephone or receive calls into the home environment at the same time. The speed of the Internet was nothing like it is today, and for many people reflecting back on this technology, Internet speeds were very slow, especially if one was uploading or downloading images, while also trying to view webpages or send electronic mail (email) (Murphy, 2019). Search engines at the time included Yahoo to facilitate information searching and many Gen X'ers created their email account via Hotmail. Some may still have the same email address as they created back in the late 90s. Now only an occasional feature in today's towns and cities, the Internet Café would seem like an alien concept to many, and yet a time existed when the Internet was available as a pooled resource and access was often shared in the community.

Many people categorised as Generation X will have grown up embracing technology as they interacted with consoles and arcades (Herman, 2001). Many younger people in this cohort enjoyed, well into the 1990s, a wide variety of game consoles such as the Nintendo NES (1987 in Europe), Nintendo Game Boy (1989), the Sony PlayStation (1995), the Sega Saturn (1995) and the Nintendo 64 (1996) (N64). This era of videogames witnessed significant transitions from 2D to 3D graphics enabling games such as *Virtua Fighter* to be the inspiration for games in the future (Feit, 2012).

In the early 1990s two games, were created and released by competitors, firstly, Nintendo had the *Mario Bros* franchise, and Sega's *Sonic the Hedgehog* (1991), accessible on the Sega Gensis (1990, released in Europe) console, depicting a blue, spiky hedgehog. The GUI (graphical user interface) (Levy, n.d.; Oxford Reference, n.d.) was throughout the 1980s, and the 1990s via the videogames industry was continually pushing the boundaries within their creations because of the hardware developments (Herman, 2001). This in turn led to games such as *GoldenEye 007* (1997) based on the 1995 James Bond film, which was specifically developed and released on the Nintendo 64 and received critical acclaim (Beaumont, 2017; Stuart & Webber, 2015).

To illustrate further the phenomenal technological developments of videogames, the game *REZ* (2001) was conceived in 1994–1995 taking inspiration from how people move to the music at events such as raves (Cocker, 2007; Hawkins, 2005; Wong, 2016). The GUI of *REZ* was taken from earlier game interfaces, and while the game is viewed as an arcade shooter, with each object being hit, *REZ* enables the gamer to feel different vibrations/feedback, and not solely through the game console being held (Mielke, 2006; REZ – the Game). The diversity of available games demonstrates the ongoing changes in the video game industry. At the same time the means of installing games in devices was also changing and sometimes required gamers to insert cartridges into their console(s), while in other instances CDs have been used to accommodate the changes occurring in the GUI.

2000s–Present

More recently Millennials and Generation Z's have, like the rest of us, experienced the Coronavirus pandemic of the twenty-first century. They have witnessed the Taliban returning to Afghanistan in August 2021 and have lived through the uncertainties of Brexit since 2016. Technological advancements such as online shopping have facilitated people to 'shop' at their convenience from the comfort of their home. People in the UK started to experience another fuel crisis in September 2021 due to political decisions which resulted in fewer numbers of qualified HGV drivers and drivers of fuel tankers. Some have suggested that this fuel crisis and potential food shortages are a direct result of the Brexit referendum of 2016. This is the second fuel crisis within two decades, the first occurring in 2001 when for some weeks, people were having to limit the use of their cars and journeys. However, given the uncertainty of the future (e.g., ongoing Brexit worries) in conjunction with the fact the UK and the rest of the world are still in the pandemic and more recently the Ukraine war (24.02.2022), which has led to global price increases relating to energy and food. It may not be unreasonable to speculate that for some of the community there is a feeling of apprehension and indeed fear especially when the cost of living in the UK is increasing due to price hikes of energy, fuel (e.g., transport), food and interest rates. This in turn is leaving many people across different social classes having to make a choice on what type of products they should buy or can afford to buy. While many people who were close to the poverty line are now also having to choose whether to use their ovens to heat food because of the increase price of home energy. For many people the choice of 'heating' or 'eating' will have to be made, and at the moment there does not seem to be a reduction of energy costs. With the advent of the Internet, and mass media channels, access to 24 hour news is easier than it was back in the 1980s and beyond. This too can lead to fake news and heighten anxiety within our society.

Aims and Objectives

The purpose of this book is to demonstrate a concise, and an insightful exploration of interconnecting topics to stimulate discussion, with a view to moving existing discourse of digital technologies and practices forward into the twenty-first century. The authors are from different disciplines and approach this body of work through their respective lens, collaborating with Age NI and the business world. Also, this book aims to include the perspectives of the stakeholder – Age NI who works closely with older adults across different geographic locations (e.g., city, urban and rural) in Northern Ireland. Furthermore, we incorporate a business perspective from with in the telecommunications industry, together with social enterprises, and who works alongside private sector clients to support Apex customers in defence, humanitarian, and government markets.

This book contributes to the fields of gerontology, communications, game studies, UX design, industrial design, and social sciences. We will draw on literature from across the decades to provide case studies and exemplars to illustrate how our thinking and narratives need to be readdressed for a positive change and movement. This is seen as a means of moving away from the existing echo chambers that have inhibited societal discussions, research agendas, policy, and impact.

We believe the audience for this book will include academics and researchers from the fields of social sciences, HCI, gerontology, gerontechnology, and design, policy makers, practitioners from the areas of architecture, user experience (UX), computer science, businesses and consultancies who are already, or would in the future, be interested in collaboration with stakeholders and academia.

Coining of New Terms

As part of this book, we coin and propose five new terms:

1. *Transgenerational Technology* (TT), optimises use, adoption, autonomy, and acceptance of technology to assist and enhance the lived experience across the generations.
2. *Transgenerational Assistive/Accessible Technology* (TAT) refers to Assistive Technologies designed to be adaptive and supportive to people across the generations who experience physical and/or cognitive limitation.
3. *Transgenerational Assistive Robotic Technology* (TART) refers to Powered Robotic Orthosis (PRO) that enhance, augment ability and body connective awareness – embodiment which are adaptive across the life course and to user needs requirements.
4. *Transgenerational Living Communities and Cities* (TLCC) posits that all generations in a community experience and feel part of inclusive and autonomous ecosystems.
5. *Transgenerational Gaming* (TG) encourages optimised digital game experiences irrespective of the age or ability of the player.

These new terms are introduced to provoke and implement technology well-being and inclusive design approaches to include, and not marginalise any particular demographic. We will discuss these new approaches throughout the following chapters as a way of forging and moving this discourse as a pathway to new technology design approaches and thinking for the twenty-first century.

Overview of Chapters

Chapter 2 – The Current State of Technology and Digital Games

This chapter presents contemporary literature surrounding digital games, reviewing previous existing work, and offering recommendations for moving the narrative forward. This chapter will offer a lens to the reader of how far (geron) technology research has been extended and offer insights and proposals, with the aim of pushing the boundaries forward into the coming decades of the twenty-first century. Chapter 2 showcases a wide variety of technologies from videogames, in the context of ethnicity, gender, Generation X and people who are ageing without children (AWOC). Given the fast pace of technological developments over the last 20–30 years we provide insights into some of the areas that are continuing to grow interest and develop including mobile apps, X-reality (XR), virtual reality (VR) and augmented reality (AR), assistive technologies, and the Internet of Things (IoTs). Finally, we discuss the area of wearable and implantable devices, from the standpoint of health-related devices to innovative technologies which have explored 'digital tattoos' on pig skin to monitor diabetes.

Chapter 3 – Adoption, Benefits and Challenges of Technology: Insights from Citizens in Northern Ireland

This chapter presents a mixed methods study conducted by co-researchers through Age NI during the pandemic. Findings will be presented followed by a discussion on the role digital technologies and practices have played. Based on the evidence from Age NI and their co-researchers, this chapter will provide direct insights from a different and sometimes unreported perspective.

Chapter 4 – Technology in the Role of Stakeholders, Social Enterprise, Industry and Smart Age-friendly Ecosystems in the 21st Century

This chapter explores a myriad of ecosystems and exemplars of existing age-friendly cities and communities (AFCC) frameworks to facilitate further explorations in this area as we move forward into the 21st century. We explore the cities of Dubai and Barcelona and how AFCC has been implemented, in addition to discussing how COVID-19 has changed the built environment, exploring how businesses adapted to meet legislation. We consider and posit the need for investigations surrounding rural and coastal regions from the standpoint of technology, and AFCC and we examine the latest AFCC framework focusing on Dementia Friendly Cities and Communities. Chapter 4 considers the benefits and the challenges to this ongoing discourse, and a series of insights and recommendations are offered to move a stagnated narrative forward to benefit academe as well as citizens.

Chapter 5 – 'The Older You Get, People Get Less Active, and Then They Feel the Cold'

This chapter discusses ageing experience, emotional design and empathy documented through research to understand older adults' perceptions towards emerging technologies. Fieldwork stories are summarised and supported by a selection of comments and expression from the participants relating to everyday tasks and activities. Technologies, particularly emerging technologies that include augmenting ability benefit from User Centred Design (UCD) approaches. This chapter discusses how research and innovation opportunity that recognises lifespan and adaptable considerations to *Transgenerational Technology* will optimise user experience and enhance quality of life.

Chapter 6 – Digital Inequities and Society

This chapter explores the inequities surrounding digital technologies and practices and we discuss how technology can impact negatively on the socially disadvantaged people in our society and increase inequalities especially among citizens from different cultural and societal backgrounds. We provide a series of scenarios that are pertinent to contemporary society, and which are often overlooked with the mission to demonstrate to our readers how there are many sub-groups of people who receive little or no attention in research investigations. We draw on previous literature and contemporary studies to illustrate how societal deprivation today impacts the health, wellbeing, and digital inequity of people.

Chapter 7 – The Research Environment

This chapter discusses the barriers, challenges, and implications of conducting research for and with stakeholders, researchers, within an ever-changing society, mandated by regional and national governments. Additional discussions are planned, focusing on the application of various mixed methods research techniques within the digital context(s) and from an interdisciplinary perspective. Our discussions will include the full process of research: conception, delivery, execution, and impact.

Chapter 8 – Not a Conclusion, But a Manifesto!

This chapter collates the journey of this book and the values that the authors positioned as a new beginning and presented as a tangible tool. Our manifesto titled: *Transgenerational Technology well-being & innovation opportunity for the twenty-first century* presents 12 points as a 'call to action' for researchers, practitioners, policy makers and stakeholders. This manifesto is intended to position narratives and interdisciplinary research agendas forward into the twenty-first century and define technology innovation.

Chapter 9 – The Journey: Author Biographies and Trajectories

This chapter presents an overview of the authors, including question and answers pertaining to their respective careers and research. Although many academic books incorporate a brief overview of contributors, especially if the text is an edited collection, in books authored by a single or multiple authors, little is usually known about the writers. Therefore, we felt that the addition of an extended biographical section and a question-and-answer section, would be of interest to readers, enabling them to learn something more about the authors, their interests and experiences, and their career trajectories.

Chapter 2

The Current State of Technology and Digital Games

Introduction

As we enter the third decade of the twenty-first century, there is a greater need for and implementation of technology across different ecosystems within society. Citizens are using digital technologies for a myriad of reasons and ever more so since the COVID-19 global pandemic.

Digital technologies such as laptops, tablets, video game consoles, and smart phones, to name but a few, are all interwoven into our daily lives through various layers of society and play an integral role within the Smart Age-friendly Ecosystem (SAfE) (Marston & van Hoof, 2019).

Since 2000 scholars from various disciplines have focused on technology to understand the impact, behaviour, benefits, and challenges across many cohorts within our society. Research exemplars include lifestyle, and leisure activities (Liechty et al., 2017), and the impact of technology relating to health and well-being (Henwood & Marent, 2019; Rafalow, 2018; Shah et al., 2019). There is a growing body of research taking an international perspective, focussing on rural and urban living and ageing (Freeman et al., 2020; Genoe et al., 2018; Marston et al., 2019).

Although many people believe technology is going to be a silver bullet and will fix everything wrong in our society, unfortunately, there are (marginalised) communities that are impacted by this growing notion. Thus, itself leading to inequalities and continues the existing debate surrounding the digital divide (Cotton et al., 2009; Fernández-Ardèvol, 2019; Gallistl et al., 2020; Gilleard et al., 2015; Lagacé et al., 2015; Marston et al., 2021). Within our society there are several generations (Fry, 2018; Nielsen, 2014; Vogels, 2019), who engage and live in our society and who experience various societal and generational events across their respective life course (Elder, 1985).

This chapter showcases contemporary research surrounding various technologies that have infiltrated our society, which are now playing a pivotal role in our lives and ecosystems. We will continue our exploration of relationships with technologies from the standpoints of intergenerational relationships and

Transgenerational Technology and Interactions for the 21st Century:
Perspectives and Narratives, 13–36
Copyright © 2022 by Hannah R. Marston, Linda Shore, Laura Stoops, and Robbie S. Turner
Published under exclusive licence by Emerald Publishing Limited
doi:10.1108/978-1-83982-638-220221005

adults who are ageing without children (AWOC). In the proceeding sections of this chapter, we will delve into the current state of play surrounding digital games, and technology engagement from the standpoint of the pandemic and generally within society.

Technologies of the 20th and 21st Centuries

In 2020, the Office for National Statistics (ONS) reported 96% of households in Great Britain had access to the Internet to facilitate various activities including online banking (76%), shopping (55%), food deliveries from restaurants, fast-food outlets, or catering services (32%) (ONS, 2020b). Ofcom (2020–2021) ascertained 92% of females and 93% of males use the Internet at home, while 13% and 7% respectively access the Internet primarily through a smartphone. Whereas, 87% and 84% respectively use a smartphone. Across the four UK nations as shown in Fig. 2.1, fewer adults in Northern Ireland use the Internet at home in comparison to adults living in England, Scotland, and Wales. However, 92% and 12% of adults in Northern Ireland use a smartphone and use this device solely to access the Internet, respectively.

Various activities (Table 2.1) were conducted online in 2020 during the pandemic which is understandable given the various governmental restrictions and legislations enforced due to the COVID-19 pandemic (Ofcom, 2020–21).

Continuing with the modes of communication, 83% and 74% of people reported using WhatsApp and Facebook Messenger respectively, with 83% of people reporting using Facebook, gaining greater popularity among older users specifically 91% of adults aged 65+ years. Whereas, 69% of adults aged between 16 and 24 years were less likely to have a profile on the social networking site. Overall, 49% of adults aged 65+ years reported Facebook to be their primary social networking site, in comparison to 16% of all users (Ofcom, 2020–21).

Social media has become interwoven within our society and daily consumption, with many adults aged between 16 and 24 years prefer to use Snapchat (72%), while younger adults (83%) prefer to use Facebook, or Instagram (57%). Additionally, 23% and 22% of younger adults had a Reddit or Twitch profile

Media Use Across the Nations of the UK, 2020-2021

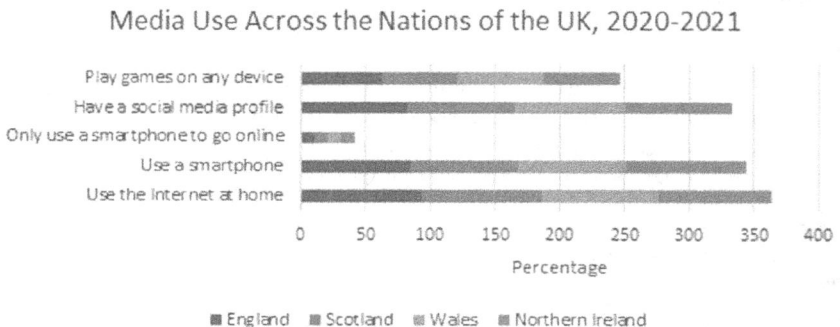

Fig. 2.1.   Media Use Across the Nations of the UK. *Source*: Ofcom (2020–21).

Table 2.1. Activities Conducted Online 2020.

Online Activities and Tasks	Percentage
Communications	92
Email	91
Government services	85
Transactions	85
Banking	83
Information	75
Watching TV content	74
Watching video clips	71
News	69
Radio/audio services	66
Civic	44
Playing games	35

Source: Ofcom (2020–2021).

respectively (Ofcom, 2020–21). TikTok (21%) usage is growing amongst social media users, specifically by users (54%) aged between 16 and 24 years, while users (27%) aged between 25 and 34 years have a profile on this platform (Ofcom, 2020–21).

Digital devices such as mobile and smartphones, have become an integral accessory for citizens, and can usually be found near the owner (Fernández-Ardèvol, 2019, 2020; Rosales, & Fernández-Ardèvol, 2016a/b). With the advent of smartphones, the development of apps and mHealth apps can be easily accessed and downloaded via the Google Play Store or iOS/App Store – depending on the operating system of the smartphone. Apps are easily downloaded via a touch of the screen and are installed onto the smartphone, this in turn enables the users to track various activities (Marston & Hall, 2016) such as dieting (Ferrara et al., 2019); fertility and menstruation cycles (e.g., Earle et al., 2020), Arrhythmia (Marston et al., 2019), smoking cessation (Haskins et al., 2017), physical activity (Laranjo et al., 2021), health and well-being from the perspective of blue light personnel (Marston et al., 2020).

Computers, the Internet, videogames, artificial intelligence (AI), and wearable devices such as Fitbits, and Smart Watches have been intertwined into the lives of many citizens for a variety of reasons and purposes. Such reasons include to increase physical activity, enhance, and maintain social connectedness via social media platforms (e.g., Freeman et al., 2020; Genoe et al., 2018) and to pass the time away. Whether you are a young person/child or a person who is ageing without children (AWOC) and abiding to respective government guidance which in turn results being isolated due to the pandemic; playing video games may offer an alternative form of entertainment, coupled with the opportunity to connect with other gamers and friends online (Marston & Kowert, 2020).

Technology Use in a Global Pandemic

COVID-19 has ripped a crevasse through Western societies and in the context of the UK exposing how the UK devolved governments were assessing and monitoring the COVID-19 pandemic (Marston, Shore, & White, 2020; White, Marston, Shore & Turner, 2020). The health of citizens has become paramount and a focus since the global pandemic erupted in 2020. A recent systematic review (Davalbhakta et al., 2020) focusses on the use of apps specifically for track and tracing during the COVID-19 pandemic. Greater emphasis was placed on technology and identifying alternative solutions for citizens during different stages of national and regional lockdowns. All devolved UK governments were monitoring the 'R' number to gain some control over COVID-19 which is not fussy on who it infects, nor is it too bothered about the level of disruption it causes across education (e.g., primary, secondary, and higher education institutes). In the spring of 2020, the UK witnessed the chasm ripping through the health and social care environments of the National Health Service (NHS), adult social care, including nursing homes, in conjunction with communities throughout the towns and cities.

COVID-19 restrictions differed across the UK and citizens had to adhere to those respective guidelines. From a UK standpoint, Christmas 2020 (Marston & Morgan, 2020b) was very different and for many citizens, they were informed by the respective devolved governments (BBC News, 2020b; UK Government, 2020) about the four differing restrictions (Marston, Shore & White, 2020). For citizens in England living in Tiers 1–3 a maximum of three households were able to form a temporary bubble for Christmas Day, while, in Scotland, a maximum of eight people from three households could meet (BBC News, 2020b/c). Wales stated a maximum of two households and in Northern Ireland three households could form a bubble between the 23rd and 27th December (BBC News, 2020b/c). Additional restrictions were also in place and included prohibition of citizens living in other areas of the UK travelling into Scotland, citizens in Tier 4 lockdown restrictions (England and Wales) were prohibited to form a bubble and Northern Irish citizens were informed that they were not allowed to travel to Scotland or a Tier four area in England (BBC News, 2020b/c).

In November 2020 at the beginning of the second lockdown, Marston and Morgan (2020b) wrote the thought piece '*Lockdown 2.0: Gunpowder Plot, Digital Christmas, Sex and Relationships*' which takes the perspective of loneliness and social isolation from the standpoint of Christmas, and how many citizens have been and were using technologies such as dating apps as a means of 'connecting' or making 'connections' during the pandemic for their social, intimate, emotional and sexual well-being (Green, 2020). At the time of writing this piece respective government narratives were changing daily and weekly. Furthermore, there was no mention or consideration for those citizens who were and are AWOC (see Chapters 3 and 6 for more information) across the life course, while the media (BBC News, 2020b) reported how many citizens would be hosting Christmas via

Zoom. This is a solution for many who already have the technology, but for many people they do not have the financial means and/or digital skills. The pandemic has highlighted and brought to the forefront the level of digital poverty (Adams, 2020; BCS, 2020; Haworth, 2020; Marston et al., 2020) and the impact of the digital divide, and inequities experienced by people in our society (Friemal, 2016; Goedhart et al., 2019; Hargittai & Dobransky, 2017; Helsper, 2021; Helsper & van Deursen, 2017; ONS, 2018, 2019a/b, 2020c; van Dijk, 2020).

In relation to mobile apps, more recently across the UK there have been various NHS related COVID-19 apps available for download onto smartphones to facilitate citizens, respective governments, and Public Health Agencies (e.g., Public Health England) to learn and understand the impact of the pandemic, and citizen behaviours. Across England and Wales citizens are able to download the NHS COVID-19 App (https://www.covid19.nhs.uk/) (Figs. 2.2a-2.2b), in Scotland citizens are able to download the 'Protect Scotland' App (https://protect.scot/) (Fig. 2.2c), and in Northern Ireland the 'StopCOVID NI' app (https://covid-19.hscni.net/stop-covid-ni-mobile-app/) (Fig. 2.2d), is available for download by citizens. Furthermore, for those citizens who are travelling from Scotland into Wales or England be-it for work related reasons or other, the Scottish government

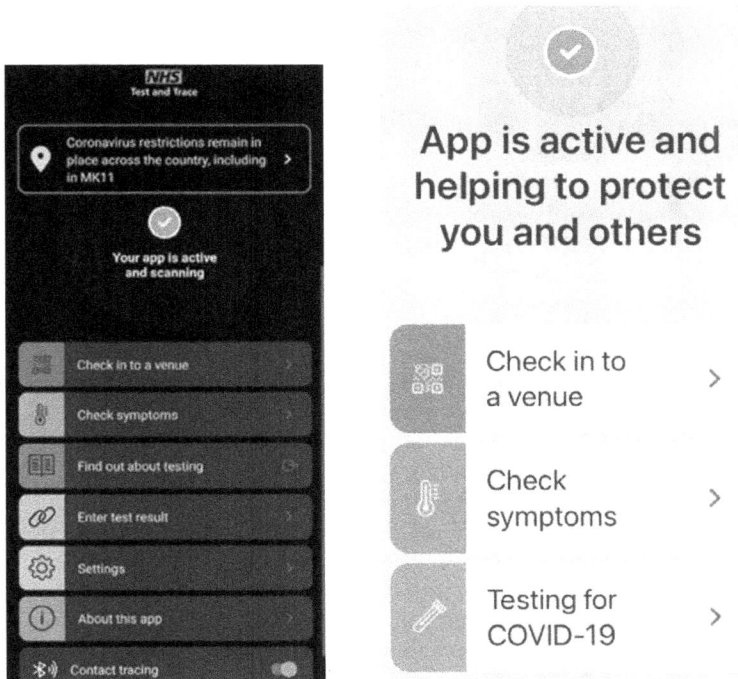

Fig. 2.2a and 2.2b.   COVID-19 App for England and Wales.
Source: Photographs taken by Dr H. R. Marston and Dr D. J. Morgan (Permission granted by Marston and Morgan).

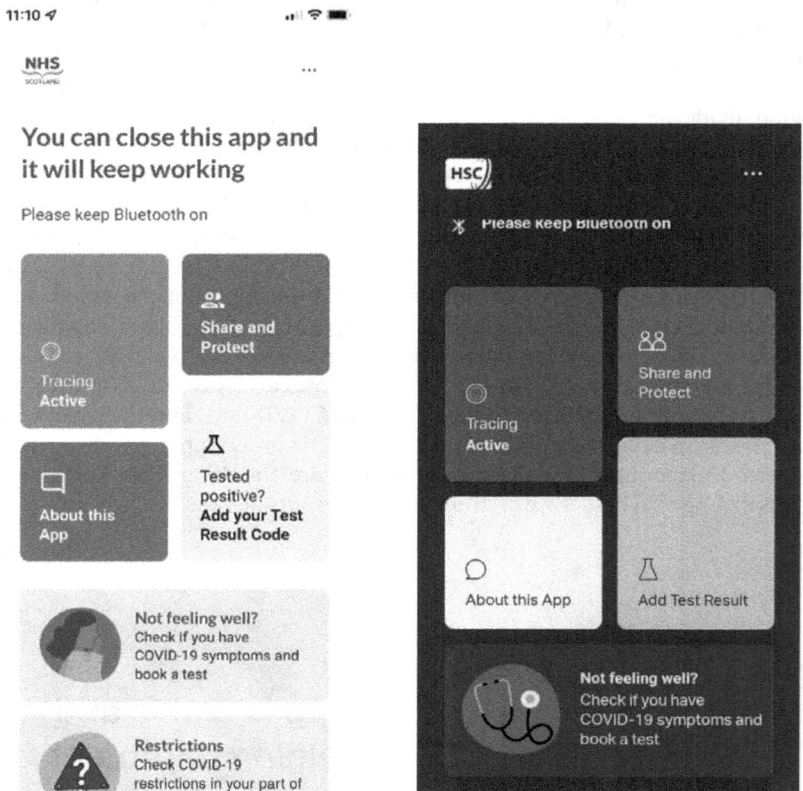

Fig. 2.2c and 2.2d.   COVID-19 App for Scotland and Northern Ireland.
Source: Photographs taken by Dr L. Shore and Dr L. Stoops (Permission granted by Shore and Stoops).

announced on the 5th of November 2020 that the 'Protect Scotland' App would be compatible with the NHS COVID-19 App used in England and Wales (Scottish Government, 2021). Similarly, the 'StopCOVID NI' app (Fig. 2.2d) can work outside of the region of NI and includes England, Jersey, the Republic of Ireland, Scotland, and Wales (NI direct government services, n.d.)

Throughout 2020 users have been able check the 'app' to review the latest government restrictions, check their symptoms, check into a venue, and more recently seek out information pertaining to testing and entering a test result. During 2020 and onwards, the apps facilitate notifications to citizens as to whether they met another citizen who may have tested positive with COVID-19. If this is the case, the individual would have to self-isolate based on the recommended guidance.

For this type of 'app' to be successful there is a level of responsibility on citizens to download and install the 'app(s)' onto their smartphone, which for many who own a smartphone is appropriate. For those citizens who do not own a smartphone and/or their digital skills are limited, downloading an important 'app' such as the COVID-19 track and trace is fruitless. Between October 7th and 23rd December 2020 in England and Wales, the growth of downloads reached 20.9 million (Statista, 2021). In Scotland, the number of downloads of the app as of 1st February 2021 on both iOS and Android devices was 1,832,346 with a total of 891,000 active users (Scottish Government, 2021). For Northern Ireland data published 14th August 2020 showed there had been 250,000 downloads of the 'StopCOVID NI' app (Department of Health, 2020).

With the advent of mobile 'apps', there are the ongoing concerns surrounding privacy and data harvesting, which can include citizens' location, images, and contact lists (Martin & Shilton, 2016). The Pew Research Centre reported 43% of smartphone users uninstalled an app(s) from their phone after discovering the amount of personal information harvested by the app (Anderson, 2015). Furthermore, 60% of users chose not to install an app on their smartphone because of their concerns associated to personal information being used by the app developer. One example is the various COVID-19 tracking apps (CTAs), which have superseded the traditional norms of track and trace to ensure the risk of transmission is reduced (Ferretti et al., 2020).

In the following section, we enter the generational overview and the demographics of digital gamers, continuing our discussion surrounding technology use in the latter part of the twentieth century and into the twenty-first century.

Generational Overview

Table 2.2 provides two descriptions of generations in society. Generations such as the Silent Generation have lived through poignant periods and episodes in society and historical events documented in twentieth century history.

Table 2.2 presents the differences across the generations and their respective years. In more recent times, the 'CoronaDiaries' project (2021) is documenting the lived experiences of citizens living through the pandemic and it can be imagined that such a project will be viewed as a piece of historical documentation enabling future generations to read how citizens coped and adapted to the changes of the first lockdown in the UK. Understanding the various generations spanning 100 years, is key to understanding how technology can, does, and will impact different cohorts of our society. For those citizens who were born in the latter part of the twentieth century and into the twenty-first century – known as Millennials and Generation Z, their approaches to technology are very different to those who are Generation X and Baby Boomers.

Digital Games and the Current State of Play

Digital games as an entertainment medium are not a new phenomenon, there has been various books presenting the history of games since their conception back in the 1950s (Herman, 2001; Kent, 2000; Newman, 2012). Since the 1950s the *Tennis for Two* game signalled the start of this medium, which motivated several

Table 2.2.   Generation Cohorts.

Nielsen			Pew Research Centre			
Cohort	**Year**	**Age in 2021**	**Cohort**	**Year**	**Age in 2016 (Years)**	**Age in 2021**
Greatest Generation	1901–1924		Greatest & Silent Generations	1945 or earlier	71 or over	
Silent Generation	1925–1945					
Baby Boomers	1946–1964		Baby Boomers	1946–1964	52–70	
Generation X	1965–1976		Generation X	1965–1980	36–51	
Millennials/Gen Y						
• Younger Millennials (18–27)	1977–1995		Millennial	1981–1996	20–35	
• Older Millennials (28–36)						
Generation Z	1995–Present		Post-Millennial	1997–Present	18–19	

Sources: Nielsen (2014), Vogels (2019) and Fry (2018).

generations of society to engage, enjoy, and share their gaming experiences with their friends, family and even strangers. Although online gaming facilitated through the advent of the Internet, enables, gamers to engage with others located anywhere in the world with games such as *Call of Duty* or other genres of games, by downloading them on to the respective hardware device.

Contemporary research in the field of game studies has explored the use and engagement of digital games in differing societal contexts for over 10 years; including sexuality and gender within game culture (Shaw, 2014); gender, gaming, and design (Graner Ray, 2004; Kafai et al., 2008; Marston & Graner Ray, 2016), the cultural (e.g., identity, agency, community and consumption) role digital games play within society (Flynn, 2003; Muriel & Crawford, 2018) and the work by Juul (2010) who explores the use and game playing habits of casual gamers between 2000 and 2010.

Gaming is not a medium solely for young people such as those who are Generation Z or Millennials (Marston, 2019), but also Baby Boomers (Marston, 2012, 2013a/b), who were the first cohort to experience this new phenomenon. Digital games are increasingly being used in the public sector (e.g., blue light personnel) (Marston et al., 2020), military personnel (Brandão, Ferreira, & Carvalho, 2012; Herz & Macedonia, 2002; Prensky, 2001a; Schulzke, 2013), as well as having the potential to afford adults who are AWOC (Woodward, 2014) the opportunity to engage with wider social networks (Marston & Kowert, 2020).

Fig. 2.3 presents data presented by the Entertainment Software Association (ESA, 2004–2020) relating to the age of gamers. Over the years the ESA have not maintained previous age groupings and have instead chosen to alter age groups accordingly. For data published in 2020, the ESA used the age grouping 35–54 years. Whereas the age groups 36- or 36–49 years were used for documenting gaming statistics between 2012 and 2018. Furthermore, in 2018 – data for this demographic is presented by gender – this has not been the case in previous years. Between the years 2004 and 2011 the ESA presented data based on gamers aged between 18 and 50 years. Since 2020 the ESA have presented data to include adults who are 65+ years, whereas previously they used the formats of 50+ years or 55–64 years, even though some gamers would be categorised as Baby Boomers (Marston, 2012, 2013a/b; Pearce, 2008) and still do continue to play. Indeed, many Baby Boomer gamers are turning 76 years in 2022, the first group of people born in this cohort.

The concept of digital gaming by older adults was first presented in the 1980s, by Weisman (1983) who explored specific video games used by adults aged between 70 and 90 years, and who were living in a nursing home environment. This work identified the benefits of digital games used by older adults living in a nursing home and results displayed positive engagement, and mental stimulation in a bid to increase self-esteem and confidence. Since Weisman's (1983) research there has been a superfluous range of national and international research covering a myriad of issues found within contemporary society.

For example, the *Games for Health* (Bean, 2018; Kowert & Quandt, 2020) movement focusses on designing, developing, and testing digital games spanning various health conditions (e.g., Duchenne Muscular Dystrophy (DMD), Heutinck et al., 2018). Several reviews have been published since 2010 in an attempt to understand the use of digital games from the context of health and the benefits

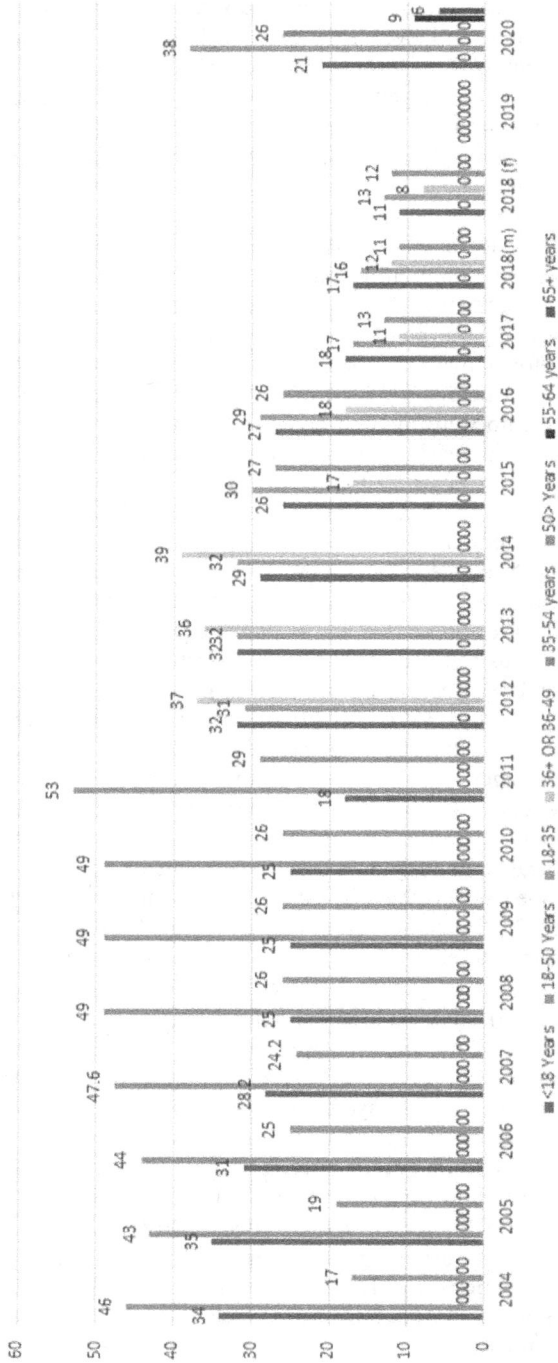

Fig. 2.3.   Video Game Statistics Published Between 2004 and 2020. *Source:* ESA.

digital games may afford users relating to health and rehabilitation (Bleakley et al., 2015; Chao et al., 2015; Hall et al., 2012; Miller et al., 2014; Marston & Smith, 2012; Marston et al., 2016).

The reviews above aimed to explore the benefits of digital game technology for rehabilitation. Looking at areas such as; stroke and fall prevention (Marston & Smith 2012); mental, physical and social health. Others factors include study design; types of measures and video game platforms (Hall et al., 2012); physical activity (Miller et al., 2014); physical and cognitive effects of digital games encompassing aerobic, strength, balance and flexibility (Bleakley et al., 2015). Chao et al. (2015) explored the effects of the Nintendo Wii exergames (games that are also a form of exercise) on older adults. While Molina et al. (2014) explored how digital game use and complimentary software (exergames) were used and deployed in randomised control trials (RCT) or controlled clinical trials (CCT) (Molina et al., 2014). Although many of these reviews focused on adults aged 50+ years, there is a paucity of literature and understanding of the benefits and challenges experienced by adults aged over 80 years (Marston et al., 2016).

Enhancing physical activity, strength and balance has garnered importance in later life as a means of reducing the risk of falling (Eichberg et al., 2015; Gschwind et al., 2015; Marston et al., 2014). Furthermore, contemporary research has explored how the relationship and potential impact of using digital games to positively aid cognition (Boot et al., 2008; Green & Bavelier, 2003; Green et al., 2010). However, there is one extensive review which focusses on the use of video games specifically aimed at cognitive tasks and enhancing performance (Simons et al., 2016), and specifically refers to games such as 'Brain Training'.

This timely review in 2016 critically analysed the positives and negatives of brain-training interventions across several areas including '1. *Marketing of brain-training products*, 2. *Learning, transfer, and the logic of brain training*, 3. *Best Practices in Intervention Design and Reporting*, 4. *The Evidence cited by Brain-Training Companies*, 5. *The evidence cited by Cognitive Training Data*, and finally *Video-Game Interventions*' (Simons et al., 2016). This detailed review explores the benefits, challenges and concerns surrounding those required in brain-training interventions and the findings detailed how interventions in this domain can 'improve performance on the trained tasks'. There is less evidence to support 'closely related tasks' with little more evidence to demonstrate how brain training can and does enhance performance or closely related tasks, or even improvement of daily cognitive performance (Simons et al., 2016, p. 103). Conclusions note there are 'major shortcomings in design or analysis that preclude definitive conclusions about the efficacy of training' (Simons et al., 2016, p. 103).

The American Association of Retired Persons (AARP) report 70% of adults are aged between 50 and 59 years, 64% are aged between 60 and 69 years, and 39% are aged over 70 years (2019a). Weekly gaming activity and more occurs across all age groups with 80% of adults aged 60+ years noting this as a form of leisure activity, while 77% of younger older adults (50–59 years) noted this form of entertainment and leisure activity is conducted on a weekly basis (AARP, 2019a).

Motivations, and gaming habits (AARP, 2019b) of older adults showed 67% of adults aged 50+ years chose to play games to keep them mentally sharp, while

33% of adults wanted to learn something. Similarly, this data supports the findings presented by Marston (2012, 2013a) who also ascertained various motivators to game playing by non-gamers and gamers.

There are several reasons for key positive motivational factors when it comes to gaming and these include, to have fun, to experience or be challenged, problem solving and to reduce stress. Both the AARP (2019b) and Marston (2012, 2013a/b) noted similar findings as to why older people choose to play games. Including specific times to play games, such as just before going to bed, or just as a person has woken up, with preference to online gaming with other gamers.

The ethnicity of gamers who are African Americans and Hispanic is recorded by the AARP (2019c/d) including their motivations for gaming (Fig. 2.4), their game genre preferences (Fig. 2.6), where and when (Fig. 2.5) these gamers choose to play games and the type of devices games are played on is also recorded.

Gender and gaming research was a popular area of study in the 1980s, 1990s and into the early part of the 2000s (Marston & del Carmen Miranda Duro, 2020) with academic conferences such as Women in Games being held at university institutions in the UK between 2004 and 2011 to share knowledge and insights pertaining to gender and gaming behaviours. In 2009, the Women in Games not for profit organisation (2009) was created to ensure there is greater representation in the Games Industry.

Within games and the industry, sexism, and misogyny (Prescott & Bogg, 2013) continue to exist, and back in 2014 the 'Gamergate' online harassment campaign was initiated (Cote, 2020). Understanding the gendered perspective of games has been studied for several years and decades (Cassell & Jenkins, 2000; Graner Ray, 2004; Kafai et al., 2008; Marston & del Carmen Miranda Duro, 2020) aimed at game designers and developers to understand the gendered differences associated to gaming behaviours, needs, and responses from this successful entertainment medium.

Motivations for Game Playing

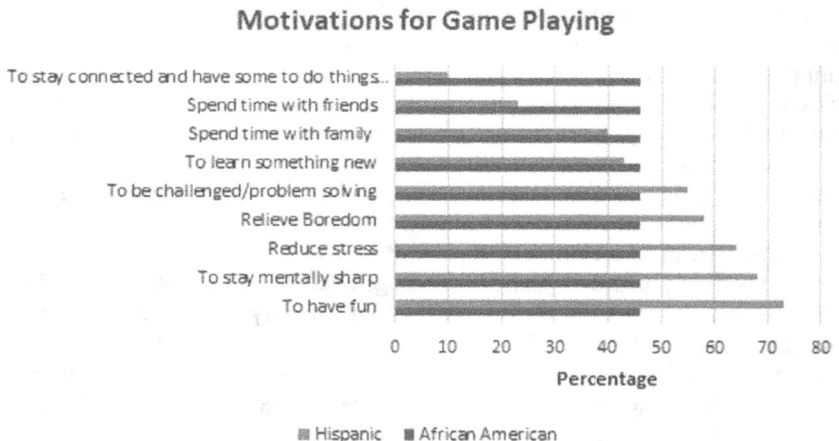

Fig. 2.4.   Motivations for Game Playing by Ethnicity. *Source*: AARP (2019c/d).

Frequency and Time of Game Playing

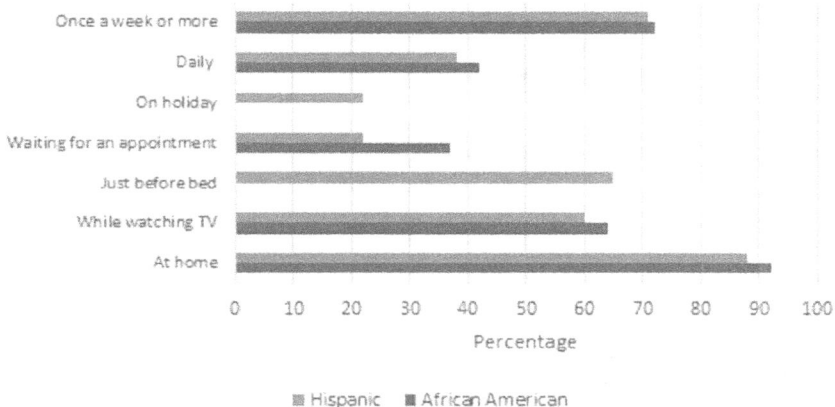

Fig. 2.5.   Frequency and Time for Game Playing by Ethnicity. *Source*: AARP (2019c/d).

Preferred Game Genres

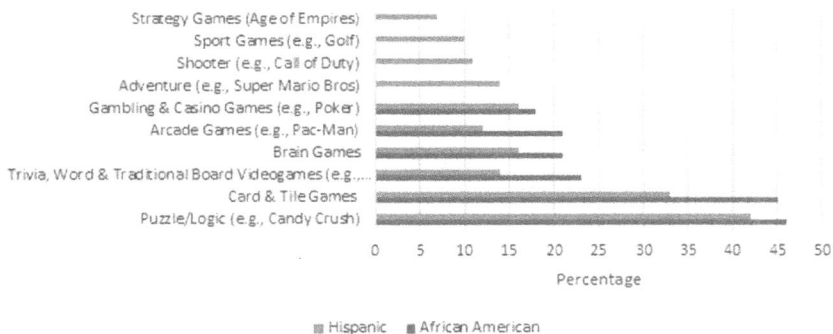

Fig. 2.6.   Game Genres played by Ethnicity. *Source*: AARP (2019c/d).

If games are to be utilised in the context of games for health, specifically targeting older adults (Marston & Graner-Ray, 2016), then understanding from a gendered perspective the motivations, needs, likes and dislikes is imperative because without this knowledge, games will not be played (Taylor, 2003). The essence of 'time' is also critical from a gendered perspective (Winn & Heeter, 2009) because for many women, they may not have as much spare time as men and instead choose to play more casual games.

Fig. 2.7 shows the primary reasons why older adults play games by gender, with women reporting a 'purpose' and aligns with the findings by Marston and Graner Ray (2016a) whereas men prefer to play games for fun.

The types of games being played by gender illustrates women prefer to play via their mobile phone or other devices, instead of a computer or console, and

Motivations for Game Playing by Gender

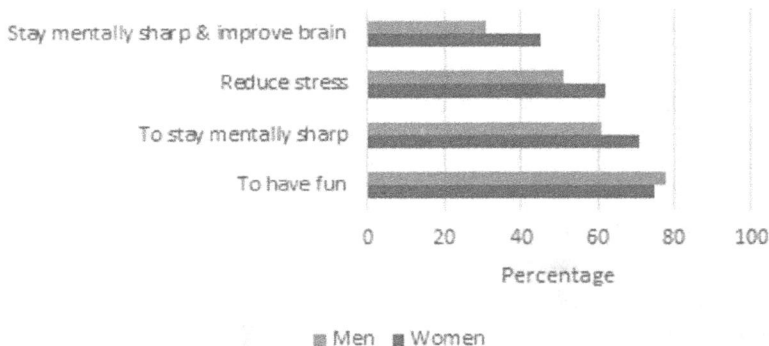

Fig. 2.7.   Motivations for Game Playing by Gender. *Source*: AARP (2019e).

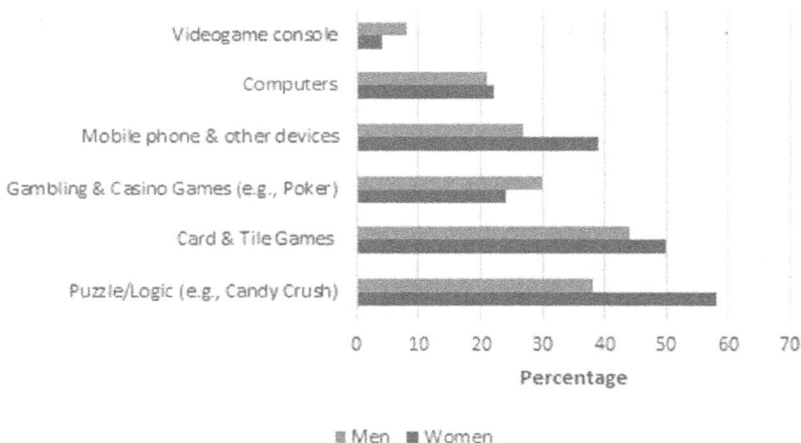

Fig. 2.8.   Preferred Game Genres and Devices Played by Gender.
Source: AARP (2019a).

as noted by literature (Marston & Graner-Ray, 2016) casual games are preferred by women.

The time of day is important for older women choosing to play games, either before bed or while watching television, this is less so for men. Although for many women their frequency can vary between daily game playing or more than once a week. What Fig. 2.9 does not show, is whether men or women play during the day, and it can be suggested, that due to other responsibilities this is not so common.

Generation X and Digital Gaming

While there has been great interest and scholarly activity from the fields of gerontology, game studies, social sciences and interdisciplinary scholars who

Frequemcy & Time for Game Play by Gender

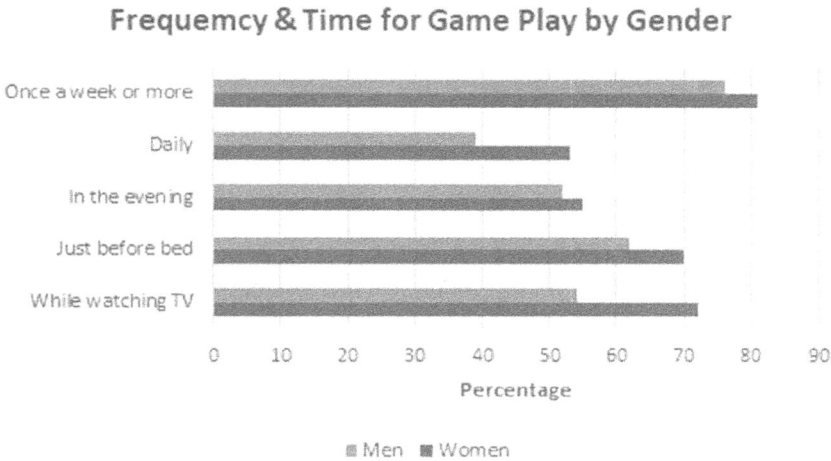

Fig. 2.9.   Frequency and Time for Game Playing by Gender. *Source*: AARP (2019a).

have recruited older adults, there is little understanding to the barriers, enablers, needs and impact from citizens of Generation X. Indeed, a recent scoping review (Marston & del Carmen Miranda Duro, 2020) explores empirical research dating from 1970 to 2000 which recruited participants that would now be categorised as Generation X. Presently, several disciplines have explored digital games from the standpoint of Generation X, to understand their needs and concerns associated with technology as they transition into later life. This scoping review specifically explores and discusses scholarly activity which recruited participants categorised as Generation X. Recommendations suggest the need for participatory workshops with people who are Generation X to fully garner insight and understanding of their needs, expectations, barriers, and challenges for videogame deployment in later life, especially in the context of games for health and social connectedness. We must start focussing our attentions on other cohorts such as Generation X because they are the next ageing population but as yet have not garnered attention from the field of gerontology.

Given the possible longevity of citizens in society, coupled with the phenomenal technological developments, there should be a call to action to conduct research to understand this cohort as well as younger generations such as Millennials. Why? Because the Generation X cohort differ significantly to both the Baby Boomers and Millennial cohorts.

Their differences lie in being exposed to technology through various means of society (e.g., work and leisure). Although, Millennials and Generation Z have received greater exposure to technology from a younger age, including access to the Internet, powerful computers/laptops, game consoles and software, Generation X have grown up learning and experiencing these new technologies as they become available on the market. Generation X are a cohort that can remember what society was like prior to the mass take-up of mobile and smartphones, the advent of the

Internet and social media platforms. Indeed, members of Generation X will have played earlier game consoles from the 1970s, 1980s and 1990s, whereas Millennials and Generation Z have not had these opportunities, nor experiences.

Generation X use technology differently due to work and family commitments, but also because they have been the cohort which to-date has been overlooked by the academy, industry and society when discussing the use and impact of technology and digital games (Brown, 2017; Brown & De Schutter, 2016; Brown & Marston, 2018; Marston & Azadvar, 2020; Marston & del Carmen Miranda Duro, 2020). Citizens in this cohort have engaged with different forms of technology and digital games which in turn differs to Baby Boomers and given that Generation X is the next ageing cohort, their needs, prior knowledge, barriers, and enablers needs to be understood.

Transgenerational Gaming

We coined the term *Transgenerational Gaming* in Chapter 1, referring to the notion of game playing behaviour being fluid throughout the life course. Previously, intergenerational gaming has been growing since Voida and Greenberg (2009, 2010, 2012) published their insights. A recent review by Marston and del Carmen Miranda Duro (2020) provides an extensive insight into the current state of play surrounding intergenerational gaming, which has received modest investigation from the fields of gerontechnology, game studies, and gerontology.

One systematic review outlines the benefits and factors impacting and shaping a previously coined term *intergenerational gaming* identifying four main classifications across 16 studies; 1. *underpin familial bonding*, 2. *enhance shared learning*, 3. *raise awareness of the other generation*, and 4. *diminish social anxiety* (De la Hera et al., 2017). Two primary factors are highlighted for consideration, 1. Player-centric and 2. Game-centric, while interactions were observed across different age groups and divided into two groups, 1. Older players (55–81 years), and 2. Younger players (4–22 years). In conjunction with additional elements such as their motivational reasons for gaming, level of ability and their differences (player-centric) as the key factors for designing intergenerational games. Findings identified both goal-oriented and space-oriented style of game interaction, concluding further work was needed to specifically understand gender, and age of participants as a way to better understand the specific benefits of gaming. We believe *Transgenerational Gaming* can play a part in this recommendation, with greater emphasis being placed on the age and sex of novice and expert gamers. As previously highlighted, greater focus is needed on Generation X, specifically in relation to understanding their needs and expectations.

Why Is There Little Insight Into Digital Games and Older Adults Who Are Ageing Without Children (AWOC)?

Technology from the standpoint of COVID-19 is affording citizens across different age cohorts to maintain social connections with friends, family, and community members (Marston & Kowert, 2020; Morgan et al., 2020; Sheerman, Marston, Musselwhite, & Morgan, 2020; White et al., 2020). We are witnessing how social media platforms such as Twitter (Marston & Morgan, 2020a) can play a role in the lives of citizens who are experiencing loneliness, social isolation and who feel their mental health is not as positive as it was pre-pandemic.

At the beginning of the pandemic from a UK standpoint (18.03.20), contemporary thoughts of how COVID-19 may impact citizens and communities were posited (Marston, Musselwhite, & Hadley, 2020); highlighting the rapid responses from communities to support vulnerable and ill residents in respective communities. This key piece by Marston et al. discusses a sub-population of older adults who are AWOC and includes childless adults who are in/voluntary experiencing childlessness (Hadley, 2018a/b, 2019, 2020a, 2021).

Currently, this sub-population of society has received little attention and is under researched by academics. Yet, there should be greater interest from the field of gerontology because this area just doesn't impact current ageing populations, but younger generations too. People who are Generation X, and Millennials, in turn should receive greater attention by the government, the third sector, and health service providers. As Hadley (2018a/b, 2019, 2020a) argues,

> While many age-related issues such as isolation, loneliness and dementia have recently gathered extensive attention (and funding) people ageing without children is a subject that remains unreported, under-researched and under-represented at all levels. (Hadley, 2018b, pp. 76–77)

Statistics published on the 17th of August 2020; by the Office for National Statistics (ONS, 2020a) highlights the impact of in/voluntary childlessness by older women. Unfortunately, the ONS did not provide data pertaining to the impact of in/voluntary childlessness on men, when it comes to informal care (or lack of) in later life. Yet, AWOC does not solely impact one sex over another, and greater recognition is needed from government departments to acknowledge and recognise this. Already, Public Health Wales (PHW), has acknowledged this sub-population in relation to the role digital technologies can play in their lives (Green et al., 2020). However, from the standpoint of older adults who are AWOC including contemporary research and social policy, greater attention and research is needed as noted in research evidence contributed to the UK government COVID-19 Committee 'Life Beyond COVID' (Hadley, 2020b). Further evidence highlights the importance of this area via written evidence published by the COVID-19 Committee 'Living online' and who noted the importance of technology use for continuing social and intergenerational interactions during the pandemic (Marston, Wilson et al., 2020). This evidence suggests the affordance and access to digital technologies is needed through various channels within communities and educational institutions; to enable and facilitate all citizens in society and especially those citizens who experience digital poverty and who are categorised as low SES.

Interaction and Engagement

The nature of engagement and interaction differs across technology devices based on existing mental models (White et al., 2020). Some game studies research focusses on the mode of interaction and engagement from the standpoint of understanding user experience (UX), enjoyment through art therapy (Paczynski et al., 2017), and engagement (e.g., motor control, wheelchair) (Gerling et al., 2010).

Over the last 15–20 years, there has been a growing body of research exploring the impact of games on gamers who may experience flow and/or immersion within various game genres (Brown & De Schutter, 2016; De Schutter & Brown, 2016; Marston, 2012, 2013a; Marston et al., 2016; Nacke & Lindley, 2008a/b, 2010; Pearce, 2008; Whitlock et al., 2014). While game design has garnered attention with the notion of contributing to existing narratives while exploring alternative viewpoints such as gender (Graner-Ray, 2004; Marston & Graner-Ray, 2016), or design features and approaches such as gamification (Deterding, Dixon et al., 2011a; Deterding, Sicart et al., 2011b), interconnecting with theoretical perspectives such as perceptual opportunities and aesthetics (Marston et al., 2014). Since 2007 (IJsselsteijn et al., 2007) the area of older adults has grown, with many scholars contributing innovative knowledge, narrative and advancing the discourse surrounding the motivators, benefits, game design recommendations and interaction experienced by older adults (De Schutter, 2011; De Schutter & Vanden Abeele, 2010; De Schutter et al., 2015; Gajadhar, de Kort & IJsselsteijn, 2010; Gerling, et al., 2015; Marston, 2012, 2013a/b; Nap et al., 2009a, b; Vanden Abeele & De Schutter 2010).

Dexterity issues (e.g., ability to conduct multiple buttons pressing) relating to old age can impact game and technology interaction; while offering alternative gaming experiences can provide innovative opportunities to expose new cohorts to this medium (Marston, 2013a; Whitlock et al., 2016). An alternative way to experience different engagement experiences is through intergenerational gaming (Voida & Greenberg, 2011, 2010, 2009); combining mutual learning and sharing of experiences, game peripherals (e.g., Wiimote) (Marston, 2013a) and knowledge to facilitate novice/older users to navigate and engage easier within the game environment than traditional handhelds.

X-Reality (XR), Virtual Reality (VR), and Augmented Reality (AR)

X-Reality (XR) is a conduit of ubiquitous technologies, sensors, networks and shared online environments in both software and hardware to facilitate the creation of content for VR and mixed reality (MR) experiences. Paradiso and Landay (2009) define XR as,

> ubiquitous mixed reality environment that comes from the fusion of these two technologies *cross reality*. (p. 14)

Virtual reality (VR) and virtual environments (VE) are not a new phenomenon of the twenty-first century. VR and VEs have been explored since the 1990s, with scholars such as Murray (2017), Turkle (1997) and Fencott (2001a) narrating and contextualizing the interconnections of VR with narrative, and storytelling, associated to the discourse and experiences of agency, and presence (van Schaik et al., 2004) of video game genre theory (Apperley, 2006).

Building on the initial developments and associations of VR and VE's, research was conducted to understand augmented exercise (van Schaik et al., 2008), and dementia (Blackman et al., 2003, 2006; Flynn et al., 2003), underpinned by theoretical concepts of media aesthetics, perceptual opportunities (Fencott, 2001b; Marston et al., 2014; van Schaik et al., 2005), and semiotics (Andersen, 1997; Chandler, 2017; Fencott et al., 2012). Moving forward with VR in the context of healthy ageing and cohorts, scholars need to review the background to VR and VEs to fully understand the implications on design methodologies (Fencott, 1999; Loftin & Kenney, 1995) while aiming to facilitate interconnections of concepts, development, user experience (UX) and engagement.

VR is now being explored by scholars (Brown, 2019; Seifert & Schlomann, 2021) with a view to the potential challenges and benefits primarily aimed at older adults. As literature in this chapter has shown, this is not a new area of investigation, especially surrounding videogames research. Brown (2019) explores the role VR can play in the lives of community dwellers (Brown, 2019), specifically to understand the usability, preferences and applications associated with mobile VR platform. Utilizing the Samsung Gear VR technology with 10 older adults (63–89 years) with the aim of understanding the perceptions of the participants in different environments (e.g., art museum, a walking path, etc.) in a local town. Findings identified three overarching themes (a) *Usability*, (b) *Video subject matter preferences*, and (c) *Application,* and highlighted the challenges and opportunities of deploying the VR technology to an older audience (Brown, 2019).

There is potential for VR technology to afford older adults who are experiencing functional limitations in later life the opportunity to experience alternative environments if they are limited to experiencing the physical environment(s) themselves (Brown, 2019). While Seifert and Schlomann (2021) connect the low take-up of VR by older adults to the digital divide, there are additional facets such as interaction, and cost of owning equipment (e.g., video game consoles, peripheral devices) (McLaughlin et al., 2012). Although the environment such as a care home can play a part. A review by Marston, Greenlay and van Hoof (2013) details the benefits of using the Nintendo Wii in long-term care facilities. Furthermore, the recommendations posited by Seifert and Schlomann (2021) align with those recommendations proposed by Marston et al. (2013) surrounding additional work being conducted to understand the physical impacts and viability of game interaction. Moreover, 'abilities' as coined by Seifert and Schlomann (2021) aligns with several earlier pieces of scholarly research (Marston, 2013; Marston, Kroll, Fink, de Rosario, & Gschwind, 2016; Marston, Kroll, Fink & Gschwind, 2016; Michailidis et al., 2018; Whitelock et al., 2011, 2014). Cognitive abilities can impact video game playing (Astell et al., 2014; Zelinski & Reyes, 2009) and there are many games developed for various health conditions (Bean, 2018; Kowert & Quandt, 2020) and disabilities (Westin et al., 2020) that can afford people to experience positive game playing. Employing co-production and user testing early in the design and development phases, and conducting player research (Drachen et al., 2018) is crucial to overcoming simulation sickness (Lewis-Evans, 2018).

Augmented reality (AR) enables users to experience interactively enhanced objects in the real world via different modalities such as visual, auditory, haptic, somatosensory, and olfactory (Ismail & Sunar, 2009). AR can be accessible via different technologies including the head-mounted display (Rolland et al., 2005), eyeglasses (Benedetti, 2014; Gannes, 2012), and a handheld display (Chowdhury et al., 2013; Sung, 2011; Wagner & Schmalstieg, 2006). AR offers users a variety of experiences based on different objects in the real world, enhancing social engagement, social connectedness and intergenerational engagement.

The game *Pokémon Go* (Niantic, Nintendo, The Pokémon Company, 2016) in a pre-pandemic society facilitated users to undertake physical activity (via searching different physical environments), intergenerational engagement and social connections, using one or several digital devices to share similar and different experiences. Learning to explore new characters throughout the physical environments in the outside world. Employing gamification techniques such as challenges in seeking out the characters, gamer customization of the avatar, and reward of points, coupled with the facilitation of exploration of new physical spaces in conjunction with enhancing and affording intergenerational gaming experiences; the *Pokémon Go* AR game is a positive example of how AR and digital games can be brought together.

Extended Reality (XR) can be useful to citizens, organisations, and many more in society to demonstrate how a particular health condition can affect someone with their day-to-day living. For example, a video available via YouTube shared by Alzheimer's Research UK demonstrates through XR how this disease affects citizens in society with tasks such as making a cup of tea (Alzheimer's Research UK, 2017).

The Rise of Apps

Since 2010, technological developments have evolved considerably which are intersecting across societal ecosystems at a phenomenal pace. Apps enable smartphone users to track, monitor and share various forms of information and feedback with interested parties such as health practitioners, friends, peers, and colleagues who have similar interests (Olmstead & Atkinson, 2015; Tang, 2019). In 2015 there were 68% of American citizens who owned a smartphone and Olmstead and Atkinson (2015) report that there were 41 different categories in the Google Play Store; enabling users of Android operating system smartphones the opportunity to download apps ranging from function (e.g., calculator) to social networking, current affairs, and gaming. Contemporary research and reviews in this domain focus on the impact and use of apps by citizens who choose to track their weight, nutrition, and diet (Aguilar-Martinez et al., 2014; Bardus et al., 2016; Ferrara et al., 2019). Other apps which are available for download can facilitate women and girls to track their menstruation cycles, (Brown et al., 2019; Earle et al., 2020), or can assist people to track their arrhythmia and palpitations (Marston, Hadley, et al., 2019), or facilitate people to track their physical activity

(Oliveira et al., 2020; Romeo et al., 2019), which can include time, altitude, calories, or distance (Marston & Hall, 2015).

In the following section we explore the different types of technology used to facilitate healthy and active ageing, drawing upon national and international research to illustrate how technology can be utilised in multi- and-inter-disciplinary domains.

Assistive Technology, and the Internet of Things (IoTs)

Since 2010 various national and international research projects have been funded to understand the implications, impacts, benefits, and challenges of employing technology in different scenarios.

The term *Assistive Technology* (AT) is used to describe devices, products, and services (Smith et al., 2018) which can assist (older) people and those with disabilities with their daily living activities (Noelker et al., 2014; Rogers et al., 1998). AT devices and services can (in some instances) meet the needs of citizens with mobility issues, visual impairments (e.g., screen readers, Braille, wearable devices), personal emergency response systems – which can be used within the home environment for people who are suffering with dementia, and hearing impairments (e.g., hearing aid, amplified telephone equipment) (UK Government Department of Health and Social Care, 2020). Although there are positive movements in this field, a recently published report by the *Smart Homes and Independent Living Commission* (Gilbert, 2022) highlights the challenges of AT within the health and social care sector of the UK and provides recommendations for a route map guiding the future.

On the international landscape, the EU has funded several projects pertaining to information communication technologies (ICT) for active and healthy ageing (Gschwind, Eichberg, Ejupi et al., 2015; Interreg Europe, 2021; Marston et al., 2015). While this domain follows the area of *Technology and Active Ageing* (Sixsmith & Gutman, 2013) exploring the role of technologies such as robotics, smart environments, and telehealth can enhance the quality of life, of older people.

Additional growth in the home automation domain is occurring via the Internet of Things (IoTs) which can be purchased off-the-shelf and installed into one's home. IoT devices include lightbulbs (Philips, n.d.), washing machines (Pantri, n.d.), kitchen appliances (e.g., coffee machine, kettles, fridges) (Smarter, n.d.), door and window sensors (HIVE), robot vacuums (Currys PC World, n.d.), exercise and gym equipment (e.g., Peloton) (Moscaritolo, 2020) and heating (HIVE, n.d.). These devices and brands (Griffith et al., 2021) can cater to all home environments depending on the needs and requirements of citizens (Marston, Niles-Yokum, & Silva, 2021; Marston & van Hoof, 2019).

One specific IoT device is the virtual assistant (VAs) a small device located throughout the home (several devices needed) and can assist people with different tasks including medication reminders, grocery shopping, listening to music, receiving answers to questions, and controlling televisions and speakers (Marston & Samuels, 2019). Adults aged between 25 and 34 years used VAs or an app more so than 17% of adults aged 65+ years, and overall, 35% of adults reported using IoTs (ONS, 2020). Presently, IoT products available on the market do vary in cost ranging from ~£50.00 to £2000.00+ depending on the product. Many of the heavy-duty kitchen appliances (e.g., washing machines, and fridge freezers) do have a higher price tag as does the robot vacuum and mops resulting in being out of reach for many citizens in society. For many of these appliances and devices, a smartphone with either an Android or iOS operating system is needed as part of the setup, and process, which if a person in a household does not own, then they incur additional expenses.

Wearable and Implantable Devices

The definition of 'Implant' by the Cambridge English Dictionary, is:

> to put an organ, group of cells, or device into the body in a medical operation: The owner's name and address is stored on a microchip and implanted in the dog's body. (Cambridge English Dictionary, n.d.)

Existing implants currently available for the purpose of health including the contraceptive device – *Implant* (NHS, n.d.a) (the size of a hair grip), is inserted by a health professional and sits underneath the skin of the upper arm. An alternative form of implantable contraceptive device is the *Intrauterine Device* (IUD) (NHS, n.d.b) which is a small plastic or copper device (T-shape) and this too requires a health professional to conduct the minor procedure of inserting the IUD into the uterus of the woman. When it is time for the implant to be replaced (usually at 5 years), the woman will have to have the implant removed and replace (if she chooses) by a health professional again.

Implantable devices are being used by humans who are choosing to self-monitor their health (Gelfand, 2019; Pratty, 2021; Science Service, 2018), or their activities of daily living (ADL). Hearables (Crum, 2019) are innovative wearables located within the ear that augment and monitor health variables that can highlight problems early or amend the listening experience through sensing technologies.

Contemporary society has witnessed individuals who have actively chosen to modify their bodies in terms of fashion, or for personal choice. Known as body modification, individuals positively choose to deliberately change their physical appearance (Featherstone, 1999), for several reasons (beauty, individuality, spirituality and cultural tradition, addiction, sexual motivation etc.) (Wohlrab et al., 2007), religious beliefs (i.e. circumcision), or sexual enhancement, as a means of body art or for shock value and self-expression across different cultures in Asia, Africa, America and Oceania (Jonaitis, 1988). Tattooing by sub-cultures in society such as sailors, bikers or prisoners is perceived to be a form of identification (DeMello, 1995, 1993; Sanders, 2010) and in some cultures has been perceived as initiation rites or fashionable (Jonaitis, 1988; Sanders, 2010). Wohlrab et al. (2007) note across societal sub-groups such as the punk and gay movements, the concept of body modification 'was mainly as a protest against the conservative middle-class norms of society' (p. 87, Pitts, 2003).

Tim Cannon, is a known bio-hacker and has previously implanted magnetic implants into his finger and wrist (Bort, 2014) and electrical components (i.e. electronic chip) into his arm (Lallanilla, 2013) to record data. The purpose for this implant was to facilitate data transmission between a mobile device and an Android operating system, but it should be noted this procedure was not conducted by a health professional but instead by a professional tattooist and piercing specialist.

In another example, 'micro chipping' was conducted by an Australian man who chose to implant a travel card under his skin to facilitate easier access to travelling on public transport BBC Newsbeat (2017). The justification for this procedure was rationalised by the individual who noted how the new implant gave him 'an ability not everyone else has' and 'if someone stole my wallet I could still get home' (BBC Newsbeat, (2017). Although this approach for many people could be perceived as unusual or not the norm, another example is whereby a Wisconsin technology company offered their employees the opportunity to be 'microchipped' (Bowerman, 2017). Offering employees to be microchipped enables the employee to gain access into the building, or purchase food. Taking a sceptical viewpoint, this approach could be abused by the company by taking a 'Big Brother' approach to spying on their employees. Although, employees are not forced to be 'microchipped' (Bowerman, 2017).

Wearables and the 'quantified self' community (Nafus, 2016) is a growing area and community whereby people come together to share their experiences of wearables and the quantified self. Within the context of wearable devices and self-monitoring research (Price et al., 2017; Rawassizadeh et al., 2015; Spiller et al., 2018) has shown the approach to monitoring of long-term conditions such as diabetes. In 2017, Diabetes UK reported technology developments to facilitate diabetics to assess their blood glucose levels via a tattoo device (Vega et al., 2017). The respective authors note this technology is not yet available on the open market, but has already been tested on pig skin, showing positive results; and the colour of the tattoo changes in response to different biomarkers (Fig. 2.10). This research was conducted by academics at Harvard University and the Massachusetts Institute of Technology (MIT) and has aimed to overcome existing problems associated with blood glucose monitoring devices.

For several years, digital tattoos (The Medical Futurist, 2021) have been experimented by companies and in the fields of health (Digital Health Central, 2020) as a way of monitoring one's health, considering the design and development of innovative and future considerations of wearables/implantable devices.

The potential benefits for using implantable/injectable devices to monitor one's health in real time and especially if we look to the future, assistive technology and techniques become more sophisticated and accurate, are quite likely to become the norm. For example, health monitoring may prove to be more cost-effective, placing greater ownership and responsibility into the hands of the individual, while alleviating any stressors within health service delivery.

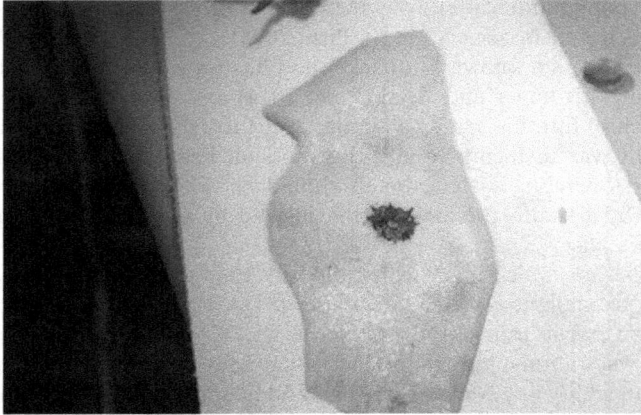

Fig. 2.10.   Diabetes Tattoo from the DermalAbyss Project. *Source*: Permission granted by Dr Viirj Kan.

However, there is a sticking point with this type of technology surrounding data privacy and breaches, security, and ownership of the data (Camara et al., 2015; Isler et al., 2018) and rightly so. But we must look beyond the next decade, and look to the future, of *Transgenerational Technology* being utilised by existing and future younger cohorts who will in 30-, 40- and 50-years' time, be older adults themselves. This means empirical research needs to start now to ascertain the opinions of younger generations including Generation X and Millennials because they are the future ageing population(s).

Summary

Technology throughout the last 40–60 years has made phenomenal advancements which for many of us today we have come to rely on whether it is for work, leisure activities and entertainment or to take ownership and improve one's health and well-being. This chapter illustrates how there is a growing domain of *Transgenerational Technology* in society whereby relationships can be fostered and transitioned throughout the life course as one ages. We have shown how contemporary developments have the potential to refine and equip future ageing cohorts such as Generation X and the Millennials, with many technologies being tested by Baby Boomers and the Silent Generation.

Technology research must reach outside of the confines and echo chambers of academia, with real life impact. Greater efforts are needed from actors, and developers to ensure this is met.

Chapter 3

Adoption, Benefits and Challenges of Technology: Insights from Citizens in Northern Ireland

Introduction

One the of aims of this book is to provide an insight into the role of the stakeholder and the integral role(s) that a stakeholder can play in research projects, and with co-researchers. The stakeholder involvement is important because they are a bridge between researchers and the participants, and often the stakeholder has different insights into the concerns and benefits of many issues experienced by participants.

Chapter 3 explores technology use by adults living across Northern Ireland (NI) during the pandemic. Building on an existing relationship with Age NI, we believe it is important that the stakeholder can share their knowledge, expertise, and experiences with readers of this book. Age NI has vast experience with co-researchers across NI.

Background

Age NI is the leading charity for older people in Northern Ireland. Their vision is a world where everyone can love later life and their mission is to help people enjoy a better later life. For over 30 years, Age NI has provided advice and vital support to thousands of older people, their families, and carers, by supporting them to remain independent and connected to their communities.

Age NI has four strategic pillars:

1. **People**: Provide and develop quality services and support to improve the independence and well-being of older people,
2. **Places:** Prepare for our ageing demographic by creating an age-friendly society,
3. **Policy:** Protect and promote the rights of older people,
4. **Progressive Organisation:** Age NI is a professional, sustainable, well-governed organisation driven by the voice of older people.

Transgenerational Technology and Interactions for the 21st Century: Perspectives and Narratives, 37–74
Copyright © 2022 by Hannah R. Marston, Linda Shore, Laura Stoops, and Robbie S. Turner
Published under exclusive licence by Emerald Publishing Limited
doi:10.1108/978-1-83982-638-220221006

The Age NI Team

Age NI employs 125 staff and involve a circa of 590 volunteers to deliver their diverse portfolio of activity. Led by Age NI Chief Executive, Linda Robinson alongside three directors, Age NI Senior Management Team (2021a) are responsible for the strategic and operational implementation of the Age NI strategy. This Senior Management Team then report to the Age NI Board of Trustees (2021b).

There are currently 14 Age NI Board of Trustee (2021b) members who meet quarterly to agree strategy and provide overall governance and leadership for Age NI, based on a shared vision, mission and values, ensuring the charity fulfils its financial and legal responsibilities and promotes best practice. They have extensive experience, specialising in corporate governance and accountability, business planning, economics and accounting, project management, accountancy, government and law, research, strategic development, public policy, public health, commissioning, and co-design methodology.

Engagement with Older People and Service Provision

In 2020 Age NI had 122,974 direct engagements with older people across their services and identified over £1 million in unclaimed benefits for older people. Age NI are passionate about having older people at the heart of everything they do. In 2010 the Age NI Consultative Forum (CF) (2021c) was formed, and a key focus of the forum is to identify the needs and concerns of older people in relation to issues such as poverty, health, equality, technology, and many other issues. Age NI's CF engages with, advises, and challenges Age NI on policy issues and on its strategic direction.

The work of the Forum covers the whole region of Northern Ireland and focusses on issues affecting people over the age of 50. It works collaboratively with, and in support of, Age NI. Members of Age NI's CF often engage in research projects of interest to them and their life experiences. In recent years members of the CF have engaged in research with academic institutions to explore issues such as social isolation and loneliness, digital exclusion/inclusion, and apps for older people.

Working With Members of the Community

The work that Age NI conducts relies on support from members of the community and that includes recruiting participants for research development groups (RDG), playing a role as co-researchers and participants in workshops.

Informed Consent and Recruitment

Informed consent was collected by Age NI from all participants who were recruited to take part in the workshops to inform this chapter. Age NI moved to a digital form of informed consent, in response to the government COVID-19 guidelines in NI at the time informed consent was obtained (August 2020), coupled with the concerns older people were voicing around receiving post and the possibility of it transmitting COVID-19. Prior to the workshops commencing, all participants were emailed a consent form to review, and the consent form was addressed again at the beginning of the initial workshop whereby each participant was asked to clearly state that they understood the information and to give their consent. As each workshop was recorded, this became the digital evidence of informed consent.

Anonymisation of all participants and quotes align to the guidelines pertaining to Emerald's guidance of informed consent and ethical approval. Participant recruitment for this work involved Stoops joining an Age NI CF online meeting (via Zoom) and presenting the project concept. A participant brief was provided via email to members who demonstrated a potential interest in participating and was circulated across Age NI networks to reach a wide range of people.

Beyond Age NI and their focus on older people, a connection was formed with Mencap NI (n.d.) (based on a previously formed relationship with Stoops and Mencap NI). The motivation for this connection was to gain a younger generation perspective along with insight in relation to disability. Mencap NI strive to improve the lives of people with a learning disability and their families now, and work alongside them for a better future. As part of Mencap's Big Plan, their six strategic priorities are (Mencap NI)

1. Early intervention,
2. Friendships and relationships,
3. Health and social care,
4. Employment,
5. Reducing stigma, and
6. Discrimination.

Project information was reshaped in an Easy Read format and shared with Mencap NI to circulate across their services. This resulted in the recruitment of three cohorts; young people with a learning disability, people with a learning disability being supported to gain employment and staff who support people with a learning disability.

Data Collection

A mixed methods data collection approach was employed, to gain a snapshot of a specific time, while qualitative data (Miller & Glassmer, 2011) can bring additional richness and understanding to a problem(s) that needs greater understanding or possible solution(s). All online workshops were recorded using the Zoom platform and transcribed by one person (Stoops). Data analysis was conducted by Stoops, Shore and Marston and the authors discussed the various themes identified and presented in the following sections.

Quantitative data was also collected between November 2020 and January 2021 which coincided with the second government mandated lockdown in Northern Ireland.

Topic Guide and Questions for Focus Groups

A topic guide was created based on sections used within the COVID-19: Technology, Social Connections, Loneliness and Leisure Activities online survey (Marston, Ivan et al., 2020) and selected questions (below) show the type of questioning,

- 'Do you find that you're using technology differently? And if so, can you give some examples'
- 'Does technology play a role in your relationship? If so, has this always been the case?'
- 'Does technology enhance your relationship or create barriers?'
- 'If you needed to use technology that you were not familiar with, where would you go for support?'
- 'Does technology have a positive or negative impact on your life? Why do you feel like this?'
- 'Do you feel there is a digital divide in society? If so, why do you think this the case?'
- 'Has COVID-19 changed your feelings towards technology? If so, in what ways?'
- 'Are you more, or less, willing to learn how to use technology because of COVID-19? Why do you think this might be?'

Findings from Online Survey

Online Survey by Respondents: Characteristics

A total of 130 people completed the online survey aged between 16 and 85+ years (Table 3.1) and the average age range of respondents is 53–62 years. For context 1.8% (32,400) of people in NI belong to minority ethnic groups. NI remains the least ethnically diverse region in the UK (Northern Ireland Assembly, 2013)

For many COVID-19 resulted in a change in how people lived their lives and the roles they fulfilled. In Table 3.2 we present the various activities and roles respondents report having since COVID-19.

Readers should take into consideration not all survey respondents answered each question.

Table 3.1.   Participant Characteristics.

Characteristics	% (n=111/130)
Ethnicity	
White	96.4 (107)
Chinese	1.8 (2)
Pakistani	0.9 (1)
White/Black African	0.9 (1)

Table 3.1.　(*Continued*)

Characteristics	% (n=111/130)
Age group – years	
16–24	1.8 (2)
25–34	11.7 (13)
35–44	11.7 (13)
45–54	12.6 (14)
55–64	21.6 (24)
65–74	22.5 (25)
75–84	13.5 (15)
85+	4.5 (5)
Gender	**% (n=111/130)**
Male	29.4 (33)
Female	69.4 (77)
Prefer not to say	0.9 (1)
Living circumstances	**% (n=110/130)**
Lived with other people (e.g., partner, friends, family, children, informal carer)	70.0 (77)
Lived alone	24.6 (27)
Live alone with a care package in place	5.5 (6)
Type of community	**% (n=110/130)**
Town	39.1 (43)
City	19.1 (21)
Rural (countryside/village)	41.8 (46)

Table 3.2.　Leisure Activities and Roles Since COVID-19, as reported by survey respondents.

Role/activity*	% (n=109/130)
Outdoor activities (e.g., walking/running)	53.2 (58)
Connecting with friends/family virtually	45.0 (49)
Watching TV or films on streaming services	41.3 (45)
Spending more time in nature (e.g., garden, forests, parks)	38.5 (42)
Attending work-related meetings on communication tools	35.8 (39)
Continuing to work (e.g., WFH, or in the office)	34.9 (38)

(*Continued*)

Table 3.2. (*Continued*)

Role/activity*	% (n=109/130)
Reading	33.0 (36)
Online grocery shopping	31.2 (34)
I am a key worker	29.4 (32)
Baking	22.0 (24)
Attending to spiritual needs (e.g., church services/mass) online	22.0 (24)
Creative activities (e.g., knitting, crocheting drawing, painting, writing)	21.1 (23)
DIY projects	18.4 (20)
Attending virtual exercises sessions (e.g., yoga, Pilates/Joe Wicks)	16.5 (18)
Sharing information on social media sites	14.7 (16)
Gardening/allotment	14.7 (16)
Sleeping more/less	14.7 (16)
Attending virtual educational classes	13.8 (15)
Catching up on reading books	12.8 (14)
Home schooling my children	12.8 (14)
Attending virtual community meetings (e.g., WI, Men's Sheds, or similar community groups)	11.9 (13)
Self-isolating due to vulnerable loved ones	11.0 (12)
Virtually connecting with community support groups	8.3 (9)
Casual selling (e.g., Gumtree, Ebay)	6.4 (7)
Online creative activities with others (e.g., drawing, painting, writing)	6.4 (7)
Searching for activities for my child/children	4.6 (5)
I am a carer	3.7 (4)
Communicating with specific COVID-19 support group(s) for my area	3.7 (4)

*Note: some respondents selected more than one option on some of the questions therefore exceeding 130.

Some respondents noted additional activities including housework, conducting pastoral care – phone calls within the context of the church, attending a day centre, recovering from illness, tidying out wardrobes and cupboards, and genealogy activities.

In addition, respondents were asked how often they are in contact with others since COVID-19 and the majority of respondents (36.4%) reported to have been in contact with someone 'some of the time' (n=40) since the start of the pandemic. While 30.0% reported 'not often' (n=33), 19.1% of people reported 'a lot' (n=21), 13.6% of people reported 'all of the time' (n=15) and one person (0.9%) reported that they had not been in contact with anyone.

Access to the Internet and Purpose

To better understand respondents' level and type of Internet use they were invited to share insights into their usage and level of engagement. In the following table (Table 3.3), we present findings relating to respondent's use and associated characteristics of the Internet.

Table 3.3 presents an insight into how technology is accessed (e.g., physical space), the length and frequency of accessing technology, the purpose for and

Table 3.3.   Internet Characteristics.

Access to the internet*	**% (n=127/130)**
In the home	87.4 (111)
Friends and family home	15.0 (19)
Use public space (e.g., libraries, cafes, Wi-Fi hotspots)	21.3 (27)
Use mobile phone data	55.1 (70)
I do not have access, but I would like to	2.4 (3)
I do not have access; I have no interest in it	9.5 (12)
Other (via employment)	0.8 (1)
Length of time using the Internet/digital devices	**% (n=107)**
>10 years	86.9 (93)
>5 years	13.1 (14)
Frequency of using the Internet/digital devices	**% (n=107)**
More than once a day	92.5 (99)
About once a day	5.6 (6)
More than once a week	0.9 (1)
Less than once a month	0.9 (1)
Purpose*	**% (n=108)**
Social media sites	80.6 (87)
Fact checking	73.2 (79)
Online shopping	74.1 (80)
Online banking	71.3 (77)
Communication (e.g., video/calls, text messages, email)	70.4 (76)
Work-related activities	61.1 (66)
Online learning	55.6 (60)
Streaming	54.6 (59)
Connecting with the community	43.5 (47)
Reading	40.7 (44)
Spiritual needs (e.g., attending services/mass virtually)	26.9 (29)
Recording data (e.g., health, finances)	26.9 (29)

(Continued)

Table 3.3. (*Continued*)

Purpose*	% (n=108)
Casual selling (eBay)	25.9 (28)
Play games with others	9.3 (10)
Creative activities (e.g., drawing, painting, etc.)	9.3 (10)
Dating websites or apps	3.7 (4)
Other (ancestry, listening to music, volunteering, farming)	3.7 (4)
Reasons for not using the Internet/digital devices*	**% (n=115/130)**
I have no interest	66.7 (10)
I don't feel I need it	40.0 (6)
I cannot afford it	33.3 (5)
I have had a bad experience using it	6.7 (1)
I don't feel it is secure	26.7 (4)
I feel nervous to use it	6.7 (1)
Reasons for using the Internet/digital devices in the future*	**% (n=100/130)**
Reduce cost	69.0 (69)
Better access to the Internet	50.0 (50)
Improved accessibility in user manuals (e.g., less jargon)	26.0 (26)
Improved ease of use	34.0 (34)
Better access to learning resources	28.0 (28)
Better accessibility options for people with additional needs	19.0 (19)
Improved information to avoid scam/information theft	35.0 (35)

Note: some respondents selected more than one option on some of the questions therefore exceeding 130.

against using technologies and suggestions to improve accessible technology. Findings show in some instances that many survey respondents believe the cost of technology needs to be reduced, while for those people who do not engage with technology it is because they choose not to. While many people access the Internet in the home, there are other options where technology is accessed such as via data usage via the mobile phone.

Digital Device Ownership, Use and Purpose

In Table 3.4 we present findings relating to respondent's use of digital devices.

Table 3.4 shows various devices are owned by respondents, while 88.2% (n=60) of people also report not using any types of digital devices, and the most frequent device used is a smartphone (74.6%, n=85), while only one person reported to use a smart home device. The reasons for using digital devices are varied and include both personal (including leisure activities) and professional tasks, with 84.2% (n=96) of people using devices for the purpose of communication.

Table 3.4. Digital Device Characteristics.

Digital device ownership*	**% (n=129/130)**
Smartphone	91.9 (102)
Smartwatch/Fitbit	88.2 (60)
Laptop	81.1 (90)
Smart TV	85.5 (71)
Smart home device (e.g., Alexa)	86.6 (58)
Mobile phone	79.8 (71)
Tablet	77.0 (77)
Kindle/e-book	66.7 (46)
Desktop computer	60.4 (58)
Video game console	49.0 (24)
Handheld game console	43.2 (19)
Personal digital assistant (e.g., pager/Blackberry)	29.4 (10)
I have not used any of the above	87.5 (21)
Digital device used most often	**% (n=114/130)**
Smartphone	74.6 (85)
Laptop	7.0 (8)
Tablet	4.4 (5)
Mobile phone	3.5 (4)
Desktop computer	2.6 (3)
Smart TV	2.6 (3)
Handheld game console	1.8 (2)
Smart home device	0.9 (1)
Kindle/e-book	0.9 (1)
Smart Watch/Fitbit	0.9 (1)
Other	0.9 (1)
Purpose for using digital devices*	**% (n=114/130)**
Communication (e.g., video/calls, text messages, email)	84.2 (96)
Fact checking	79.0 (90)
Social networking	79.0 (90)
Online banking	72.8 (83)
Online shopping	72.8 (83)
Work-related activities	53.5 (61)
Online learning/training	52.6 (60)

(Continued)

Table 3.4.   (*Continued*)

Purpose for using digital devices*	% (n=114/130)
Streaming activities	47.4 (54)
Word processing	43.9 (50)
Excel/databases	31.6 (36)
Tracking data (e.g., health/finances)	31.6 (36)
Virtual church services	26.3 (30)
Reading	47.4 (54)
Playing games (individually)	28.1 (32)
Internet (playing games with others	13.2 (15)
Internet (research, e.g., family history)	24.5 (28)
Internet (casual selling, e.g., Gumtree)	26.3 (30)
Creative activities	9.7 (11)
Online dating/apps	6.1 (7)
Other	7.0 (8)

Note: some respondents selected more than one option on some of the questions therefore exceeding 130.

To further explore respondents' opinions on digital skills, they were asked about any difference in the level of digital skills across the generations. Overall, 93.7% of survey respondents thought younger generations have greater or higher digital skills, and 6.3% of respondents thought there was no difference between generations' digital skills.

Learning and Motivations to Technology Use

In the following table, we provide an overview of the findings associated with survey respondents' motivations and learning preferences towards technology.

Highlights from Table 3.5 shows the majority of respondents request assistance from a friend or family member who is younger and from a different generation to themselves (70.4%, n=76), while other responses including trial and error and seeking out online materials provided assistance. The pandemic also changed the motivations of using technology for some respondents, while others reported little change, with 71.2% (n=71) of people using technology to reduce loneliness and stay in touch with friends and family. Although, 17.2% (n=17) of people found the use of technology more stressful and 68.8% (n=75) of people reported how the pandemic did lead them to using technology more frequently.

Changes in Technology Usability in the Home and the Workplace

Given the phenomenal technological developments over the last 10–20 years, the way in which people interact with various technologies can vary from holding a device and multiple button pressing (if playing a videogame) (Marston, 2013b) to swiping left or right on a smartphone screen (Marston, 2010). The survey invited respondents to share their views on how technology has changed in both the home and work environments, as outlined in the Tables 3.5, 3.6.

Table 3.5.   Learning and Motivation Characteristics.

Learning approaches to technology (seeking assistance)*	% (n=108/130)
From a friend/family member from a younger generation than me	70.4 (76)
Trial by error	50.0 (54)
Online materials (e.g., videos/manuals)	50.0 (54)
User manual	22.2 (24)
Online forum	17.6 (19)
Friend/family member from the same generation as me	13.9 (15)
In-store	13.9 (15)
Friend/family member from an older generation than me	2.8 (3)
Other	3.7 (4)
Motivations changed since COVID-19	**% (n=107/130)**
Yes	48.6 (52)
Stayed the same	40.2 (43)
No	11.2 (12)
Has COVID-19 led to you using technology more often?	**% (n=109/130)**
Yes	68.8 (75)
Sometimes	8.3 (9)
No	22.9 (25)
Staying in contact with friends, family, support groups	**% (n=111/130)**
All of the time	49.6 (55)
A lot of the time	31.5 (35)
Some of the time	10.8 (12)
None of the time	7.2 (8)
Motivations (advantages) to using technology to keep in touch with others*	**% (n=99/130)**
Reduced loneliness	71.7 (71)
Improved mental well-being	45.5 (45)
Increased happiness	40.4 (40)
Less worry/stress	30.3 (30)
Feeling more safe and secure	25.3 (25)
Improved health	23.2 (23)

(Continued)

Table 3.5. (*Continued*)

Motivations (disadvantages) to using technology to keep in touch with others	% (n=99/130)
More stress/worry	17.2 (17)
Reduced level of mental well-being	14.1 (14)
Increased loneliness	8.1 (8)
Reduced happiness	7.1 (7)
Feeling less safe and secure	6.1 (6)
I have not experienced any	39.4 (39)

Note: some respondents selected more than one option on some of the questions therefore exceeding 130.

Overall, many of the survey respondents perceived technology usability (Table 3.6) to have become easier, while for some, they perceived usability has become more difficult and, in some instances, has stayed the same. From a workplace perspective, usability was perceived easier while fewer respondents perceived it has become more difficult.

Survey respondents were asked whether in their opinion technology can lead to inequalities (Table 3.7). Additional comments were shared and highlight how technology can increase the digital inequity of people in our society.

Further responses relating to this question include, not being able to afford technology, people are 'made to feel wrong when you don't use it', 'people like me are left behind. I don't want to use it but so many places now try to make you use it', 'Online learning and home schooling are the big issues at the moment', 'not everyone has good network coverage', 'yes, can make younger generations feel unequal if they haven't up to date technology', 'they are unable to access information', 'Without access to certain technology it is much more difficult to apply for jobs, to market one's self, to gain access to better deals when shopping, to book accommodation etc.', 'Although I see the overwhelming benefits of

Table 3.6. Technology Usability.

How has usability of technology in the home (e.g., TVs, game consoles, ovens etc.) changed over the years*	% (n=106/130)
Easier to use	81.6 (62)
More difficult to use	79.0 (30)
Stayed much the same	78.3 (18)
How has usability of technology in the workplace (e.g., computers, photocopiers, fax machines, etc.) changed over the years	**% (n=106/130)**
Easier to use	75.0 (57)
More difficult to use	65.8 (25)
Stayed much the same	69.6 (16)

Table 3.7. Inequalities and Technology.

In your opinion does technology lead to inequalities	% (n=109/130)
Yes	62.4 (68)
Sometimes	30.3 (33)
No	7.3 (8)

technology not everyone has access to it for a variety of reasons. Some can't afford the device or the Internet connection, others just don't want to use it and therefore end up missing out on certain opportunities'.

Sharing Information

The activity of 'sharing' can vary between people and for some sharing information is not only a regular activity across platforms, but it can also generate negative feelings and/or perceptions too. In Table 3.8 we present findings relating to survey respondents' activities around sharing information.

Table 3.8. Sharing Information Via Technology – Characteristics.

Digital devices used to share information	% (n=111/130)
Some of the time	29.7 (33)
None of the time	27.0 (30)
Not often	23.4 (26)
A lot of the time	10.8 (12)
All of the time	9.0 (10)
Why do you share information about yourself*	**% (n=79/130)**
Common interests	48.1 (38)
Start or continue conversations with friends	46.8 (37)
To increase communication in friendships	30.4 (24)
To inform others of my activities	27.9 (22)
Others could evaluate me negatively	11.7 (13)
Because I enjoy it	7.6 (6)
To gain others' opinions	7.6 (6)
To feel better	5.1 (4)
Because I like sharing information	2.5 (2)
To build my confidence	1.3 (1)
Other (e.g., career achievements, event registration, record activities for the future, bank/health/shopping services requirement, communication with friends, etc.)	19.0 (15)

(Continued)

Table 3.8.   (*Continued*)

Concerns about sharing information	
Information being stolen	68.5 (76)
Falling victim to a scam	66.7 (74)
Increase of telephone/mail solicitation	34.2 (38)
Loss of control over who knows this information	27.9 (31)
My choice not to share my information	26.1 (29)
People wouldn't be interested	13.5 (15)
I don't have any concerns	6.3 (7)
People might laugh at me	5.4 (6)
Because it is embarrassing	0.9 (1)
Other (fear of people joining bits of information up, only share face to face, monitoring for health reasons, selective about information sharing)	7.2 (8)

*Note: Some respondents selected more than one option on some of the questions, therefore exceeding 130.

Overall, very few people used devices to share information about themselves, albeit ten people did report 'a lot of the time' and 'all of the time' and their rationale for this activity was primarily associated to common interests (48.1%, n=38) or to start a conversation with friends (46.8%, n=37). Most of the survey respondents (68.5%, n=76) reported their concerns about sharing information are connected to their information/data being stolen, and 66.7% (n=74) of people were concerned about becoming a victim of a scam.

Workshops

Nine workshops were conducted in total. Six workshops involved older people from Age NI and three workshops involved people from Mencap NI. In addition, five interviews were carried out with older people. All interviews were recorded and transcribed by LST and coding was conducted by two members of the team [HM, LST]. We have provided the ages of the participants against the quotes and in some instances some people were not comfortable in specifically detailing their age. Instead, we have provided an age range. Overall, the average age of workshop participants was 71.2 years, Median = 70.5 ± SD = 7.4.

Data analysis shows there are many overlaps between the participants from the two organisations and with this in mind, we are presenting the discussions in a collective format. The overarching themes include '*Technology impact and the role in the pandemic*' with corresponding themes of '*Benefits to using technology*' and '*Challenges to using technology*'. Within each of these, sub-themes emerged through interviewees highlighting additional thoughts and perceptions pertaining to technology learning styles, future perspectives, social connections with friends and family members, and this is visually represented through a mind map (Fig. 3.1).

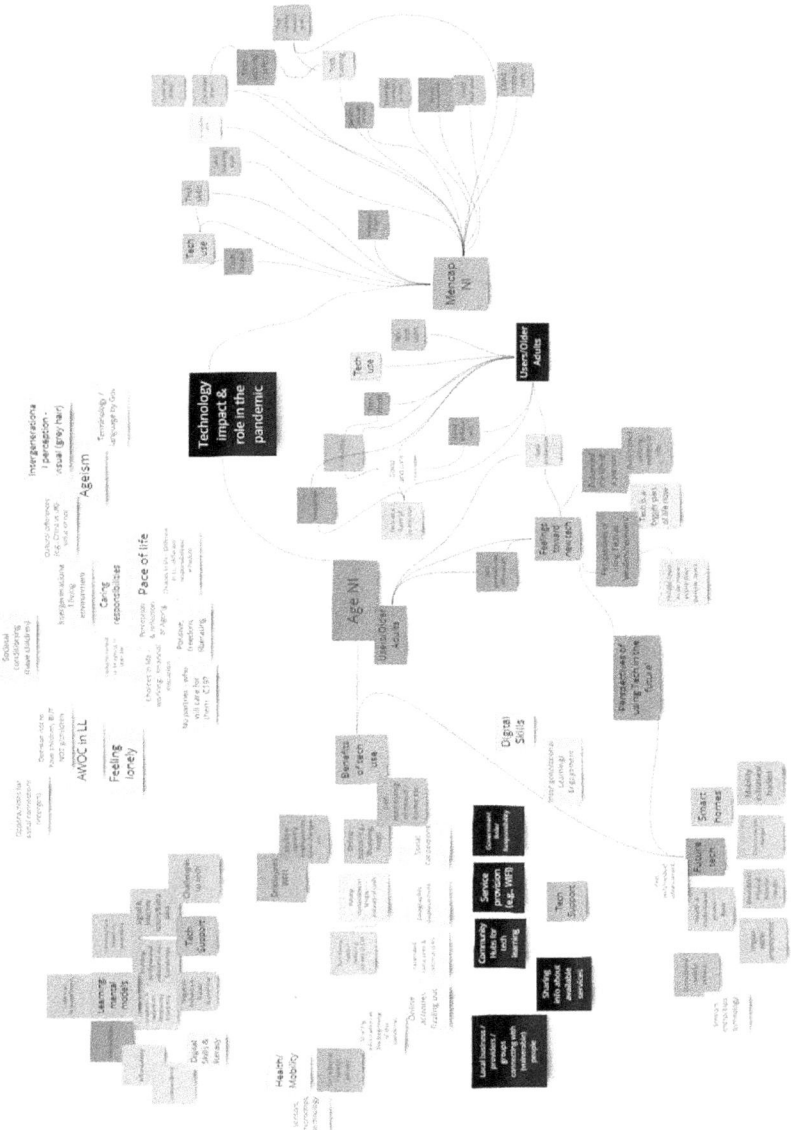

Fig. 3.1.   Concept Mapping From Workshops.

In the following sections, we will explore and unpack the identified themes in a bid to understand how adults across different generations relate to and connect with technology.

Benefits to Using Technology

Enhancing Social Connections, Geography Displacement and Interactions

There are positive responses in relation to using technology during the pandemic to enhance social connections. For some participants their use of online platforms was their first time engaging with online communication platforms whereas for younger participants they regularly use social media platforms to communicate with their friends and family.

> [...] my sons live overseas, and they are both mad into technology, so I use it more for keeping in touch with them on video calls and online games with them. It has even helped during COVID – they can't come home so seeing their faces on video has kept me going. [Female, 65 years]

And for some older people, this new form of communication facilitates greater conversations with their loved ones:

> I get to speak to her more often which is lovely [...]. [Female, 89 years]

For one older person, she describes how technology facilitates her social connections with family members living abroad, and in turn, makes her more cheerful and alert,

> Well, as I've mentioned before, I don't have family here in Northern Ireland, so the use of technology has enabled me to keep in contact with my family members who are in other countries, other parts of the world, and I've used it more since the lockdown to keep in touch with them, and that has just made me feel more cheerful, more alert, more interested, even though I'm living a much more restricted life. [Female, 78]

> [...] Because I do live well away from my family members. They're scattered all around the world. Because of modern technology, I can keep close to people in Australia, in America, in various parts of Britain and Ireland. And you know that feeling of being left out and isolated is considerably improved by the fact that I can get in touch with them at any time and have just even the silly conversations. They don't have to be serious conversations, just to know what they're doing, and to hear their news and to hear their voices. And at times I actually do see them through Zoom. Indeed,

I think that is a wonderful asset and I'm very, very grateful for that. [Female, 78]

Throughout the pandemic we have heard little information about how technology is playing a role in the lives of citizens, who are in their 30s and 40s. The following quote illustrates how technology plays a role in the life of a 42 year old male participant specifically when communicating with family members or others who are abroad:

> Technology, especially now with COVID playing such a large part in our lives, has become more prevalent within our everyday relationships. It has reached a point wherein we can instantly talk to any family member, be they 5 miles from me, or on the other side of the world. It has replaced the older postal methods, the snail mail system which took days or weeks to arrive, or fax which relied heavily on phone networks, allowing us to have a fully connected life. [Male, 42]

The quote above is not so dissimilar from older participants who were interviewed, and illustrates how technology facilitates this Gen X'er to maintain their social connections, and leisure activities,

> During COVID it has certainly enhanced relationships, allowing video calls, or games with people who are not with you, or cannot see. It has enhanced our ability to spend time with family around us from the point of connections with family and friends. [Male, 42]

The same Gen'xer describes how if he did not have access to technology, his 'world' would be a lot smaller,

> Without the ability to contact some other family members or friends who live on the other side of the world, my world would be that much smaller. Having family further afield that can be contacted is amazing. [Male, 42]

A mother [89 years] and daughter [65 years] describe how their use of technology plays a role in their daily lives, while offering reassurance to the daughter knowing that her mum can easily connect to her via the device:

> Mum would be on her own a lot more as I can't be up at the house with her all the time. I think the tablet helps her feel like she has company even if she is just watching cooking videos or attending online mass. Because I know she has this company I don't feel as worried about her living on her own. Now that she is getting better at using the tablet and mobile, she gets in touch with me more to ask questions about them. So, without this we might not speak just as often. [Female, 65]

In a pre-pandemic world many people may not have been familiar with online communication platforms. However, because of the pandemic many people transitioned quickly to using online platforms for various reasons,

> [...] I never would have used Zoom to meet, talk to my family, or see my family but because of COVID I use it a lot I'm very close to my sisters. They live quite a distance away, so we've used it an awful lot. But even my phone I'm using for exercise, for yoga, I wouldn't ever have done that prior to COVID. [Female, 35–45]

Adoption of (New) Platforms and Devices

Adopting new technologies can be both exciting, as well as daunting, especially when there are numerous platforms available, adopted by both individuals and organisations alike. For some people, the prospect of using a new platform can be a positive experience, especially when a person is already familiar with existing platforms,

> [...] That was what happened to me with computers that I'm using much more Zoom and other platforms. Yesterday I was on a platform called WebEx and with a three-hour workshop and it was like, oh, but it was so sophisticated. They had breakout groups and all sorts of stuff going on. And I mean, it really was amazing. And so, I think I've used WhatsApp, FaceTime, Skype, and other platforms for quite a few years now. I belong to different things, but certainly C19 has a much more focused and improved version of all of those happening. So, it's a much bigger part of my life now than it has ever been. [Female, 65]

The ability to 'tap' one's debit/credit card in a shop while purchasing goods is a popular method of payment today. Yet, for some older people, this approach of tapping one's card for small purchases was unfamiliar and suspicious:

> [...] I never paid for the small purchases by tapping and I never shopped with my card. I always either paid cash or if I had to use a card, I would just use my pin to authorise it. I always felt the tapping, it seemed like a bit sort of slightly dodgy. And I didn't really want to have a long list of my purchases on my on my bank card anyway. [Male, 74]

The same person realises during the pandemic how paying for goods by 'tapping' the card against the reader, was a safer option for retail employees, himself and for other members of the community, instead of handing cash over, because of the possibility of virus transmission,

> But then it dawned on me at the beginning of this pandemic, when I did go, very rarely, but I was actually paying by cash and then suddenly realised that for the people behind the till this wasn't a good

idea. And for their safety, I needed to forget about paying by cash and actually use my card, just tap it and got on with it. So that's an example of actually my realisation that other people needed me to do this rather than that I needed to do it. Yeah, it was for the greater good of others I suppose as a way to prevent the spread. [Male, 74]

People who were categorised as most vulnerable by the UK government were advised to shield and use online grocery stores to order food. The quote above illustrates how the mindset of the participant changed because of the societal situation. Similarly, this is true for many people during COVID-19 who have switched to online shopping.

Additionally, another participant describes how they had 'to get a grip' of changing their behaviour, even though initially they struggled with a specific retail outlet,

[…] is getting my entire food supply online. And I never, ever thought of doing that before. And I've had various times of poor health, feeling less well and therefore unable to go shopping. But I've always managed one way or another without ever thinking of going online. But I just thought I got to get a grip on this. And I'm not a shopper. I don't like shopping. I regard it as a chore. But I mean, I did come to grips with that with the Tesco website. It just took a bit of a struggle. But I was absolutely determined this is going to have to be something I could do. And, of course, it's I just find it relatively straightforward. I've learnt how to do it and what I was forced to learn. I forced myself to learn, but it did so well, that it's fine. And I'm certain I'm not going to go back to my old ways. Not now, I'm definitely going to continue with the online shop. And that's not to say I won't occasionally visit shops, but I don't need to now. [Male, 74]

This quote is a key example of how the relationship between technology and people has evolved during the pandemic, even though there was apprehension and a reluctance to learn and use online shopping platforms for groceries.

This approach to shopping could and is having a catastrophic effect on the high street and stores as described by Philips et al. (2021), who ask in their timely paper whether the WHO age-friendly cities and communities' framework should consider greater expansion in a post-pandemic society, relating to the revival of the high streets and town centres. Many people were required to use online shopping sites during the pandemic, for some people, this ease will be beneficial, because there is the ability to select convenient deliveries, manage the household budget and only buy products that are needed.

Generation X are a cohort that is overlooked in society, sandwiched between the Baby Boomers and the Millennials; and people who are Generation X are a cohort that for some have grown up with technology, and video games (Brown & Marston, 2018; Marston & del Carmen Miranda Duro, 2020). For many Gen X'ers they use technology for various reasons including work, leisure, and day-to-day activities. One participant describes his rationale for using technology to facilitate greater opportunities to continue working and connecting with colleagues during the pandemic,

> I would probably use either my smart phone or my laptop more than anything, my laptop is my main workplace tool, allowing me to complete my daily tasks whilst remaining in contact with other team members. In the same vein, my smart phone is a source of contact for work, personal, and also a source of entertainment. [Male, 42]

This quote illustrates how a smartphone in his life is integral for their daily activities, while his laptop acts as a portal for him to connect to his work colleagues, enabling him to work from home and carry out other daily and leisure activities.

Leisure Activities

Throughout 2020 the UK devolved governments mandated lockdowns reducing citizens opportunities to continue their leisure pursuits in the way they did in a pre-pandemic society. In our workshops, some participants shared their experiences of using technology to maintain their leisure activities and spiritual needs,

> [...] I think that if we're going to be in a long period of COVID-19, I think it is important that people start focusing on these ideas of wellbeing and maybe spirituality and particularly amongst our age group, because my guess is that a lot of older people have still got good connections with the church. [Male, 77]

Another interviewee describes how both virtual and physical church services continued to function in her (surrounding) area, enabling members of the congregation to maintain connection to fellow worshipers:

> [...] because I am a very active member of the local church, and we have a whole cluster of churches around here where I live. And I can assure you that we are very active. We do have our services online. We do speak to one another. We have all kinds of ways of meeting although the churches are not actively having their Sunday services again.
>
> They are obviously following regulations that are keeping spaced out and they have gone to tremendous lengths to make sure that it's going to be safe attending their own local services. They have overflow into their own church halls and other parts of their buildings to make sure that anybody who wants can come along. And admittedly, when you are actually inside the building for worship, you can't be less than two meters. But people tend to then go out into the car parks afterwards. And although, again, you can't be near them two meters, I can assure you there's any amount of

supportive conversations go on. And because we tend to think of ourselves as church families and we tend to sort of do a lot of what you might call social intermingling as well. And that can't happen physically. But it certainly can happen in other ways. [Female, 78]

This quote shows how members of the church are still able to support one another, be-it in the physical environment of a car park or by online platforms, the quote demonstrates how support is shared with wider members of one's family who are geographically displaced. For many people, during the pandemic, receiving support regardless of the format will have been and continues to be comforting:

So, I think people who belong to churches do feel supported now and the take up on the online services is immense. You know that the members of the congregation actually forward our online services to members of their family who are living somewhere entirely different, indeed in different parts of the world. So, there's tremendous outreach going on through that particular way. [Female, 78]

However, as the female participant below notes she is not a religious person herself, but she can understand why some citizens may seek comfort:

I'm not a religious person at all. And I never go to church nor would I ever set foot in the church if I can possibly avoid it. But I do have a lot of friends and family who are deeply into church activities and their presence online is tremendous. So, I think if you already have a connection to a particular church, they've done amazing work, you know, and all across social media and everything. It's just unbelievable, people do get a lot from them and what they need from them I believe. But I also make the point that there's other ways and other methods of spirituality that doesn't have to be connected to God or church or whatever, and that's where I would get a lot of my sense of well-being from these other ways. And there's a huge Internet presence for that. But really, I take the point what you're saying, GB, if you're not already connected to it, you may not know this is happening. [Female, 65]

The description above shows how there are alternative ways to receiving spiritual well-being which is more suitable for her and possibly others who are not aware of virtual meetings, and this is positively acknowledged by a male participant who notes:

That is a really good point of access to these things. I acknowledge. It's also quite interesting too that it is growing. There's a growing awareness, of the offering of churches. You know, there's a lot of people out there who don't have any connection to churches and aren't aware of all of this. [Male, 77]

Offering virtual church services across (different) communities (White, Marston, Shore, & Turner, 2020), can enable people to attend them, from the comfort of their home (White et al., 2020), without having to travel,

> My tablet, I use it for lots of things. I like to watch mass, sometimes from different parishes and watching cooking videos on it. When we do the video calls, I use the tablet so I can see everyone better. [Female, 89]

Conversely, for some older female participants in the workshops, using their devices to access social media channels gave them the opportunity to engage with leisure groups:

> […] I use it for phoning and texting but can watch videos on it and do video calls. I sometimes play games on it and use it to keep in touch with the sewing group I am in on Facebook. [Female, 65]

Routine was for many people important during the pandemic, and one interviewee describes how she uses her Kindle to read the newspapers in the morning,

> I read on Kindle a lot, I also get my two newspapers every day on online. I will read one before I even get out of bed in the morning. I would lie and read one of them and read the other one later in the day. So, I actually do a lot of reading. Yes, but it tends to be on my Kindle. [Female, 78]

Yet, members of staff at Mencap NI describe how technology plays a role in their leisure time, which for some interviewees has resulted in behaviour changes during the pandemic:

> But even my phone I'm using for exercise, for yoga, I wouldn't ever have done that prior to COVID. And even podcasts, I never listened to a podcast prior to COVID and now I love them. I cannot get enough podcasts. So, there are a lot of benefits and environmentally I think it's better we're not traveling the same. That's a big thing that tends to be neglected. And certainly, I would think it is a big benefit. [Female, 35–45]

> I would never even have humoured the likes of a virtual concert; I would never have gone on YouTube to sit and watch a concert or anything but do now. I have really enjoyed having access to the likes of the National Theatre and other things that you've been able to do, but it's very much as a better than nothing kind of situation. So as this all goes over, I will increasingly go back to as much face to face as I can. [Female 25–35]

However, one interviewee describes how she would prefer to spend her leisure time outside, or baking instead of constantly being on her smartphone:

I would rather be outside, I think because I spend so much time on a screen, I would be like give me the garden, do a bit of baking, do a bit of art in my free time. So that's how I sort of balance it out. I'm a big mobile phone at the dinner table is definitely a no, no. It is my pet hate; they go in the drawer and that's it. [Female, 35–45]

Positive Aspirations for Technology – Thoughts and Attitudes

During the workshops, participants posited concepts surrounding community led initiatives and hubs as a way for members of the community to drop-in and attend classes, seek out informal advice and enhance their knowledge and digital skills:

> [...] I'm just wondering if it goes down to the real basics, you know, about people getting to know about the technology and being introduced to it. Would it be through the churches? You know, the library has the computers there that you can use for free advertising, maybe have a class there. You're probably thinking, well, you couldn't have one to one maybe. But after COVID, after things are sorted a wee bit better and, you know, advertising in the day centres having something there to introduce people, you know, where you can have a one to one with somebody and introduce people into it that way. [Male, 74]

Another participant concurs and highlights the need for greater one-to-one support to facilitate their learning in the respective environment,

> Yeah. To make the information more readily available. And those services that are already there and people there to actually show people what to do. And because X we're only able to learn if we see it, you know. [Female, 66]

And another interviewee describes a local initiative – an introductory course for people who wish to learn about technology, while suitable course advertisement is needed to ensure everyone is aware of these courses,

> [...] Engage with Age do run introductory classes on technology. You know, for people who have had no experience at all, only it's not happening now, but it's a very useful course. They do run them periodically. You know, it's something for anybody who wishes to know about technology. It'll be in the newsletter or something, giving people information about technology. People need to know where to go and what to do. And it needs to be advertised. And, you know, if you aren't familiar with it, people can see it, maybe in a shop window or with a local newsletter going round or something. That's the way to go. [Male, 74]

Taking an intergenerational standpoint, one interviewee describes and suggests the possibility of bringing younger and older people together to share knowledge and to assist with various skills and methods of learning new technologies,

> [...] I think the idea of maybe having a focused program where intergenerational, direct mentoring, to young people mentoring older people or older people mentoring younger people. That would sort of work in a way, would be of some interaction and some learning in it and it would be maybe more face to face and rather than doing everything online. [Female, 67]

The following quotes strengthen this notion of intergenerational learning and support, and provides real life examples of how access to the Internet is available in the community using Internet cafes,

> What we could do if/when we come out of COVID or even during it, is maybe set up something on the style of Internet cafes where people who want to learn would come in and learn maybe less formally, they won't be taught directly. The focus has to be on learning, not on somebody teaching you something. So, we could maybe use that idea of maybe where there's people who volunteer to help people get their hands on experience. Again, this happens in a library anyway. I think that most librarians do, but it might be a way of maybe getting it more formalised if you like. Subsidies are worked out as a proper response to help people get online. [Male, 77]

> Can I just quickly say, Internet cafes, when I was working in Eastern Europe, they were an essential life support system because you couldn't get a connection anywhere else in your hotel. I would have to go. [Male, 74]

The availability and access to Internet cafes in Europe, as suggested by the male participant above illustrates how possible community hubs could serve members of the community, be-it as residents or visitors. who used them due to the poor connectivity in the hotel.

> I do have a family member who I rely on all the time who is over in Yorkshire. Just yesterday, because there's some complicated thing with my email provider, they were doing funny things and we had to do stuff and I couldn't really understand what I was supposed to do. I had my son on FaceTime and on my phone. He's looking at my screen and he's telling me what to do. And I'm older so the multiple use of technology saved his time on the phone. I love doing all these things with it. Took us ten minutes what would take me three hours to do. Doing this was my son's idea, I'd have to say. Of course, it was his idea. [Male, 74]

Utilising multiple platforms by the son was the best approach because of geographic displacement and the most appropriate way to rectify the problem was to share the platform, enabling the son to solve the technical issues. This too alleviated any stress and apprehension by his father.

The quote below highlights how modern technology and platforms can facilitate a 'hands-on experience' for people who are volunteering in public and community spaces such as libraries.

> It's just this idea of linking in with all the groups and all the people where they are and delivering training and things like that. They used to do the Workers Education Association, and of course, the government pulled the funding about 15 years ago and they closed down in Northern Ireland. It's a huge loss. It would have filled the gap. It would have contributed to filling the gap, certainly. [Female, 67]

However, because of funding cuts community initiatives such as training hubs have ceased, but instead could act not only as training for residents in the community but wider afield, these kinds of initiatives could act as a way of connecting people together who are isolated and have skills and knowledge to share.

From an entertainment perspective one young interviewee describes how his game playing equipment can interact with him via haptic feedback, as he sits in a gaming chair:

> I have a chair which uses technology – it is a gaming chair (showed the chair). You can connect to Switch; you can play music you can play the sounds on the chair speakers. It is a purely game chair, it doesn't help you to get fit. It can vibrate when you do certain actions on certain Switch games. [Male, 17–23]

Haptic feedback is common throughout game playing practices, and depending on the type of game being played coupled with the actions and interactions being conducted by the gamer/player, the haptic/vibrations feedback will differ and will be felt through the chair or the game pad (Marston, 2010).

Intergenerational Engagements

We continue the notion of learning and engagement from the standpoint of intergenerational relationships and technology. Some interviewees note how they do not have extended family members to call upon and are ageing without children (AWOC):

> Well with me not having any younger generation to call on when it comes to new things, I try to blunder along on my own and try to get instructions. I try to understand what all these things that are referred to by their initials are, I just get up in despair. [Female, 78]

The same interviewee posits how a 'buddy system' may afford those older adults who are single and do not have younger people to call upon when needing assistance:

> If there was some system or somebody's got to put together a system where you could kind of buddy up as a single older person, you could buddy up with somebody younger, who had the time and the interest to actually be available to help you. If you've got stuck, I would love to be able to lift the phone to somebody and say I don't know how to do this, could you possibly pop over and tell me? Tell me how to do it or show me how to do it. That would be absolutely wonderful. If somebody would think of some sort of scheme where you got to be buddied up with a younger person who is competent, and also willing and interested. A lot of young people wouldn't be bothered helping but some would, and I just wish I knew one. [Female, 78]

Similarly, another interviewee describes how younger people in his community are reaching out and asking him for technical solutions,

> I'm going to take you up on the point of the younger people, I actually get younger people knocking on my door asking me how do we do this on my computer? I have young people that will come along with their new things and say I don't know how to use this; can you help me? So, I don't think it's about age, I think I am in the position I am in because I've grown up with this and I've adopted it as a challenge along the way. I mean, I'm looking on my phone now and I've got 70 different little buttons to press. [Male, 82]

One interviewee describes how using the Zoom platform facilitated a regular family quiz night, enabling members of the family who live across different regions of Ireland to join in, to bridge and enhance social connections,

> Since last year me and my family on a Saturday night do a quiz and we all kind of take it in turns each week on who is going be the quizmaster this week. Sometimes if there is a holiday coming up there will be a theme for it. Mum had done one for Easter this year for the last quiz and it was pretty good. I ended up finding out that the tallest Easter egg ever made was 10ft tall. I have learnt a bunch of random did you know facts that my brain probably doesn't need but it is a good conversation starter. We have been doing that for over a year now and some of my mums' cousins down in Wicklow were able to join us on Zoom so that was pretty good. Learning a bunch of random facts and getting to see some relatives who I wouldn't normally see. [Female, 17–23]

> I showed my granny how to use technology about two years ago. She didn't know how to use it, like her phone. I taught her how to use the phone and after that she used it and she has two technologies now. I was able to show her but now my cousin, she is 9, shows granny how to do everything so I don't have to do much. [Female,17–23]

Digital Skills, Confidence, and Training

As we will discuss in greater detail in Chapter 6, digital skills can be a common issue surrounding digital take-up. For many people, the pandemic thrusted them into using various types of platforms which were unfamiliar to them. In the following quote, a member of staff from Mencap NI describes her learning experience with two different platforms,

> I have to say when the pandemic started and there was talk of Teams and Zoom, I am a technophobe and I put my hand up to that. I don't even know where to start, but it has been good just to learn and the trainees laugh when they see that it's me in control because they go, okay so you're just going to disconnect us. And I went, yeah. There's just been a real ease I guess with it. You know there'll be bumps where you hit the wrong button. A lot of our guys have accepted that and don't want it to be a performance, all singing, all dancing. [Female, 35–45]

And with learning anything new, one's confidence needs to be maintained. Yet, with technology there are always new platforms or features being rolled out and for some people, word of mouth is usually how this information is shared,

> My personal habits I wouldn't say have overly changed I'm maybe a wee bit more confident using say the odd video call or voice notes and things on WhatsApp. But I have a friend who's an early adopter of technology and always tells us, oh there's this new app, oh you can do this, or you can do that. And that kind of helps me decide on whether or not I want to bother with them. I tend not to. [Female, 25–35]

Additionally, younger interviewees share their experiences of learning new software and devices, for educational purposes,

> Microsoft Access is so difficult; you should try to learn it. I had to use it for my course, but I am not a big fan. I was doing essential skills ICT in college there and the course has ended now. But I had to use Microsoft Access and Excel and like things I wouldn't have used before. It was just all numbers everywhere and it was talking about all these complex terms and things like that. My teacher helped which you know was very appreciated, but I hadn't a clue really. I had trouble finding out where the currency button was, it was just small things like that. [Female, 17–23]

Learning to set up new hardware can be difficult and may result in seeking out assistance from a family friend as one interviewee describes,

> The first time I got my iPad brand new, and I had to set it up. My cousins got me to put it on and they helped as I had no idea how to set it up and they were very good. [Female, 17–23]

Another interviewee describes how she feels apprehensive using her sister's computer for fear of deleting an item, and how using older computers can result in slower processing times, and accessing programs,

> My computer was second hand from my dad's work, so it is much slower than it is usually. So, when my assignments were due, I wasn't allowed to type on the page, and I couldn't get into Microsoft Word on Teams, so I had to get my teachers to email me the work. My younger sister is doing her exams at the minute for A-Levels. So, I can use her computer, but I feel like if I use her computer, I could delete something. [Female, 17–23]

This quote illustrates the complexity of language for some people across the generations, while for some people, they may only think it is older adults who struggle with understanding the language and jargon.

Surveillance

There has been growing discourse surrounding surveillance cameras in care homes (Care Quality Commission, 2015; Fisk, 2015; Fisk & Flórez-Revuelta, 2016; Learner, 2018). However, some young interviewees, describe how cameras are installed across the family's farm to enable their respective fathers to maintain surveillance on livestock and the property,

> My dad has the cameras up the farm and it's like that it is very good checking on the phone how the cattle is. It is to check on when they are having babies. [Female, 17–23]

Additionally, one young person describes how their father can make payments to the vet via the phone,

> My dad has this thing on his phone too so he can check in on all his cows and on payments like vets' cheques and stuff like that. [Female, 17–23]

Challenges to Using Technology

Adopting New Technologies and Safety Concerns

Some interviewees describe how their children have concerns about their safety within the home, which may impact upon the integration of new devices. One interviewee describes how she was reluctant to engage with new specific devices, but relented based on her children's concerns for her safety when they were not around:

> If I need it, I will try it but most things I don't really need. My children keep saying about getting me one of those Alexa things, but it sounds a bit silly to me. Why would I want to talk to it and tell it what to do? I like the tablet and mobile, but some of these other things seem silly. You don't want to be lazy and just tell a machine what you want. I told them I don't want one. They think it would be good if I fall to ring someone. I agreed to an emergency button that I wear round my neck, and I don't like it. The one time I did fall a few weeks ago I didn't have it on – it is too hard to remember to always wear it. [Female, 89]

This quote offers intergenerational insights, from the perspective of children who are concerned about their mother falling in the home environment. While their mother does not see the importance of integrating such a device into the home because, for her (the mother), integrating this type of technology has the potential to make her and others lazy.

This interviewee [Female, 89] notes how she negotiated with her children to wear a device around her neck which in turn appeases the children's apprehension to her safety and health. Similar safety concerns were identified in workshops conducted in the *Technology In Later Life* (*TILL*) study. Participants from the TILL study, Freeman and colleagues (2020) identified similar safety concerns by children, and the attitudes of their children towards their parents. However, in this context, this participant specifically describes how when she did fall, she was not wearing the device around her neck as she forgets to wear the device. Therefore, her children could argue had their mother agreed to installing a virtual assistant (VA) device (e.g., Alexa/Google Home) into the home, she could have raised the alarm.

Conversely, White and colleagues (2020) propose a concept through a unified modelling language (UML) diagram of a system which may have assisted this participant to select her primary contact (PC) at the time of falling, and had the PC not been available, the system would move to the next contact in the stored list and so on. Similarly, such a concept could also be integrated into the VA device, once the initial setup of the VA device had been conducted in the home.

Social media use is reportedly common and popular with younger cohorts (Marston, 2019). However, for one young interviewee she describes her reluctance and hesitancy of using certain social media platforms and instead prefers to send text messages,

> I would mainly choose WhatsApp and Instagram to text people. I don't know about the rest of you, but I am not so comfortable using Facetime, but I am OK using Zoom. I am not 100% sure why that is but I think it has something to do with camera angles, but yeah, I would really text people much more than Facetime. [Female, 17–23]

Opening and setting up a new device or computer can be daunting for anyone, especially because it can be common for new models of smartphones not to come with an instruction booklet. In the following conversation, interviewees describe the complexities of learning a new device and share some positive advice to everyone during the workshop:

> [...] I have good advice, if you don't know how to set up a phone or laptop or whatever use YouTube. There are always handy videos there. They have photos, everything you need. They even say what all the stuff is. [Male, 17–23]

> --I might try that next time. [Female, 17–23]

> --YouTube have a lot of videos like green screen or photos of what you have to do. You know accessibility or any of that. When I first got my phone, I was very confused about how to turn it off. It turns out the button I thought turned it off was an emergency SOS. So, you have to hold two buttons to switch it off, not sure why Apple did that. [Male, 17–23]

> --Yeah, I have one where you have to turn it off with two buttons. My other iPad you just turn it off with one button which is easier. [Female, 17–23]

This conversation is rich, insightful, and informative, because it highlights issues that are true to novice users of technology. However, solutions such as YouTube videos which offer visual examples can provide vital information to solving the problem. Additionally, changes to hardware devices can also be problematic with the placement of buttons changing and may in some instances result in the SOS button being pressed.

Health and Technology

The use of technology also known as telehealth/medicine (Fisk et al., 2020), and which can include online consultations were rolled out as a way of reducing the risk of virus transmission. Older interviewees describe how they were informed via health professionals of the impact technology was having,

> [...] I have a friend who is a GP and was using it during the early stages of the pandemic and one of the problems that she had was that when you see someone walking into your surgery you're making an assessment, even before they sit down on the chair. She finds it really stressful trying to assess someone's needs or make a diagnosis over zoom and this was trained professional GP in the job for 25 years. Her concerns were that hopefully this is not the way we're going down, maybe for a triage or something. But yeah, to try and make a full diagnosis she said she finds it very, very

stressful. Even things like unsaid cues, body language, things that were not being said, as opposed to things that were being said, and expanding upon that. So, it's more difficult to pick those up, on a virtual platform. [Female, 55–65]

Additionally, for some people, the notion of using online resources to identify possible health ailments in particular older adults, brought greater concern for one medical professional (a GP) who describes how this method is accelerating, leading to the respective patient 'demanding' medication for treatment,

> My eldest son is a GP. And his biggest problem at the present moment is that there are elderly people who go online to look for symptoms and things like that, and then come into the surgery and tell him what's wrong with them. And he said, it's getting worse and worse. He said, they go online, and they've got a spot on their arm then suddenly they've got a major illness and they're coming in demanding this medication, demanding everything else it is a pain in the butt for many doctors. [Male, 82]

However, two female interviewees describe their positive experiences of using technology to ascertain their health issue,

> No, it went completely the other way for me because I had a rash on my stomach and when I looked on Google, I saw that it was exactly where shingles normally is. And the fact that I felt numb across that area for a few days, meant it was quite likely to be shingles. So instead of waiting a few days to see whether anything developed and what happened with this rash, I phoned the doctor. I got the rash in the evening, and I phoned the doctor the next morning and I was on antivirals by lunchtime. If I'd have delayed it, I would have had a lot of pain that I didn't have so it can work very much in your favour. [Female, 67]

> In my case I would say that Google was actually lifesaving because several years ago I had felt very sick all of a sudden, developed a very stiff neck and a headache. And I sat on the edge of the bed thinking maybe if I lie down, I will be OK. But I had my phone with me, and I googled the symptoms, and it came up with meningitis or brain haemorrhage. [...] in that instance I looked and thought right I'm not going to lie down even though I really wanted to. Without having Googled it I think I may have lay down and had a sleep. It spurred me into action. [Female, 65]

Continuing from the description above, another interviewee describes the importance of being listened to by their health practitioner, while describing how the GP is the overall 'gatekeeper' to referrals,

> I think with any consultation, whether it's virtual or whether it's face to face, if you feel you've been listened to, you're more likely

to take onboard what they're saying. But if you feel that sort of dismissing, you're not really listened to, it doesn't matter whether it's virtual or face to face, it affects your confidence. I mean, the face to face is very important. But at the end of the day a lot of the face to face is just referring you to somewhere else. For example, I've been trying to get a blood test done. And I have to get a GP to do that. But I've been ringing the receptionist and saying could I have a blood test but no I can't do that unless the GP refers me. So often, the GP is a gatekeeper to another person. You can't go and get yourself an X-ray without going to a GP, but the GP doesn't need the other records. And then they'll agree to whatever X ray. I mean obviously Google Health is gonna happen. But we need to actually be part of the process of saying what will work and what won't work. That's what we can do for our representative groups. But I don't think we can stop it. [Male, 77]

These quotes illustrate the differing relationships between patient, health professional, and technology, and while technology is not a quick fix for diagnosis, the quotes presented here show how some older adults are positive towards using technology.

Learning and Training

While there have been notions and mooting's by interviewees to instil greater access to community courses, in community spaces such as libraries. Access is just one facet that can act as a barrier, whereas language/jargon can be another barrier and challenge,

I have tried technology courses in the library a couple of times, never very satisfactorily. They're always run by younger people. Obviously, they take a lot for granted that I just don't understand particularly the use of the jargon. As J has said, the words they use. I'm saying, what's that? I also find that as I get older, I don't want to learn on the day. Yes, that's fine. I understand it and so on. But see, twenty-four hours later, a week after, a month after, I'm afraid it's not there it's not quite sticking one way or the other. But I think I just don't take things in that way. And as a result, when I'm in a class like that, I need to be writing it down on paper all the time and to be shown how to do things. I'm writing down steps, that's one step, two steps. And they're looking at me in amazement, you know, because it's obvious to them that you click there and then you click that and so on and so forth. But I actually have to break it all down on paper and it's very difficult for the younger generation to understand that they're still there showing you this wonderful system. But at the end of the day, I'm writing it down with pen and paper. I know if I don't do so, I'll not remember it. [Female, 78]

This quote highlights several concerns including terminology and jargon being used, while many courses are run by younger people which as noted in the quote, the participant feels there is a sense and lack of understanding to the needs and issues experienced by older users who are wanting to learn how to use technology. The participant continues to describe her learning styles, and while she may have understood the various processes in the session, it is not until later, in her home whereby, she has forgotten how to execute a task. This participant describes how a step-by-step approach suits her learning style, being shown how to do a task, while making notes.

Moreover, designers of technology could apply learning mode features that are easily accessible by users who seek a 'refresh' for example, reminder of how to access/send text messages, like the approach conducted in the '*Adapt Tech, Accessible Technology*' (ATAT) project (Marston, Morgan et al., 2021; Morgan et al., 2020). Another interviewee describes how he finds classes and training intimidating given his limited experience. He describes his preferred learning style, including the instructor being external to his familial network and having someone who can sit next to him. Specifically, this interviewee describes how he has ceased seeking support from his family members, because of how he feels – intimidated and describes how he uses various platforms, all of which vary with their interface and task-related processors:

> […] I find that most of the training is a bit intimidating if you are coming cold to it and I've always learnt better by sitting beside someone. I have to say that I've learnt from others, but it has to be somebody who is not in the family. I find my family very intimidating when I ask them anything about technology. So, I've stopped asking them because they haven't got the skills to actually understand that I may be coming from a very crude sort of understanding of things. So, I need a stranger really. But sitting beside them, I think that is a good way of picking up on technology because they can use shortcuts and stuff like that. Maybe you take a note in a book and that will help you the next time. I mean, I'm working across five different systems and every one of them have slightly different modifications within the system. And I miss that. The most important site for me is the one that gives me my pay. Because I've got to go on or whatever, so I've learnt to use those ones, I'm not working for nothing. […]. [Male, 77]

These two powerful quotes present the reality of feelings, needs, impact and requirements of older adults situated within the learning/educational context,

> […] Sometimes when you're making a phone call, and you're putting the text in, the text is ahead of you. It's putting in things you didn't want. But I think we're moving into an era where you could have echo devices. For instance, P could talk to his washing machine, you could say look, I want a mixed wash with a short spin, can you do that? And talk to it. [Male, 77]

Technology development is advancing at a fast pace and for many people, this is not only off-putting but intimidating, and realising how the future of technology will continue to change. As described above, whereby a person will be able to talk to a washing machine.

Technology Barriers and Negative Experiences

The following quote describes how technology for a Gen X'er has both positive and negative detractors based on the input device(s) associated with the respective device,

> I am more than happy to work with any technology, no matter what the requirement for it is, with a fair amount of ease. It does not mean that there are some technologies that I believe are not as important as others, there are some items that are more useful to me in everyday life than others, and therefore do not see the need of using or owning other. I suppose an example of that would be a technology that allows you to write on a screen using a stylus pen or a tablet or surface computer and have the freehand writing convert to computer generated text. To me this is not as useful, computing, or smart devices allow for keyboard inputs, and I see that type of usage as more complex than is required, one that I don't feel helps a user achieve a difficult task. [Male, 42]

Older adult's *negative* experiences of technology are associated with customer service support, terminology, and the provision of directions over the telephone:

> You know, when I phoned, they go through a recorded message and it says, if your Internet isn't working, try rebooting the router. And when I finally got through to a human being, I said they told me to reboot my router, but they didn't tell me how to do that. I wasn't sure whether it was switch it off and switch it on again. And they said, yes, it was. But why then I said, didn't they say that? [Female, 67]

This quote illustrates how many citizens are lacking in digital skills, understanding of terminology, and training for activities that many find straight forward, associated with technology integration in the home. Also, the following quote highlights how people with limited or no digital skills may feel, using a personal example, describing the term 'roaming':

> [...] I feel that there's still a large group of people out there who are totally overwhelmed by taking on the technology, who need help to access and, you know, to get into this and that. We benefit so much from technology. But there's still out there an overwhelming feeling because there are things that you guys (we) talk about that goes well over my head, you know, because I haven't got quite into

it. And, you know, like you're talking about your phone there, MC, and problems with it. And, you know, the words, the usage of the words that they would say to you, you know, about the roaming for example. I wouldn't have a clue about that. I know when I am on the phone with support like that and they were talking about my roaming ability, I wouldn't know. [Female, 66]

During this interview, the mother describes how the easing of restrictions in the future may impact on her familial connections and being able to continue the frequency of connection(s) with her daughter and family members:

I would still see her when she comes to the house. It might just be that I speak to her less and won't really know what she is doing. For all of my children I wouldn't know how they are or what their children are doing. I think I would feel more alone and lonelier. [Female, 89]

An alternative viewpoint is presented by a young person who notes how technology development facilitates greater opportunity for bullying and harassment online, while maintaining a positive notion of technology to maintain friendships:

I think technology is good in a good way for that. But I think it is bad because people can bully you, I've been bullied in the past and that was online too. It was two years ago now, so I am OK. I think it can be good as well. I have been to Kenya twice and have some friends over there, so it is good to keep in touch with them. [Female, 17–23]

Although we have presented the barriers and challenges to using technology in this section, we continue this theme focussing more on privacy, data and scamming activities found via technology and online presence.

Privacy, Data, Scamming and Information

New technologies can afford dubious and scrupulous behaviour such as scamming, or in some instances may instil apprehension in people because of the behaviour that the device can (perceive) undertake. One interviewee describes her apprehension and (potential) fear that her technology is 'listening' in,

[…] I'm very suspicious about a lot of technology. So, I don't have any Alexa's or any of that kind of stuff. I get very wary when my work phone makes recommendations that it couldn't possibly make unless it was listening to me. So, I am a wee bit uncomfortable around technology, but I kind of knew I needed it. [Female, 25–35]

Another interviewee describes how he experienced people trying to scam him, but did not fall victim to the scam,

> I was on a bunch of group calls as well this year and people were trying to scam me, they thought they were pro hackers trying to break into debit cards and all. I could have just reported them to Microsoft, and they would have had them banned. [Male, 17–23]

It is likely, the male interviewee did not fall victim to the scam because he was tech savvy and had pre-existing knowledge of how some scammers work. Whereas, for many people (old and young), this is not the case.

Summary

This chapter presents an insight into technology use by older and younger adults from two stakeholders located in Northern Ireland. Findings presented here, illustrate how participants utilise technology, and have similar concerns and trends, albeit of different generations, age groups and abilities.

During the pandemic, the need for Internet access to take part in some leisure activities was important with many types of leisure activities being recorded by the survey respondents. While others reported using their smartphone data, or public spaces, or their friends and family Internet. A small number of people (2.36%) report not to have any form of Internet access while 9.45% report similar and were not interested in gaining access.

Similarly, the reasons for using the Internet are comparable to findings published prior to the pandemic (Genoe et al., 2018; Marston, Genoe et al., 2019) and include social networking, online shopping and banking, fact checking, streaming, and watching television shows, and carrying out work-related activities. However, what differs is the ability to use technology to access spiritual welfare services, not only provided by a single house of worship but for many individuals, being able to remotely access facilitated them to virtually 'attend' services in other towns and communities.

Since the pandemic there has been greater insights into the feeling of loneliness and social isolation and the role which technology and social networks play within this sphere (House of Lords, 2021; Marston, Wilson et al., 2020; Morgan et al., 2020; Pennington, 2021). The data here narrates how many people use the Internet as a mechanism to maintain social connections (Pennington, 2021) and for some people, their perspective of technology enhances the feeling of loneliness and being less happy, while one's mental health and well-being was also viewed as a negative.

Another interesting although not surprising aspect is how 48.60% of our respondent's motivation to engage with technology was because of the pandemic, while 40.19% of people, reported their use of technology had remained the same. Similarly, other pieces of evidence (Cotten et al., 2013; Pancani et al., 2021; Schlomann et al., 2020), show how respondents' purpose for engaging with technology was to stay connected with friends and family. Survey findings show respondents do feel a greater sense of isolation and loneliness during lockdowns, and we must keep in mind, residents in Northern Ireland – a devolved nation, did have different COVID-19 restrictions to the other three regions of the UK. In some instances, the pandemic restrictions were greater at differing times in comparison to elsewhere.

For people living in Northern Ireland, being digitally connected facilitated social gatherings online, purely because there were no alternative activities to choose from. With many people noting how passing the time was the primary mechanism to connect with other people. Similar discourse was purported, and this data aligns with findings by Nguyen et al. (2020) who explore digital engagement while Hargittai et al. (2020) explore the willingness to install the US version of 'Track and Trace' apps. Findings from the former respective study ascertain a reduction in online activity (e.g., social media use, video calls and online gaming), with women living alone and younger generations who had concerns about their Internet access increased their digital engagement during the first wave of the pandemic. Gender was not equally split amongst survey respondents, suggesting the data presented here follows a trend similar to existing data of women experiencing a greater sense of loneliness.

Learning new technologies can be difficult especially for individuals who are not tech savvy. As the data suggests survey respondents rely upon a friend or a younger family member to assist them with their new device. Although 50% of respondents report to use some form of online information/guide(s), or, for others, they learn by doing. This data suggests and highlights there is a possibility of a 'sense of ownership and autonomy'. For example, those individuals who choose to learn and understand how their device operates through trial and error, may want to feel ownership towards the device. While other people who seek out assistance may not feel the same way. Previous works (Freeman et al., 2020; Marston et al., 2019) highlight how jargon can be a barrier to learning and using technologies, and this data continues to support this notion. A greater conscious effort is required by multiple actors in our ecosystems from the macro to the micro levels, including education providers and within the miso levels surrounding our more intimate support networks and communities to reduce the use of jargon and provide greater assistance and support.

The qualitative data is rich and insightful and demonstrates how residents in this region experience similar challenges, barriers, and enablers to using and adopting technology in their daily lives. To date, there is little understanding of the implications and impact technology plays in the lives of residents from a *Transgenerational* perspective. However, as we have shown, there are similarities in the concerns and issues between service users of the two organisations. Therefore, we believe the notion of conducting future research from a *Transgenerational* standpoint would be more advantageous instead of focussing primarily on one cohort in later life. If we truly want to change our understanding of digital inequities then we need to recalibrate our approaches and processes. Although life course theory (Elder, 1985) can facilitate this, it does not push the discourse, and research still primarily focusses on specific cohort experiences. Whereas, *Transgenerational* approaches and perspectives would afford researchers the opportunity to be fluid in recognising the experiences of a young person in their twenties can and are likely to be different in their thirties.

Currently, there is a paucity of statistical data published by the Northern Ireland Assembly (NIA) surrounding digital and Internet engagement. Although the Office for National Statistics (ONS) does provide some insight (See Chapter 6) for this region, the ONS primarily concerns itself with England and Wales. Previously Marston and colleagues recommended to the NIA via the *Knowledge Exchange Seminar Series* (KESS, 2012–2018) the need to start collecting data relating to this field (Marston, Freeman et al., 2018). This recommendation still stands, and greater effort is needed for this type of data to be collected, because it would facilitate and serve organisations such Age NI and Mencap NI, researchers and policy makers to track and understand digital engagement and practices at a regional level. Such data would assist actors to understand the *Transgenerational Technology* ecosystem in this context and in a post-pandemic society. We do not know how society is going to evolve in a post-pandemic society and recording data sooner rather than later would facilitate 'tracking' of future trends and concerns.

Chapter 3 provides a snapshot of a historical period from one specific region of the UK to understand how technology plays a role in the lives of older and younger people. We provide a series of recommendations which will feed into our manifesto (Chapter 8), and we posit how these recommendations facilitate the proposal of *Transgenerational* approaches and processes. The qualitative data presented here is rich and it is impossible to present it all in this chapter, which in turn lends itself for further dissemination and outputs. Given the nature of discourse here, these findings can support Age NI and the NIA to understand the affects and impacts in which technology has and continues to play.

Chapter 4

Technology in the Role of Stakeholders, Social Enterprise, Industry and Smart Age-friendly Ecosystems in the 21st Century

Introduction

Within and across our society lies a myriad of ecosystems and infrastructures that we engage and live in. Ecosystems are not solely aimed at one organisation, or one cohort in society, but should encompass all businesses, organisations, and citizens (regardless of age) with a view to adding benefits while reducing and eliminating the challenges and issues concerned respectively (Marston et al., 2020; Marston & van Hoof, 2019). The role which technology is playing within our communities is being rolled out across the meso, micro and macro levels (Shin & Park, 2017), starting from within our homes and expanding outwards to incorporate municipalities, government, health, and public services.

Ecosystems impact the different physical environments (e.g., rural, urban) within our society and communities, which in turn directly impact the various actors residing in them. For example, closure of the village/high-street banks or post offices leads to unemployment, increased difficulty of accessing services, especially for people who are disabled and/or ageing and rely on the convenience of a village post office or bank, rather than having to travel to a larger town or city via limited/poor public transport services.

In this chapter we explore the various ecosystems surrounding the concept of ageing in place, and age-friendly cities and communities (AFCC) drawing on existing frameworks and discourse. Expanding this discussion, we explore how coastal regions and other cities such as Dubai and Barcelona are implementing AFCC design into their environments. We expand our discourse from the standpoint of the pandemic, illustrating how businesses, and highstreets deployed and employed a design hack approach taking an agile method. Woven throughout this chapter is technology discourse, as we consider and reflect on how digital

Transgenerational Technology and Interactions for the 21st Century:
Perspectives and Narratives, 75–111
Copyright © 2022 by Hannah R. Marston, Linda Shore, Laura Stoops, and Robbie S. Turner
Published under exclusive licence by Emerald Publishing Limited
doi:10.1108/978-1-83982-638-220221007

engagement facilitates people from the standpoints of AFCC, during the pandemic and in a post-pandemic society.

Setting the Scene

The ecosystems created and inhabited by people across the generations rely on many services and systems to enable interactivity and productivity. In turn unmet needs of people can be identified and supported by various technologies. Ageing experience can present a challenge, resulting in reliance on assistive technologies (AT) or new approaches to accessing services.

The field of gerontechnology is not new. If we look back at the history of this field to the 1990s, contemporary scholars came together in a bid to collaborate and showcase a growing body of work with the sole aim of utilising technology to benefit ageing populations. Instilling creative approaches such as 'Design for All' to ensure inclusive design is implemented and adhered to when designing and developing technologies can lead to rich input from older adult users (Merkel & Kucharski, 2019).

The relationship(s) between gerontechnology, AFCC, design and citizens are integral within our contemporary society, and we believe this will be ever more important as we move forward into the twenty-first century. For many years, scholars have and continue to conduct interdisciplinary research (UKRI, n.d.a) bridging disciplines from the standpoint of application and/or theoretical perspective, the two approaches are very much interwind.

However, guaranteeing the 'applied' perspective within research projects (large or small, un/funded) is critical if technology is to be adopted and rolled out across our society. This is usually termed co-design and co-production and is popular across many disciplines especially within the social sciences. Collaborating with target audiences who are involved in a project from the beginning facilitates real-time feedback and is vital to ensuring the service or product being designed and/or developed meets the needs and expectations of the audiences it is targeting.

For many years and decades, audience participation has primarily listened to the familiar voices that always volunteer for research projects, which in turn may not reflect the voices of people who differ in socioeconomic status (SES) groups. This in turn limits the insights, and breadth of challenges and benefits of those people who truly could gain from digital transformation and/or support. Citizens in our society all have a part to play, and everyone's voice is important regardless of their SES, whether one is connected by an organisation or not. Albeit, the latter, in some instances can and do reach members within communities that are not easily accessible to research teams. Similarly, organisations such as Age NI play a critical role within research projects because they too understand the issues and concerns of respective audiences.

Designing and developing gerontechnology/AT services and products, with the aim of being integrated into our respective AFCCs requires commitment from different actors, without creating echo chambers, and acknowledging, and realising that every person old or young is a key player.

As described in Chapter 1, several terms were coined taking the perspective of technologies and services being recognised as 'Transgenerational' rather than pitted for 'later life'. Current discourse surrounding healthy ageing, suggests there is the drive to add greater importance of technology within our day-to-day lives, and this requires the mindset of actors to recalibrate our approaches across and within different sectors to design, test and evaluate TT, TAT, TART, and TLCC products and services across different SES groups.

Gerontechnology/AT and AFCC discourse needs to keep up to date with contemporary issues, and concerns, and this can be achieved by collaborative approaches from actors. Each actor should draw on and work together with a view to making a positive change and should be viewed through the lens of a long-term strategy and not solely a short-term fashionable, tick box exercise. This would require a cultural change within our society, and this is where a *Transgenerational* approach would be implemented.

In the following section, we explore where the field of gerontechnology started, coupled with the aims and objectives detailed over 30 years ago in the latter part of the twentieth century.

Gerontechnology from the Beginning

Approximately 30 years ago the field of gerontechnology was cultivated by several founding members and many of them were the founders of the 'International Society of Gerontechnology' (ISG) (Graafmans et al., 1998; Harrington & Harrington, 2000; Pieper et al., 2002), a new field of interdisciplinary research was born. An editorial published in 2012, describes how,

> Gerontechnology (GT) is concerned with technology for ageing persons. At the start of GT, some 20 years ago, the field 'Technology and Ageing' existed already. It was directed at ageing people with physical restrictions, providing them with compensatory aids: electric nerve stimulation for paralysed nerves, electric typewriters controlled by eye movements, closed circuit television circuits for blowing up texts. Some mental functions were also covered, such as training-algorithms after cerebral accidents. Today this area of R&D is as important as it was before: cochlear, retinal and neural implants, robot arms, legs and vehicles, speech handling systems, and iPads.
>
> GT extended this field to include the total technological environment serving all needs and aspirations of ageing people; technology supporting ageing people in all aspects of their lives, just as it is for younger people. It was clear that this would not happen any time soon by itself: the gap between technological innovation in society and ageing people was already substantial. The first international conference on GT in 1991 indicated how to approach the problem: searching for scientific insight into the origins of this gap, while trusting that such a knowledge base would guide us toward promising pragmatic actions for improvement. (Bouma, 2012, p. 1)

This editorial outlines the 20 year history of the field of gerontechnology, referencing the first and consecutive gerontechnology conference(s) held in, Eindhoven, the Netherlands (1991), Helsinki, Finland (1996) and in Munich, Germany (1999). In the new millennium and succeeding these conferences, additional outputs were rolled out including a quarterly journal, and additional conferences (International Society of Gerontechnology, n.d.). The endeavour of these activities coupled with the release of the first volume of the *Gerontechnology* journal was knowledge translation, sharing and exchange of innovative approaches to new multi-and-trans disciplinary research. The *Gerontechnology* journal is still operating, and the archives are open access and are available via the ISG website (ISG, n.d.).

At the time gerontechnology was becoming a field in itself, with respective scholars (ISG, 2016) setting the benchmark(s) for future research, and discourse, sharing a vision between scholars and founders facilitated collaborative insights and developments acknowledging it was, and still is necessary to bridge innovative and conceptual processes.

> The combinations of insight from two different types of scientific discipline are crucial to understanding GT: (i) Human ageing: theories, concepts and methods of physiology, psychology, sociology, epidemiology; (ii) Technological innovation: theories, concepts, and methods of physics and chemistry, building, communication and information, transport, industrial design, and business. Each of these two clusters concerns an extended area of knowledge and research. Understanding the combination and the interaction between them seemed a difficult and complex journey into the unknown. But, this is what science is for and we started from a solid base, or rather, a number of unconnected solid bases. We might call this the theoretical approach. (Bouma, 2012, p. 1)

This ethos continues to live on in contemporary research today with many projects combining the spirit of the gerontechnology founders, with many gerontological theories aligning to this field with the aim of understanding how older adults can and do remain independent, autonomous, and active. van Bronswijk et al. (2002) propose a model targeting older adults, research, and development (Table 4.1) to illustrate how actors are and can be aligned to gerontechnology whilst re-emphasising how it is not solely made up of one field.

van Bronswijk and colleagues (2002) acknowledge at the time of this model, additional indirect disciplines were impacting this field within our ecosystems (e.g., medicine and agriculture), with a view of advancing impacts and goals within our society. van Bronswijk and colleagues (2002) note,

> [O]nly when all matrix cells are equally covered by research, development, design and distribution (RDD&D) may we hope to reach our ultimate aim of a sustainable high quality of daily life in the knowledge-based society for older persons. (p. 4)

Table 4.1. Matrix Displaying Five Application Domains and Four Types of Technology Impact. *Source:* van Bronzwij et al. (2002).

		Application Domain				
		Health and Self-esteem	**Housing and Daily Living**	**Mobility and Transport**	**Communication and Governance**	**Work and Leisure**	**Total**
Technology impact	Enhancement & satisfaction	0	1	0	1	1	3
	Prevention & engagement	1	2	4	0	0	7
	Compensation & assistance	1	5	7	4	1	18
	Care support & organisation	0	1	0	1	0	2
Totals		2	9	11	6	2	

Twenty years on from this publication, the quote still seems pertinent – and possibly more so now in contemporary society with technology developments, changes, design, and discourse surrounding AFCC. Yet, can we, as researchers, and the research, development, design, and distribution (RDD & D) communities say that sustainability has been met? Technological developments coupled with the shifts and movements associated to inclusivity (stakeholder and audience engagement) such a matrix is still contingent now and possibly more so than ever. Especially as there is an ever-growing need for healthy and independent living.

Researchers should consider applying a *Transgenerational* approach to further and facilitate exploration and understanding of the paradigm (in this context technology) of people's lives, but also their structural contexts, and societal changes (Elder, 1985; Elder et al., 2003). This 'applied' approach would serve and benefit inter-and multi-disciplinary researchers well to 'design services and products for all' not just for use in later life but as a continuum. Especially as societal changes occur and impact different age cohorts.

Therefore, designing services and products for Baby Boomers (1946–1964), Generation X (1965–1980), Millennials (1981–1996) and Generation Z (1997–2012) should consider all of these age cohorts (Dimock, 2019), because the lifecycle of being born, growing older and death, differ at different segment or periods of time within our society; thus, in turn each cohort supersedes the next cohort (Phillipson & Baars, 2007). This notion is reinstated further by Riley et al. (1999) who detail how differences between cohorts can lead and change throughout society,

> Because society changes, members of different cohorts (i.e. born at different times) age in different ways [authors' emphasis]. Over their lives, from birth to death, people move through structures that are continually altered with the course of history; thus, the lives of those who are growing old today cannot be the same as the lives of those who grew old in the past or of those who will grow old in the future. (p. 333)

Employing this ethos and approach, the impact of *Transgenerational Technology* is certainly representative of the notion of younger cohorts in today's society (e.g., Gen X, Millennials and Gen Z) (Loos et al., 2012; Marston & del Carmen Miranda Duro, 2020) who are perceived as being, more tech savvy than existing older cohorts (Freeman et al., 2020; Helsper, 2010; Neves et al., 2013; Neves et al., 2018). Technology use and adoption continues to grow by older cohorts (Anderson & Perrin, 2017), the discourse surrounding the barriers to adoption by people in later life (Shore et al., 2020) continues. This includes computer anxiety (Beckers et al., 2008; Richardson et al., 2011), low self-efficacy (Bozionelos, 2004), learning and use (Kim, 2008), and yet, Fernández-Ardèvol and Ivan (2015) ascertain age was not the primary factor when understanding computer anxiety. The notion of *Transgenerational Technology* applications is still not remedied. Associated technology factors should be considered because of the current societal environment, impacting on citizens who are ageing in place.

More recently, devices such as virtual assistants (Marston & Samuels, 2019), AT solutions (Department of Health and Social Care, 2019), telehealth and telecare (Fisk et al., 2020; Greenhalgh et al., 2021) and the Internet of Things (IoTs) are facilitating opportunities to be integrated into the home environment and wider societal ecosystems. This in turn is offering some level of positive autonomy, and independence (van Hoof et al., 2021). What is pivotal in reaching and realising the narrative(s) of van Bronswijk and colleagues (2002) is greater collaboration, co-production factors are needed in the research design process. Recruiting end-users from different SES groups can be and should be imperative to the rollout of *Transgenerational Technologies* given that products and services will not be solely used by one specific cohort in our society.

Looking to the future, by applying these approaches while embracing diverse actors to RDD &D has the potential to move gerontechnology discourse forward, building on the foundation blocks set out by the founders of gerontechnology and ISG. These foundations can and should be taken seriously, and reviewing past research activities, learning from the limitations, and building on the findings can offer substantial reward.

More recently, the Socio-Gerontechnology Nework has been growing since its inaugural meeting in Vienna, Austria in 2017. The mission of the Socio-Gerontechnology Nework states,

> [...] Socio-gerontechnology offers empirically grounded new and more 'realistic' ideas about older users, formulates advice and examples for involving social science and humanities perspectives in co-creation processes, and leverages ground-breaking interdisciplinary scholarship to theorise about the increasing relevance of technology in later life. (Socio-Gerontechnology Nework, 2021)

Members of the Socio-Gerontechnology Network published the *Socio-gerontechnology – Interdisciplinary Critical Studies of Ageing and Technologies* (Peine et al., 2021) book. This compilation of works rooted in several fields aims to understand the relationships between ageing and technology from the standpoints of theory, methods, and conceptual notions is a positive step forward to building on the ISG foundations. However, there is still a lot more work to be conducted, and this in our opinion must take an applied approach, to be truly meaningful. In the following section we explore contemporary literature and concepts from the standpoint of AFCC, and age in place.

Ageing in Place, Age-friendly Cities, and Communities (AFCC) Ecosystems and Frameworks

The concept of 'ageing in place' within the field of gerontology is not a new phenomenon given the breadth and depth of literature spanning over 40 years (Altman et al., 1984; Burholt & Dobbs, 2012; Burholt et al., 2018; Laws, 1993; Means, 2007; Oswald et al., 2010; Peace et al., 2007; Rowles & Bernard, 2013;

Rubinstein, 1989; Scharf et al., 2016; Sixsmith, 1990, 2006; Sixsmith & Sixsmith, 1991). Definitions of 'ageing in place' include,

> the ability to live in one's own home and community safely, independently, and comfortably, regardless of age, income, or ability level. (CDC, 2013)

> remaining living in the community, with some level of independence, rather than in residential care. (Davey et al., 2004, p. 133)

And in the context of ageing in place, Sixsmith and Sixsmith (2008) note their definition,

> Ageing in Place has become an important issue in redefining health and social care policy for older people in recent years. The basic premise of Ageing in Place is that helping older people to remain living at home fundamentally and positively contributes to an increase in well-being, independence, social participation and healthy ageing. (pp. 219–220)

Another term 'age in place' (Golant, 2015) is preferred (Frank, 2002), because it relates to, and facilitates older adults maintaining and continuing their levels of autonomy, their independence and connections to social support mechanisms including friends and familial relationships (Keeling, 1999).

The notion of 'ageing in place' or 'age in place' has seen several frameworks which bridge this ethos outlined by van Bronswijk and colleagues (2002), architects, environmental gerontologists and (geron) technologists. Regarding the environment and technology domains, Mollenkopf (2004) states,

> The view that the environment in which people live today is much more stamped by technology than it was just 50 years ago is no doubt undisputed. [...] the idea that the increased use of technology is also affecting social competencies and behavior in very different spheres of life. (pp. 60–61)

The quote above (Mollenkopf, 2004) still rings true as we move into the third decade of this new century, especially as our social competencies and behaviours are more intertwined, albeit in different spheres because of technology facilitating these relationships. Previously, various technologies (e.g., IoTs, apps, virtual assistants, smartphones, etc.) were not easily accessible to citizens. However, it could be argued how this statement is very much relevant to contemporary society.

Exploring ageing in place we present different frameworks and models pertaining to AFCC, in a bid to understand existing and future relationships of (*Transgenerational*) technology, environment and citizens. Much has been written surrounding AFCC since the World Health Organization (WHO) published their guide to global age-friendly cities in 2007.

AFCC culminates several domains outlined by the World Health Organization (2007) (Fig. 4.1) to afford our global ageing populations independent living. This growing body of work facilitates actors to understand the differences, issues and concerns surrounding ageing populations from this perspective (Buffel, Handler, & Phillipson, 2019; Chaudhury & Oswald, 2019; van Hoof & Kazak, 2018; van Hoof et al., 2018; van Hoof et al., 2021).

In a bid to move current AFCC discourse forward, literature (Marston, & van Hoof, 2019; Marston et al., 2020; van Hoof et al., 2021; White et al., 2020) extends existing frameworks to theoretically posit how technology is critical in this domain,

> Many cities and communities, albeit mainly in high income countries, have benefitted from the planning, implementation and evaluation cycle of the AFCs' agenda. However, this does not mean that the work is done. Actually, the work is far from over. (van Hoof et al., 2021, p. 20)

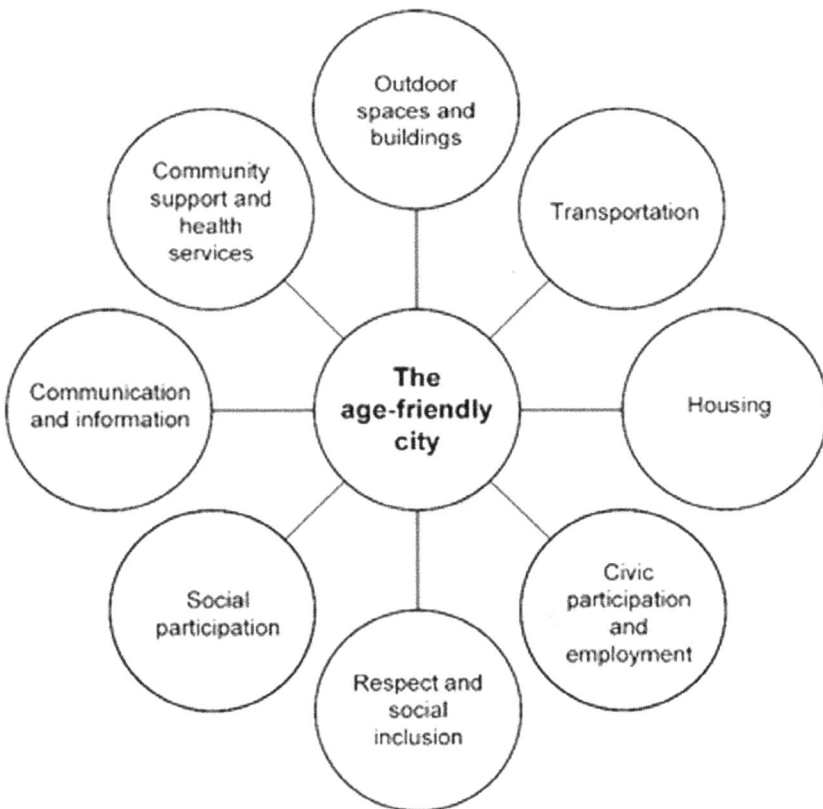

Fig. 4.1.   Eight Domains of the Age-friendly City set out by the WHO.
Source: World Health Organization (2007).

Moving forward with this new discourse, it is crucial to identify and form new partnerships, understand the impact of intersectionalities, employing a co-production ethos to improve the AFCC domain,

> Future roll outs should avoid the notion of tokenism and this could be avoided by forming new partnerships with organisations from the third sector in areas and regions where there are variable levels of socioeconomic status among citizens. Future research projects should consider involving various intersectionalities rather than just age, and gender. This itself would provide greater understanding and richness to data collections, project outputs, public engagement, and knowledge transfer activities – but more importantly it would demonstrate to the organisations and the individuals the seriousness and the real need for change and voices to be heard. Finally, multi-and-transdisciplinary teams have the opportunity to conduct impactful work that can be replicated in other towns, cities, and communities which may have not being recruited. Employing a co-design, and co-production approach from the onset affords everyone the opportunity to learn and share knowledge and experiences to make greater strides and lasting legacies – both from the standpoint of the individual as well as at a municipality level. (van Hoof et al., 2021, p. 20)

van Hoof et al. (2021) describe in detail several frameworks including a model proposed by Fulmer et al. (2020) (Fig. 4.2), and focusses on the social

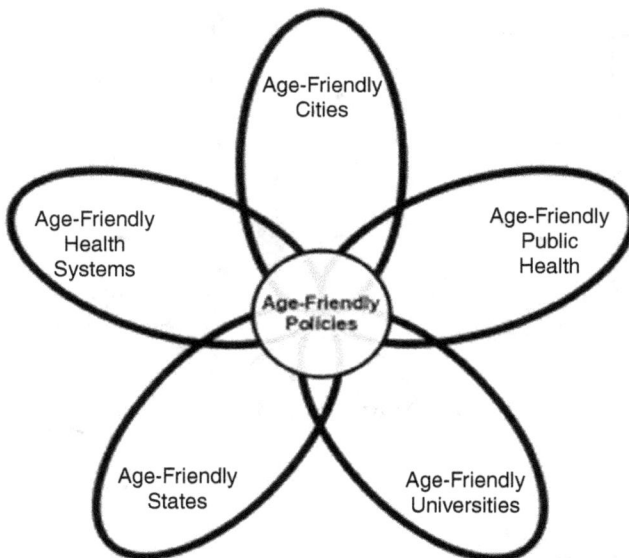

Fig. 4.2.   The Age-friendly ecosystem: A Synthesis of Age-friendly Programmes. *Source*: Taken and adapted from Fulmer et al. (2020).

determinants of health, public health systems coupled with the lived environment. Disappointingly, technology is missing from this framework and there are new domains posited such as 'age-friendly universities', and 'age-friendly public health'. There should be initial considerations evolving and employing 'age-friendly service provision'. This would capture many actors with the view to training future health professionals and educationalists.

Building on the WHO framework (2007), the 'Smart Age-friendly Ecosystem' (SAfE) (Marston & van Hoof, 2019) (see Fig. 4.3) clearly illustrates how technology can be implemented into the physical space.

The 'Concept of Age-friendly Smart Ecologies' (CASE) framework (see Fig. 4.4), extends the SAfE framework (Marston & van Hoof, 2019) and has the potential to afford 'flexibility to adapt and future proof respective environments, where necessary' (Marston et al., 2020, p. 23). Taking an ecological approach, the *CASE* framework integrates sustainability within the environment, and accessibility which has seldom featured in previous models. Placing people at the centre, surrounded by outlining technological environments, proposes how adaptations can be made across the meso, micro levels within the AFCC.

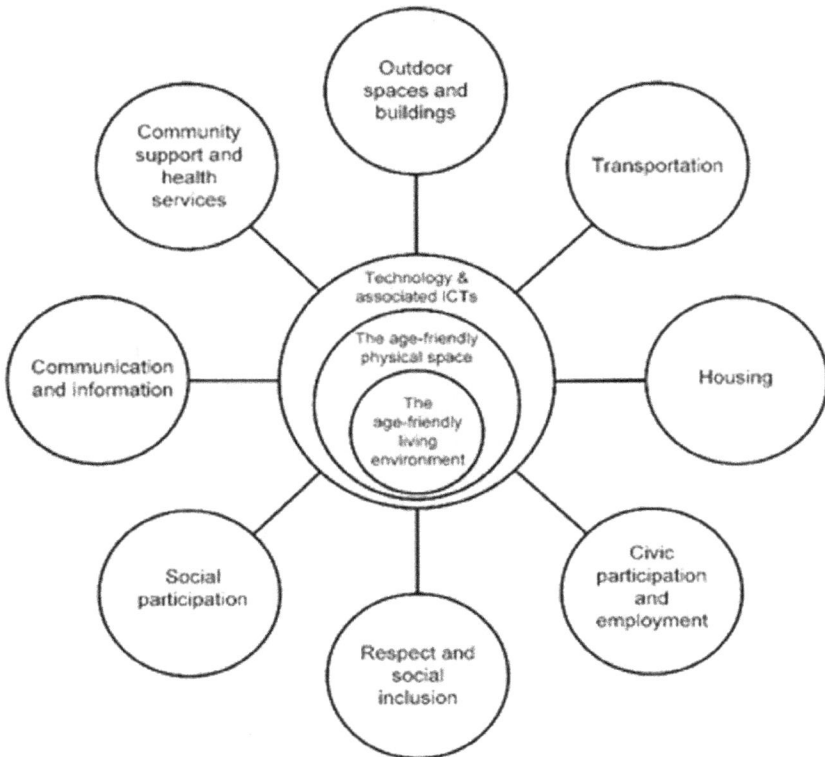

Fig. 4.3. The Smart Age-friendly Ecosystem (SAfE) Framework. *Source*: Marston and van Hoof (2019).

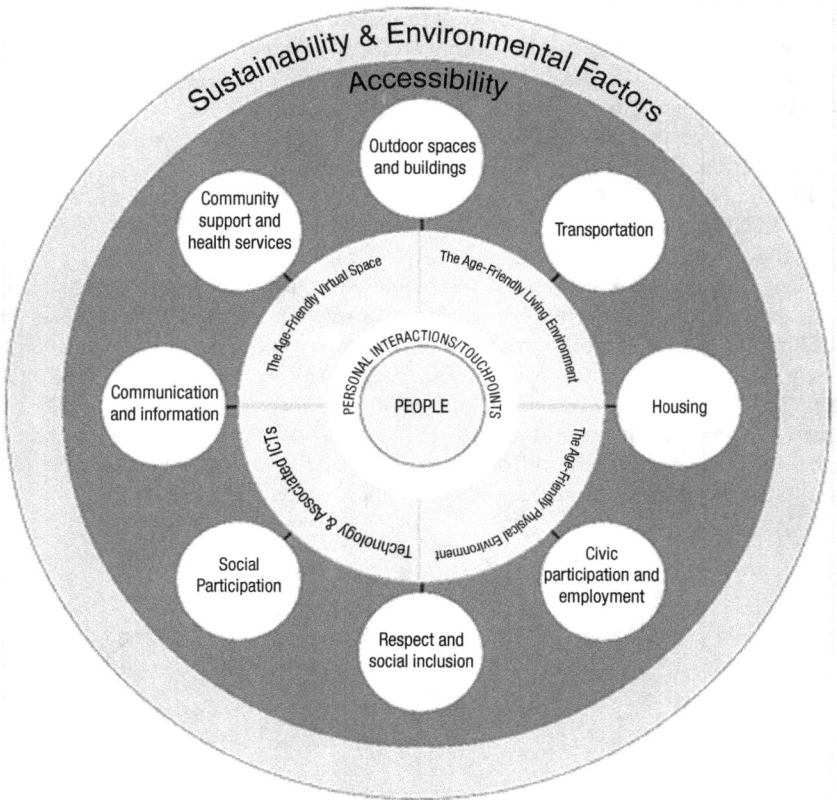

Fig. 4.4.   The Concept of Age-friendly Smart Ecologies (CASE) framework.
Source: Taken and adapted from Marston et al. (2020).

It is staggering to understand how the WHO age-friendly framework underrepresents the importance of technology (2007), especially how the Internet was accessible to citizens for approximately 10 years at the time of the framework being developed. Yet, we can only speculate that this exclusion was deemed unimportant and not on the radar of contributors whose background can be from the medical and/or social science fields to be included as a separate domain and in consecutive years. Very few scholars and organisations have rarely considered the importance of technology in day-to-day living.

AFCC Design Implementation from Dubai and Barcelona

It is seldom to see how other international cities employ AFCC approaches. However, exploring Dubai (Figs. 4.5 – 4.6) we can see a pedestrian crossing with both green and red solar-powered lights. These lights not only correspond with the traffic lights but inform drivers that this is a designated road crossing. All drivers must abide by the laws and if a driver ignores the laws/pedestrian crossing

Fig. 4.5. Pedestrian Crossing in Dubai, Displaying Red Traffic Lights, and Sensors Marking out the Pedestrian Crossing. *Source*: Permission granted by R. Turner.

Fig. 4.6. Pedestrian Crossing in Dubai, Displaying Green Traffic Lights, and Sensors Marking out the Pedestrian Crossing. *Source*: Permission granted by R. Turner.

then a fine is issued (Bayut, 2021). Figs. 4.5 and 4.6, display emojis on the traffic lights to drivers who are waiting to proceed and is a method of communicating messages with drivers relating to their own respective behaviours (e.g., their speed) (Gulf news, 2017).

These signs are specifically used in areas where there are schools, acting as a traffic warning measure to inform drivers of their speed and to reduce the risks of accidents and fatalities (Zain, 2018). In the UK many pedestrian crossings rely on audible 'beeps' to assist people with visual impairments to cross the road safely, it is unclear whether similar approaches are used in this respective region, and whether using emojis would work in the UK or not. There are cultural differences between both Western and Middle Eastern societies, but this semiotic approach is a commonality between the two regions and can facilitate travellers and tourists alike to drive safely with their pre-existing knowledge, surrounding the meaning of emojis and the meaning of colours (red – danger/stop, green – good/go).

If we turn our attention to the city of Barcelona, across many aspects of public transport and streets there is blended accessibility and age-friendly features. Fig. 4.7a illustrates an accessibility ramp on the tube system that helps people relying on wheelchairs or children in buggies/prams. The ramp is elevated slightly and marked to distinguish the elevation and safety features.

Additional features are found on the floor of the tube station and include various colours, textures, and tactile tiles (Figs. 4.7a – 4.7b) in certain formats, coupled with different textures (e.g., smooth vs blocked tiling), we assume this is to facilitate accessibility of visually impaired people and to distinguish between the edge of the platform for all travellers. Further changes can be seen in the texture of the ramp, which differs from the tiles, enabling individuals to identify through their feet whether they are still walking on the ramp or not. Given how the world is still in a pandemic (at the time of writing this), countries are still open to visitors, many public spaces such as tube stations are requesting people to keep an orderly format (Fig. 4.8).

Accessibility and age-friendly features can be seen at the street level in the district of El Poblenau (Barcelona), whereby pedestrians crossing the road at certain areas in the district will see changes in the pavement, and visual

Figs. 4.7a & 4.7b.   Accessibility Ramp in a Barcelona Tube Station.
Source: Permission granted and taken (November 2021) by H. R. Marston.

Fig. 4.8.   Specific Route(s) for Commuters/users in a Barcelona Tube Station.
Source: Permission granted and taken (November 2021) by H. R. Marston.

aesthetics surrounding the joining of the pavement and the road. Accessibility and age-friendly features are considered in the design of public spaces and more importantly, intersections pertaining to transport and mobility (Fig. 4.9).

Sustainability and eco-friendly approaches to travel are becoming popular across European cities such as Copenhagen (Marston et al., 2020). The company YEGO (2021) integrates technology into transport coupled with sustainability ethos, operating across several cities in Spain (Barcelona) and France. People can hire an electric moped (Fig. 4.10) if they hold a driver's license and have connected their bank account to their smartphone (Figs. 4.11a – 4.11b), they are able to commute across the city and are charged by the minute (Fig. 4.11b).

The illustrations depicting contemporary life across cities aims to provoke readers to contemplate *Transgenerational Living Cities and Communities* (TLCC) and how considering this approach may be a positive step forward for future living arrangements, employing the CASE framework (Marston et al., 2020) to underpin applied rollouts. Demonstrating how simple design implementations and ecological changes can impact citizens who would benefit from a *Transgenerational* approach.

The CASE framework (Marston et al., 2020) does not specifically include 'age-friendly universities', 'age-friendly public health', 'age-friendly health systems' or even 'age-friendly states' what it does present is several ecosystems, which can be viewed at the miso, micro and macro levels, and one could argue health-related

Fig. 4.9.   Pavement and Road Markings and Textures in the El Poblenau District of Barcelona. *Source*: Permission granted and taken (November 2021) by H. R. Marston.

Fig. 4.10.   Electric Moped in the El Poblenau District of Barcelona. *Source*: Photograph taken (November 2021) and permission granted by H. R. Marston.

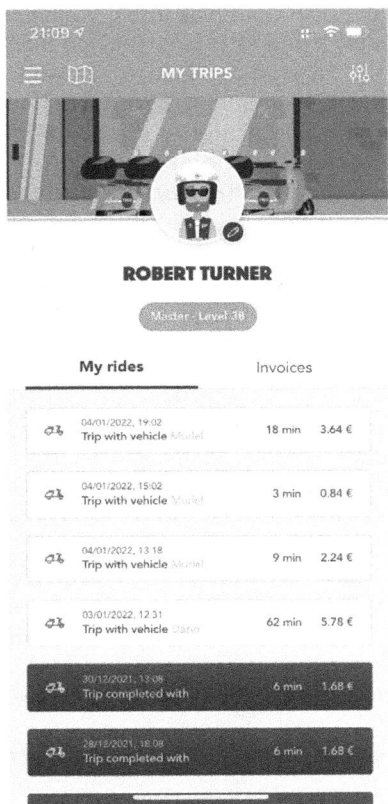

Figs. 4.11a and 4.11b Overview of the YEGO Journeys, Costs, and Location(s) of Moped Throughout the District of el Poblenou. *Source*: Photograph taken and permission granted by R. S. Turner.

environments and universities could be reviewed at these different levels. We explore in the following section a new model posited by the WHO focussing on dementia friendly cities and communities.

Dementia Friendly Cities and Communities

In August 2021 the WHO published the report '*Towards a dementia inclusive society*' which aims to act as a toolkit to ensure cities and communities are dementia friendly (WHO, 2021). This new model is an extension from the original age-friendly model posited in 2007 (Fig. 4.1) and illustrates two additional domains or 'petals', 1. *Safety* and 2. *Carer support*. However, it is disappointing to see how technology is not recognised in this new model given the growing body of research surrounding how assistive technologies (AT) are playing a part in the lives of people who have dementia.

For over ten years, scholarly activity and literature has been growing, focussing on the benefits of AT to support people living with dementia and their carers (Gibson et al., 2016; Gibson et al., 2019; Newton et al., 2016; Orpwood et al., 2010; Sixsmith et al., 2007). More recently, attentions have turned to understanding how virtual assistants and social media platforms (Shu & Woo, 2021) are facilitating people to access and share information (Shu, & Woo, 2020). Utilising social media platforms affords organisations and researchers alike the opportunity to raise Alzheimer-related awareness (Cheng et al., 2019).

Conversely, robotic pets such as 'PARO' are garnering (Lane et al., 2016; Pu et al., 2020) attention with a view to affording older adults and people with dementia (Petersen et al., 2017) the opportunity to reduce negative emotional and behavioural symptoms, while enhancing one's mood, social engagement and potentially improving the quality-of-care experience that an individual is receiving (Hung et al., 2019). However, as with many types of technology there are barriers and challenges, and robotic pets are no different. Factors that should be considered include the cost of purchasing the device, infection concerns, stigma associated to owning a robotic pet, ethical issues, and workload (Hung et al., 2019).

Another positive factor introduced within the extended dementia-friendly model is the acknowledgement of 'carers' and their role in caring and supporting an individual with dementia. Carers UK (n.d.a) is a national charity offering support (network) to carers and advocates for a movement of change. There are 6.5 million carers across the UK, many of whom are friends, immediate and extended family members, and in many cases are unpaid (Carers UK, 2014a). This charity affords existing and new carers the opportunity to access resources, and to connect, which in turn affords additional support (Carers UK, 2014b).

The role of being a carer may not start in later life and for many younger people, they too can find themselves being a carer for a parent or even a child with disabilities (Carers UK, 2013). Using technology to support carers varies across different age groups, with 28% of people aged between 18 and 24 years, 35 and 44 years, and 45 and 54 years, 35% of people and 31% of people are aged between 25 and 34 years and 55+ years, respectively (Carers UK, 2013). While 30% of the 'general population' use technology in this context, with moderate use of social media by Facebook (32%) and Twitter (40%) users (Carers UK, 2013).

From a societal class standpoint, Carers UK (2013) ascertain 35% of middle-class people were more likely to use technology than 25% of working-class people. It is unclear from the report why there is a discrepancy, but we consider and posit those people who are from a working-class background may not have the financial resources to afford the necessary technology, or the digital skills and knowledge to understand the benefits of using technology. Similarly, older adults from low SES backgrounds describe their experiences of using technology, and enhancing their confidence (Morgan, 2021), while for some people technology use can instil fear, and apprehension (Freeman et al., 2020).

Technology can be alien to older adults and even more so for those individuals with dementia. Yet, at the same time, technology can be truly supportive (Nygård & Starkhammar, 2007; Rosenberg & Nygård, 2012). We believe the discourse could have been pushed further by the WHO and the new dementia-friendly model (WHO, 2021) leading by example, and truly acknowledging the integral role technology plays in this area (Starkhammer & Nygård, 2008; Topo, 2009; Topo, Saarikalle, Begley, Cahill, Holthe, & Macijauskiene, 2007). Therefore, we posit two critical questions,

1. Where is the scientific basis and merit for proposing the model?
2. Why is 'Technology' not listed as a separate domain or area of focus?

Positing these questions seeks a response, because there is existing evidence (Dikken et al., 2020), and discourse to the role and impact of technology in this area and it is not being recognised as a major player or component in the dementia-friendly initiative. Instead, the WHO (2021) should have consulted the existing evidence and investigated the impact of technology in AFCC (Dikken et al., 2020). Instead, it seems this recent published report (WHO, 2021) takes a more policy driven approach instead of creating an innovative evidence-based framework that can be adapted for different (global) ecosystems.

We change our shift at this point and in the following section we explore how and if theoretical concepts in the existing AFCC literature have considered the impact pertaining to coastal regions and communities.

Coastal Regions

Presently there are 34 age-friendly cities and towns across the British Isles (Centre for Ageing Better, n.d.). From the perspective of the WHO and the Pan American Health Organization (PAHO), there are over 500 cities across 37 different countries forming the 'WHO Global Network of Age-Friendly Cities and Communities' (PAHO, n.d.).

What is missing from the existing list, and diagrams is a framework that encapsulates and acknowledges rural villages (e.g., Hawes in the Yorkshire Dales), smaller towns (e.g., Pontefract, Swansea, Inverness, etc.) and larger cities (e.g., Wakefield, Plymouth, Norwich, and Edinburgh). Although it could be mooted that existing towns and cities within the existing network can and do, represent other towns and cities that are not listed. We should keep in mind a one size does not fit all, and therefore, exploring other towns and cities to determine if they meet age-friendly requirements should be considered. There is a lack of acknowledgement towards coastal regions (e.g., St Ives, Bamburgh, Cromer, Salcomb, etc.), and towns (e.g., Whitby, Falmouth, Penzance, etc.), which for many residents, and tourists alike, the level of age-friendliness is likely to differ somewhat to urban and city regions.

From a AFCC standpoint, little work surrounds the impact or even in-depth understanding of the challenges, barriers, and impacts to residents living in coastal regions and islands. Except for Burholt et al. (2013), Marston et al. (2021), Public Health England (PHE) (2019) and Atterton (2016). However, Scotland and the neighbouring islands are leading the way in employing telehealth/care approaches to afford access to improve delivery of personalised care, reducing delays and bureaucratic processes (Scottish Government, 2012). Telehealth/care can take the disguise of mobile phones, video conferencing and online communication platforms (e.g., Skype, Zoom, etc.),

> Mr X, who lives on an island in the north of Scotland, is referred by his GP to his local hospital to have an endoscopy (an internal examination using a small video camera on the end of a tube). A trained doctor at the hospital carries out an endoscopy, and the images are viewed live by a consultant in Aberdeen using video-conferencing equipment. Mr X can see the consultant on the video screen, and speak to him about the results. (Auditor General for Scotland, 2011, p. 3)

Previous studies (PHE, 2019) examined the risk and opportunities for advancing digital connectivity across rural and coastal regions, and the coverage of broadband across these areas was ascertained as a barrier even though technology and associated communications show potential ways of delivering treatment. Additional barriers highlighted a reluctance by older adults to adopt services including telephone advice lines, although NHS highland (Scotland) utilises a video conferencing service across older adult psychiatry clinics, leading to faster assessments, treatment reviews and patient monitoring (PHE, 2019, p. 10).

Greater access to technology by health professionals is delivering services and care provision but there is still the physical infrastructure which is problematic, '[A] balance where digital interaction could enhance rather than replace face-to-face care may be most appropriate' (PHE, 2019, p. 14). For many health professionals, they lack the skills, knowledge, and self-confidence to use technology, which is detrimental to service delivery, especially in a post-pandemic society, whereby many tasks and responsibilities transitioned online. The *Smart Homes and Independent Commission* has highlighted several barriers surrounding technology use and rollout within the health and social care sector (Gilbert, 2022). One of the main findings from a series of roundtables and evidence highlights the lack of digital skills by health professionals, and several recommendations are proposed including, the implementation of technology into national curriculums.

Conversely, a recent news article (Plater, 2022) describes how the virtual assistant device 'Alexa' could offer people the opportunity to connect to a health professional (who are seeking nonemergency assistance) via the device, through the partnership with the 'Teledoc' company. For some people, privacy and access to data will be a concern by individuals who are seeking medical assistance and cybersecurity experts, however, as Plater describes,

> Amazon cannot access, record, or store the content of your conversations with Teladoc. Alexa only logs that a call took place, not what health information was discussed during the call. And all of your telehealth interactions with Alexa – such as your requests to speak with a doctor – will be redacted in your voice history.

> Any protected health information you share with Teladoc will be handled pursuant to HIPAA Trusted Source [Health Insurance Portability and Accountability Act of 1996] and Teladoc's Notice of Privacy Practices. (Plater, 2022)

Further considerations should be considered also, and this news piece mentions 'health insurance', and for those people in the US who do have health insurance, access to this service will be free, while for those people without insurance the charge will be $75. There are many different health insurance models worldwide, and especially in the UK whereby, the National Health Service provides healthcare at the point of access. Therefore, if such a service was to be rolled out across the UK, would it be expected that prospective users would need additional health insurance? How could this type of telehealth run alongside the existing health provisions across the UK?

Currently, 'Push Doctor' (n.d.a) offers virtual appointments seven days a week, via the app, and for people who do not have a smartphone, they can access the services via the website on a laptop/computer. Previously, 'Push Doctor' required users to subscribe/pay for online appointments and more recently, their website details how this service is now being integrated into surgeries to enable patients to request an online appointment free of charge (PushDoctor, n.d.b). For surgeries registered with 'Push Doctor' patients of this service will not be required to pay for the consultation (PushDoctor, n.d.b). However, if a surgery is registered, then there are additional charges for the individual who is categorised as a private patiend. This additional charge is £45.00 for the appointment (PushDoctor, n.d.c).

Although this service is available seven days a week, it does come at a price especially for people whose surgery is not connected to this telehealth provider. For some people who are on low/fixed incomes and who are in desperate need of seeing a health professional, the cost for a 10-minute online consultation is financially out of their reach. This approach could be perceived as the early stages of NHS privatisation and instilling a 2-tier health service, for the haves against the have nots. The latter referring to the cost, and that is after considering people who have access to Internet connectivity and hardware. For those people who do not own a computer/smartphone and/or have suitable Internet connectivity there are additional barriers and a greater sense of the 'haves vs the have nots'.

A Global Pandemic

Since 2020 towns and communities have been affected by government directives, with many high-street shops closing during the first several months of the pandemic (Philips et al., 2021), and expansion of existing pavements to accommodate social distancing rules (van Hoof et al., 2021). During the first year of the pandemic, physical adjustments to the pavements were conducted (Figs. 4.12a-4.12b) to adhere to the 2-metre government guidance. Many businesses placed notices on the doors and windows informing customers of the current situation (Figs. 4.13a-4.13b).

Fig. 4.12a.   Construction Work on the High Street of Stony Stratford to Enable the Extension of the Pavement to Facilitate Appropriate 2-metre Distancing Outside. *Source*: Ownership and permission granted by H. R. Marston.

Fig. 4.13a/b.   Shop Signage in Stony Stratford. *Source*: Ownership and permission granted by H. R. Marston

It was not unusual to see sticky tape on the floors of grocery stores (Fig. 4.14) to ensure the 2-metre social distancing (Figs. 4.14 – 4.15) guidelines were maintained.

Fig. 4.14.   DIY 2-metre Distance Inside a Grocery Store at the Counter.
Source: Ownership and permission granted by H. R. Marston

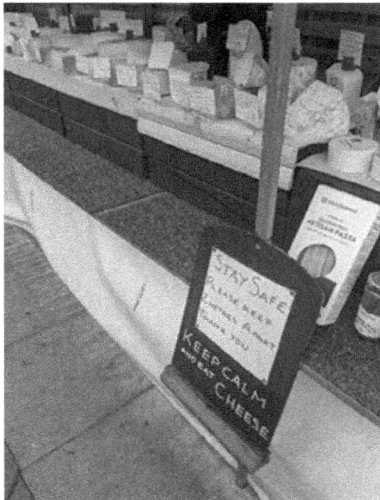

Fig. 4.15.   Homemade Signage at a Farmer's Market Stall. *Source*: Ownership
and permission granted by H. R. Marston.

Many homes chose to decorate their windows with rainbows and other images
connected to the NHS (Fig. 4.16). Residents in the town of Stony Stratford
(Buckinghamshire) created the 'teddy bear trail' to offer people on their daily
walks an additional game (Fig. 4.17).

Fig. 4.16.   Homemade Visuals in Windows. *Source*: Ownership and permission granted by H. R. Marston.

Fig. 4.17.   Displays a Teddy Bear Which was Part of a Trail for the Residents of Stony Stratford. *Source*: Ownership and permission granted by H. R. Marston.

Although many hospitality venues were able to open during 2020 they conducted several forms of 'design hacking' (White et al., 2020) to ensure their venues were adhering to social distancing and hygiene guidelines (Figs. 4.18 – 4.21), utilising hazard tape and stickers to outline appropriate distance at the counter (Figs. 4.18 – 4.19).

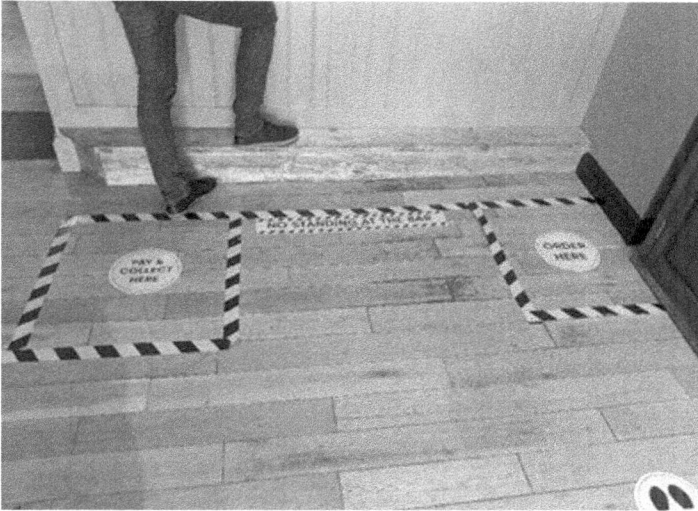

Fig. 4.18.   How Customers can Order and Collect Alcohol at a Counter in a Pub. *Source*: Permission granted by Mr Dobson.

Fig. 4.19.   How the 'Old Grocer's' Maintained 2-metre Distance Between Tables on a Bench. *Source*: Permission granted by Mr Dobson.

Technology Use in the Pandemic

The perception of technology changed quickly at the beginning of the pandemic, with institutions, individuals and businesses taking an agile approach to work, education, and socialising, recognising the necessity and importance of *technology* as the major player in our day-to-day lives. Throughout 2020 technology facilitated people to order groceries online, learn new hobbies, stay connected and

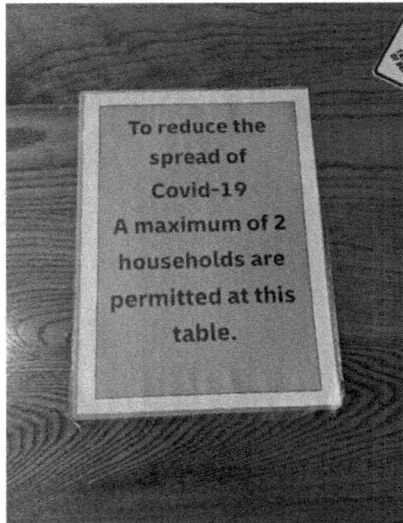

Fig. 4.20.   Notice Located on all Tables and in the Toilet Space of the 'Old Grocer's' as a Gentle Reminder to all Customers to Adhere to Respective Guidance. *Source*: Permission granted by Mr Dobson.

Fig. 4.21.   Notice Located on all Tables and in the Toilet Space of the 'Old Grocer's' as a Gentle Reminder to All Customers to Adhere to Respective Guidance. *Source*: Permission granted by Mr Dobson.

share information with friends and family (e.g., Friday night Quizzes on Zoom) (Fig. 4.22).

Social media platforms such as Facebook and Messenger offer friends the opportunity to share food pictures/recipes with one another (Figs. 4.23a/b – 4.24), while trying to maintain normality during the pandemic.

In the years and decades to follow, we will all reflect on this period including the changes to our work routines (e.g., hybrid) and wearing facemasks. The pandemic demonstrates how mandated rules present innovative responses that result in new life patterns, rituals, and activities.

Digital Communities Wales (DCW) (n.d.a) presents several case studies implemented to assist people in different communities (urban and rural) across Wales, including a befriending service for residents in the county of Powys, the Mothers Union supporting digital champions, while the Ty Gwyn care home in Penarth facilitates technology confidence for both residents and employees in a bid to improve the health and wellbeing (DCW, n.d.b).

Across the UK each devolved government implemented their own approaches, directives, and guidance for care homes (Department of Health, Northern Ireland, 2021; Public Health England, 2021; Public Health Wales, 2021a; Scottish Government, 2020), leading to families and friends being separated from one another, confusing information, especially if visitors were travelling into different tiers (or whether they could or not) for work or caring responsibilities. Residents in care homes (Booth, 2020; Vincent, 2020) may have seen their relatives through the windows, and in some instances care home staff chose to stay in the care home environment to reduce the risk of bringing COVID-19 into the environment (Murray, 2020a/b). In the spring of 2021, restrictions started to ease across the nations, but for many people in England they were still unable to visit their relatives (Booth & Blackall, 2021), whilst Public Health Wales (PHW) provided an 'Action Care' for visitors to care homes (Public Health Wales, 2021b).

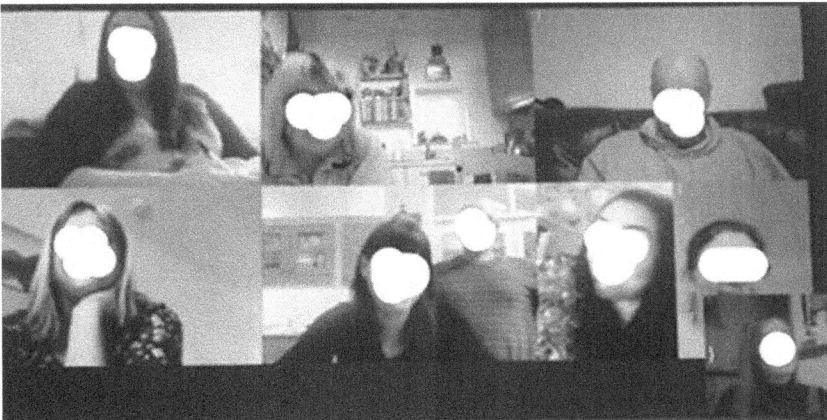

Fig. 4.22.   Group Zoom Call During the Pandemic of Friends and Family.
Source: Ownership and permission granted by L. Cairns.

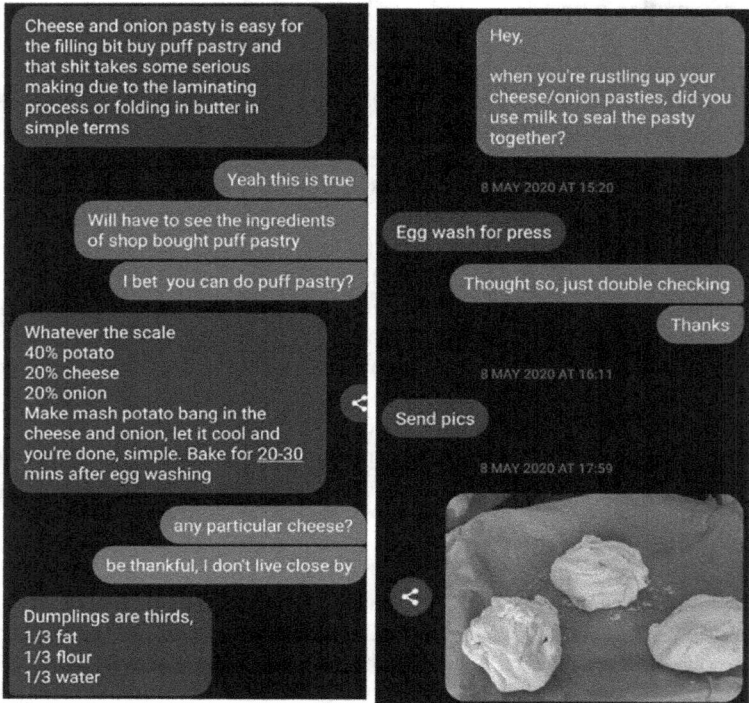

Fig. 4.23a/b. Friends Sharing Pictures of Food via the Messenger Platform During the Pandemic. *Source*: Ownership and permission granted by H. R. Marston & R. S. Turner.

Fig. 4.24. Friends Sharing a Recipe via the Messenger Platform.
Source: Ownership and permission granted by H. R. Marston & R. S. Turner.

Geographic displacement because of restrictions led people to seek alternative leisure activities to maintain a social connection, including cooking/sharing recipes and attending quizzes together (Figs. 4.22–4.24) during lockdowns. These simple activities that many of us took for granted in a pre-pandemic society, have been experienced through screen(s). During the lockdowns, technology facilitated the ability to socially connect with each other – for those people who have access to the Internet and devices. Whereas, for those people who live in care homes or do not own such devices and hardware, they either relied upon external assistance and/or caring staff to facilitate communication with their loved ones via a screen. For some people, this approach facilitated stronger friendship bonds (e.g., between friends) but for many families, this was not the preferred choice or way of connecting with loved ones. And by no means a replacement for physical face-to-face socialising, and contact, which can impact upon citizen's mental health (Mental Health Foundation, 2021).

Taking a different perspective, we explore in the following sections how technology plays a role from the stakeholder and industry perspectives.

Age NI and the Role Digital Technology Plays in this Stakeholder

Technology can enrich the lives of older people and Age NI have experienced this particularly during the COVID-19 global pandemic.

For many older people, devices such as tablets, and smartphones have been the only connection they have had with services, family, and loved ones. Technology offered some people the opportunity to enjoy reminiscing through listening to songs they used to love or to experience virtual travel to places they have never been. Technology facilitated older people to connect and engage with others, including their peers, advocacy organisations, policy, and decision makers. To illustrate the shift Age NI experienced in relation to technology and stakeholder engagement, the information below outlines the transition of the Age NI Consultative Forum (CF) in their journey to adopting digital technology as a means of connection and engagement during the early months of COVID-19.

Age NI Consultative Forum

Co-design and the concept of meaningful engagement with older people in the work of Age NI is something the CF strives for. The work of the CF covers the whole of Northern Ireland and focusses on issues affecting people over the age of 50 and it works collaboratively with, and in support of, Age NI.

Formed in 2010, the purpose of the CF is to identify the needs and concerns of older people and to communicate these to Age NI. The CF engages with, advises, and challenges Age NI on policy issues and on its strategic direction. The CF has been involved in a wide range of initiatives, from shaping Age NI's organisational strategy, to being media spokespeople on issues that matter to older people, to acting as a sounding board for other organisations wishing to engage with older people.

Currently, the CF comprises of 30–40 individual older people from across Northern Ireland. The CF Terms of Reference indicates that it should meet four times a year, to discuss standing business items, featuring topical and current issues. Pre-pandemic, these meetings were held in-person, in an accessible venue, for a half day and had an informal, but important, business as well as social element.

Transition to Digital Technology in the Context of COVID-19

Prior to the COVID-19 pandemic, digital technology didn't feature strongly when engaging with the CF. Beyond a basic use of technology, for example, PowerPoint presentations to support briefings, offering online access to members to participate in meetings had never been considered or offered. The onset of the global pandemic resulted in Age NI having to re-consider its approach to engaging with CF members. This meant a swift transition from engaging with people who came together in the same physical location, to embracing digital solutions. As digital technology did not feature strongly in the CF pre-COVID-19, the move to digital technology, when the first lockdown began in March 2020, was significant for the CF. A chronological journey of this change in the method of engagement with older people who are members of the CF is outlined below.

March 2020 – the Start of Lockdown

It was clear that in person meetings could no longer continue given the restrictions set out by government. The unsettling and uncertain nature of the pandemic coupled with isolation experienced by CF members highlighted the need to maintain personal connections through virtual means. Zoom was chosen as the most accessible platform for members of the CF to continue to meet, and the process of introducing and familiarising CF members with using Zoom was to use old fashioned telephone calls. These telephone calls were made to each individual member of the CF to brief them on the planned switch to using Zoom and to give them some guidance on how to use the communication platform. To complement the telephone calls, emails were also sent to members containing details of the move to Zoom and details on how to use it.

The shift to meetings on Zoom evolved quickly, with meetings taking place more frequently, on a fortnightly basis as opposed to the usual quarterly meetings. Recognising that interacting online with others could be exhausting, meetings were initially restricted to one hour. The motivation behind this increase in frequency of meetings in the early days of COVID-19 was to retain personal and social connections and to gradually ease members of the CF into this new way of interacting and working.

In the initial three months of COVID-19 the CF agenda was flexible and responsive, focussed on what Forum members wished to speak about, including their experiences and concerns around COVID-19 and impacts on older people. Time was spent supporting people to navigate Zoom and learn new digital skills, such as how to mute/unmute or to see others on the screen. Additionally, attention was paid by the meeting facilitator to how individuals were finding the transition.

Aware of how members would usually interact when at an in-person meeting, the facilitator on Zoom was able to observe and offer support online or by telephone if a member's level or style of participation changed significantly.

Overall, the initial three-month period of the pandemic resulted in a very agile, flexible response from Age NI. Early on, the emphasis was on facilitating and encouraging connection and on COVID-19, but ultimately members of the CF retained their important role as key stakeholders, highlighting issues and matters of concern to older people.

June to August 2020 – Easing of Restrictions

During June and August 2020 there was an easing of some restrictions whereby non-essential retail stores and restaurants were allowed to re-open. Restrictions on larger groups coming together continued. In response to this general easing and first real sense of hope since the onset of the pandemic, CF members agreed to move their meeting frequency from fortnightly to monthly. Members had started to embrace the technology much more and had developed confidence and competency in using it. Although meeting in person was still something many members wished for, fears remained, and members appreciated the value of embracing digital at a time when anxieties persisted about coming together in groups.

Over this period there was a change in CF focus and agendas. While discussions about COVID-19 continued, other issues began to be considered. CF members spoke about the voices of older people not being heard by decision makers during the emergency response to COVID-19. In response Age NI produced a report, '*Lived Experienced: Voices of Older People on the COVID-19 Pandemic*' (2020), drawing on the experiences and views of older people, including members of the CF, people who use Age NI services and the wider age sector. This publication helped highlight the issues that mattered most to older people at this time and contained action points for the government and others to take forward.

Furthermore, external organisations began, once more, to contact Age NI about engaging directly with older people. An example of such work include contact by the Department for Communities who wished to consult older people on how to effectively roll out digital connection. This was a genuine engagement, with COVID-19 being an important context for the engagement rather than the sole focus of discussions.

September to November 2020 – Uncertainty and Lockdown

This period brought with it a second wave of COVID-19 and a new lockdown. At this point the CF meetings remained on Zoom and continued to take place monthly. While the more formal business of the CF continued to be taken forward, it was recognised that the Zoom meeting format resulted in a loss of the more informal social networking and peer support that had previously been a feature of the CF meetings. Prior to COVID-19 CF members had an opportunity to mix and chat informally with some hospitality prior to the meeting commencing. To fill this void, a separate 'Zoom for the craic' meeting was introduced that took place once every 6 weeks, providing a light-hearted get together, where people sang, had some fun and connected with one another on a more personal basis. Feedback on the sessions suggested that they were a welcome outlet and helped to sustain relationships between members and support their wellbeing. This was an entirely separate initiative to the formal, business style meetings and was open to any members of the CF who wished to participate.

From this point on, engagement opportunities really picked up as government departments sought the views of older people on a range of strategies, including the older people's housing strategy, disability strategy, anti-poverty strategy, active ageing strategy and duty of candour. Engagement with these strategies involved older people participating in focus groups and meetings on Zoom and reviewing strategy documents.

In addition to the regular CF meetings, the 'Zoom for craic' and the public consultation exercises which all took place digitally (e.g., Zoom, email), members took part in focus groups with different stakeholders. Examples of this include engagement on the Bill of Rights for Northern Ireland with the Ad Hoc Committee of the Northern Ireland Assembly and involving focus groups of older people on technology use across the generations, for inclusion in Chapter 3 of this book.

November 2021 – Update

At the time of writing, it is 18 months since the first UK lockdown and the CF is still meeting via Zoom. Restrictions have continued to ease but there are significant concerns about a new COVID-19 variant, Omicron.

The CF now meets every two months. This means that the CF has still not returned to meeting once a quarter and in person, as outlined in its Terms of Reference. As the COVID-19 situation is ever changing it is difficult to have clear plans about when a return to quarterly meetings will happen. Tentative plans are being made, however, for members to meet as a group in January 2022. The situation will be monitored closely, and meetings will remain on Zoom until such time as it is safe to return to in person meetings.

Since the adoption of technology and moving to the online Zoom platform for meetings, the CF has developed confidence and skills in their usage and many now use online platforms with ease. The need to switch immediately to the use of technology did not, however, suit all CF members. Some had the ability to use technology, but simply did not want to use it for this purpose. Others did not become confident in using technology or did not find this approach accessible. Additionally, for some the issue faced was the lack of appropriate hardware to be able to effectively participate online. Age NI provided a laptop for the Chair of the CF so that they could carry out their functions effectively on an online platform and sourced some tablets for use by other CF members.

Age NI did explore alternative ways to facilitate the continued inclusion of those who did not wish to utilise digital solutions or who found them not accessible. One member, for example opted to receive papers for consideration in Braille rather than participating by Zoom. The agendas for this 18-month period are more diverse and contain a greater number of items for consideration than those before the pandemic. This could be due, in part, to the increased volume of requests for engagement on policy and legislative changes and in part to the shorter discussion times on each item as contributors give their views in turn. While members are together on screen, they do not share a physical space, which may impact on how members participate in discussions. In addition, older people, who may previously have wanted to engage in only one activity in a day are now taking on multiple engagements on a range of topics. Without the need for advanced planning around travelling, physical energy levels and so on, some older people on the CF appear willing to take on more.

Key Benefits and Challenges to Embracing Digital Technology

The adoption of technology in the context of COVID-19 resulted in several clear benefits, an increase in, and diversity of the engagement opportunities that older people were taking part in. Utilising the Zoom platform resulted in removing any potential barriers involving transport to engagement venues and reduced the physical energy and logistics of participating in several engagements in one day or week. Age NI's sense, is that while older people were participating in more engagements because they could, the stronger motivation remained their interest in the topic or issue.

Further benefits of utilising technology included the ability to maintain an element of 'business as usual' along with a sense of connection at an extremely isolating time for many older people. Members of the CF retained their role as key stakeholders. On a human level, it was important to be able to maintain connections with others and enjoy peer interactions and support.

The push towards using technology because of COVID-19 offered opportunities to further build on the co-design model of participation. Prior to COVID-19, Age NI staff acted as the main link with external organisations and provided progress updates at CF meetings. During the COVID-19 period members of the CF who were involved in the various engagement initiatives became responsible for providing updates on the ongoing work at CF meetings, placing greater value on their involvement and ownership of the process.

Age NI found that the availability of the Chat function on Zoom was hugely beneficial. It was felt that there is something very democratic about this function as it empowers people of all styles of participation to share their views when, and in a way that suits them. Chat function notes are transcribed as a supplementary document to the minutes for any CF meetings. On Zoom, the presentation of a series of individual screen images of members also meant that the focus was on the individual speaking, rather than on staff facilitating, creating equal opportunities for participation.

With any significant change to process often comes challenges. Age NI did find that there were some members of the CF who did not wish or were unable to participate using technology or any of the alternatives offered. Their contributions and insights have been missed and are a loss for Age NI, policy, and decision makers in Northern Ireland.

In the early days of COVID-19 and moving to the Zoom platform, a considerable amount of time was placed on supporting and tutoring people on the use of both the hardware and the communication platform itself. Furthermore, time was spent understanding the level of resource and hardware available to each member and plans put in place for those who required hardware such as tablets to participate.

Moving forward, technology will likely remain an important feature of stakeholder engagement. It is hoped that the CF will return to in-person quarterly meetings soon. The use of online platforms, like Zoom, are likely to remain a feature of stakeholder engagement, with a hybrid model being utilised to allow for a level and diversity of engagements to facilitate involvement and participation.

Social Enterprises and the Role Digital Technology Plays in this Segment of Society

A revolution has taken place in the sphere of social enterprises, with exposure now being possible on national and global scales only possible historically if the endeavour was made into a news feature or a significant amount of funds were spent on advertising.

We are now all familiar with phrases such as 'it has gone viral' (Klebnikov, 2022; Moreau, 2020) which not only applies to embarrassing hearsay and videos of cats but also to numerous benevolent good will projects or calls for assistance or support. A campaign or social enterprise can reach millions of people in a very short time and have its 15 minutes of fame as Andy Warhol (Nuwer, 2014) famously stated. Enabled by technology as a powerful catalyst but inherently driven by common human curiosity with a hint of bordun has resulted in obscure, local and far-flung worthy causes. It highlights plight and the need whilst subjectively pricking everyone's sympathy and empathy triggering action ranging from a 'like' to a 'share' to even a contribution of money and time in support.

Platforms such as Just Giving© have weaponised collecting donations for a social enterprise and charitable events, coming a long way from the sponsorship form that would be carried around to ambush unwitting victims, with children becoming mini debt collectors chasing people down for their 10p pledged per mile for the sponsored walk.

These intuitive platforms increase the reach and ease of the administrative burden albeit for a fee. It is bittersweet that they undoubtedly assist in raising more funds for these types of efforts and enterprise but themselves have proven to be an extremely lucrative market segment with Just Giving being worth £95m Blackbaud in 2017 (Delahunty, 2021), whilst subsequently the COVID-19 pandemic has significantly boosted social enterprises and charitable activity significantly since 2020.

How Does Technology Play a Role in Industry?

Technology is the driver of industry in the sense industry is there to sustain, maintain and enhance the current level of societal technology, and ranges from everything from a sharp stick to quantum computing.

Technology and industry are in a perpetual cause and effect loop, with technology being developed to improve major industrial outputs. For example, Amazon are the leaders in machine learning, this has been most prevalent with process efficiencies and algorithmic machine learned warehouses (Panda et al., 2020) which improved operations in dizzyingly complex facilities with Amazon warehouse robots self-learning (Edwards, 2020).

Historically, scientific discovery for the sake of knowing was a gentlemanly pursuit and known as 'Gentleman scientists' (Segen, 1992, p. 246) with the thought of using discovery for financial gain being considered vulgar. For example, these leading 'Independent Scientists' include:

- Henry Cavendish – Physics and Chemistry (numerous discoveries) (Cavendish, 2011),
- Charles Babbage – Father of Computing (first mechanical calculator) (Copeland, 2000),
- Robert Boyle – Chemist and Physicist (Boyles Law) (Principe, 2021).

Whilst it is fair to say modern science is forever in the debt of the pre-capitalism old world aristocracy. In the capitalist system technological advancement is driven by industry and industry is driven by commerce and consumerism, with all roads leading back to consumerism this has proven to be an irresistible incentive resulting in the fastest technological progression in human history.

The relationship between industry and technology is not tenuous nor is it fleeting, they are intrinsically linked. A symbiosis that shapes the world for better or for worse depending on your perspective. A growing number of earthlings live longer healthier lives, work easier and know more, with a promise from the happy couple, the marriage between technology and industry the global number of beneficiaries will continue to grow. It can be agreed in a vast majority of cases for the better we live the lives of our ancestor's wildest expectation thanks to this enduring relationship.

Summary

We provide a concise overview of how the field of gerontechnology has evolved and was pertinent in informing inter-and-multidisciplinary research agendas for over 30 years. The inclusivity of this field has been pivotal in highlighting and bringing to the forefront the issues, challenges and benefits surrounding inter-and-multidisciplinary research. Now is the time for change and the United Nations *Decade of Healthy Ageing (2021–2030)* (World Health Organization, 2020–2030) sets out priority actions for the forthcoming decade. To this chapter, Action 2 '*Ensure that communities foster the abilities of older people*' (World Health Organization, 2020–2030, p. 9) is very pivotal as we look towards the future. Although timely and welcomed there are still areas within the action points that have been overlooked regarding 'Action 2'. The WHO (2018) state,

> guidance and tools are needed to support cities and communities
> to make decisions around which actions are most likely to ensure
> these outcomes and not leave any groups behind in the process of
> development. (World Health Organization, 2018, p. 20)

Scholarly research (see Dikken et al., 2020; van Hoof et al., 2021) specifically details and presents existing models and evaluation approaches that can be deployed to monitor progress, providing scholars (should they choose to) several options and angles to monitor and evaluate progress, to achieve their objectives.

The mindset of AFCC is slowly changing given the new discourse purported by van Hoof et al. (2021), Dikken et al. (2020), Marston and van Hoof (2019), Marston et al. (2020) and White et al. (2020) but there is still a long way to go. Technology does and will continue to play a significant role as we move towards a post-pandemic society, and this includes the AFCC domain. Sadly, in the *research framework for the United Nations Decade of Healthy Ageing (2021–2030)* (World Health Organization, 2020–2030), technology is not acknowledged in this new research agenda.

In Chapter 1, we coined several new terms which we believe should be considered going forward to afford future ecosystems, the opportunity to be more inclusive across generations. Reframing terms such as 'intergenerational', 'older adults' and 'ageing populations' in association to digital technologies and instead use the term *Transgenerational* affords the notion of a journey from one generation to another. This too reduces the stigma of transgressing into old age, and instead, with reference to technology, presents a mindset of seamless (societal) transformation.

The term 'age-friendly' communities and cities could be seen as ageist, stigmatising and ableist, (Chivers, 2021), denoting old age and segregation, with the connotation that cities and communities should primarily be adapted specifically for older people. We need to start examining how our ecosystems should look in 20-30-50 years from now, because future ageing populations will comprise of different people with different needs, expectations, and opinions to that of our current ageing population(s). We posit future research agendas should involve younger generations in their consultation forums, because they will be the people living in these areas in later life.

Additionally, we posit technology will still be used in later life and currently AFCC discourse does not recognise the importance technology has within this domain except for the Socio-Gerontechnology Network. Is it the current thought by scientists and researchers alike that the needs and expectations of future ageing populations should be tackled by the future researchers in stead of tackling the needs, and expectations of the future ageing populations now? If it is then surely this approach will lead to the 'reinvetion of the wheel' because there seems to be a lack of apetite from current researchers and scientists to extend and broaden the discourse, not only to be inclusive but to ensure environments are suitable for all ages?

Why not start now, by inviting young people to join older adults into consultation forums to ascertain *ideal* 'Healthy Ageing' ecosystems? Initial steps to acknowledging this approach and inclusivity is to reframe 'AFCC' to *Transgenerational Living Cities and Communities* (TLCC). Cities and communities do not solely comprise of older people, but instead citizens of various ages, and disabilities, from different SES groups who all have a part to play in their ecosystem. The term TLCC infers that all generations in a community can and should have a part to play, instead of being marginalised. Just as AFCC was coined because of the exclusion of older age in policies and viewed as a way of placing focus on this problem. We need to work within the realities of our society, and future environmental and technology discourse(s) would encompass TLCCs.

Recognising the reality of our evolving (technological) environments stresses the diverse voices that are not represented, and the paucity between research, policies, and practice. The delivery and the adaptability of appropriate TLCCs in terms of reality and accessibility in our society, can afford several actors from within and across diverse sectors to take the preliminary steps towards reframing our thoughts and delivery. If we change our pre-existing notions to a 'design for all', including evaluation and implementation, we will have greater opportunities to achieve what we aim to set out – design and inclusion in 'Healthy Ageing' for all.

Hearing the voices of Age NI and industry are exemplars for research agendas to move forward and to understand the relationship(s) with technology and end-users. Age NI describe how their sea change in day-to-day operations depicts the issues and struggles many people and organisations faced at the start of the pandemic. Yet, the industry perspective highlights how our ancestors were pivotal in shaping contemporary society as we know it. And this is what we as scholars and actors should be doing now, for the forthcoming decades of this century.

Technology is going to continue playing a role across the meso, micro and macro levels of our ecosystems and it is the responsibility of all to ensure this transition and transformation is smooth as previously stated in this chapter

> The relationship between industry and technology is not tenuous nor is it fleeting, they are intrinsically linked. A symbiosis that shapes the world for better or for worse depending on your perspective. (p. 51).

This too can be said for all of society, and as we edge further into this century, we believe this notion will become more intrinsically linked. It is the responsibility of all of us, to ensure that no one is left behind during this *Transgenerational Technological* era.

Chapter 5

'The Older You Get, People Get Less Active, and Then They Feel the Cold'(Quote from the Field – Shore, 2019)

Introduction

The intense activity of listening back and reliving the life experiences shared by older adult participants during 'in the wild' research motivated and inspired this chapter to share and offer insights of what it feels like to age and witness great technology transformation.

The ageing population is increasing and will continue to do so until mid-way through the twenty-first century, concurrent to this birth rates and fertility are expected to decline (Bussolo et al., 2015). Emerging technologies, robots and assistive robotic devices can support and enhance quality of life (QoL) for older adults particularly in social and task-related settings (Smarr et al., 2014; Wu et al., 2014).

Gerontechnology approaches ensure that researchers, developers and design teams of technology and wearables afford understanding of the ageing experience and how these technologies can be optimised and used to enhance day-to-day living. Spending time 'in the wild' with older adult participants expands on this understanding. The participant expressions offer insights to the researcher involved, presenting surprise, generating emotional investment and broadening this understanding to feel what it is like to age. The practice of empathetic understanding of older adult's day-to-day experiences has documented the joys and pains of ageing (Moore & Conn, 1985). In addition, empathy suits such as AGNES (Lavallière et al., 2017) assist with gaining insight and understanding to the experience of ageing and its impact on everyday tasks such as shopping, dressing, and cooking.

User-centred design (UCD) approaches such as the creation of personas, scenarios, and empathy maps reflect the research, observations, and interactions with people during fieldwork (Cooper et al., 2014). Personas (personified examples of people) can be used to summarise the research and define a user type (Steen, 2008). However, the intention of good design/user research is not to create

Transgenerational Technology and Interactions for the 21st Century: Perspectives and Narratives, 113–125
Copyright © 2022 by Hannah R. Marston, Linda Shore, Laura Stoops, and Robbie S. Turner
Published under exclusive licence by Emerald Publishing Limited
doi:10.1108/978-1-83982-638-220221008

a persona, more importantly it is to understand your users' needs, goals, and experiences of their world (Travis & Hodgson, 2019). Empathetic understanding is critical to design and delivery of products and service systems that benefit and enhance peoples' lives and interactions.

Age-related conditions such as arthritis, Parkinson's disease and stroke can impose limitations of mobility and QoL. Soft robotic wearable devices can support or augment abilities of the various joints of the body (Chu & Patterson, 2018). In recent years the voice of the older adult is shared to enhance knowledge (Abdi et al., 2021) by offering insights and perceptions to emerging technology devices (Shore et al., 2018b) and apply this knowledge to the design of these devices (Shore et al., 2020). This voice is often expressed beyond the remit of a project and offers great richness which can be collaborated and engaged with further through Co-Design and Co-Creation approaches to understand challenges and opportunities and define outcomes that enhance day-to-day life experience and activities (Da Silva Júnior et al., 2021; Leask et al., 2017).

Ageing Experience and Empathy

Children born since 2011 may live to celebrate 100 years old (European Commission, 2014). How does a world look by the year 2061, or perhaps 2111? What technology and QoL will support people as they age in the future? Currently, the average life expectancy is 73 years (Bloom, 2020) with an expectation that it will exceed to the age of 77 by 2050 (United Nations, 2019). Additionally, the World Bank highlights other challenging factors such as fiscal inequality in retirement, reduced fertility rates which in turn will impact on the QoL and ageing process (Bussolo et al., 2015).

Factors related to ageing experiences and healthcare costs should motivate proactive innovation approaches that prevent or reduce age-related diseases and life changes such as cardiovascular disease, obesity, workload application and performance, with a requirement to redirect care and funding to community-based settings (Bussolo et al., 2015). Furthermore, because of caring for ageing parents, while simultaneously caring for children, 'the sandwich generation' can feel challenged and experience a reduced sense of well-being (Gillett & Crisp, 2017).

More recently the SARS-CoV-2 (COVID-19) has had a major impact on citizens at various levels of society – local, regional, national and on a global scale. This will remain a public health concern into the future (Holt et al., 2020). Social isolation has been experienced, coupled with the manifestation of loneliness due to social isolation measures (Marston & Morgan, 2020a, 2020b) undertaken to fight the pandemic (Banerjee, 2020).

The importance of good physical, emotional and mental health as we transition through adulthood to ageing can ensure a positive QoL (Singh et al., 2005). This is optimised further when we consider other factors such as meaningful engagement and self-realisation to maintain a sense of autonomy and contribution (Ryff, 2014). In addition, opportunity to remain fit and active as we age can be enhanced by health and fitness apps and video-game technologies (Gschwind et al., 2015; Marston & Hall, 2016) that are designed to accommodate older adults needs (Silva et al., 2015). Policy makers are encouraged to develop and include health technology products and services as essential features that may assist and offset some health, social care, and ageing challenges (Garçon et al., 2016). Furthermore, acceptance of health and fitness apps can be optimised through Co-Design approaches (Harrington et al., 2018).

Emotional Design and Empathy

Norman (2005) discusses *Visceral, Behavioural* and *Reflective* elements in relation to design and as crucial elements to shaping user experience by the emotion and connection they evoke. Furthermore, the importance of the *symbiotic relationship* between the person and machine, offers an exciting prospect combining *conscious, emotional, intelligent systems* (Norman, 2007).

To enhance Human Robot Interaction (HRI) emotional design approaches can enhance the interaction between individuals and robots, thereby optimising the HRI experience (Saraiva & Ayanoğlu, 2019).

The ability to map or mimic another's expression or feeling through empathy can generate emotional connection that enables; or if negative emotion, prohibit the creative process and ideation (Salminen et al., 2021).

Technology and devices such as PARO (a therapeutic robotic seal) can enable and offer emotional support to older adults as they experience social and emotional health changes due to retirement or bereavement etc., (McGlynn et al., 2017). Furthermore, emerging, and wearable technologies that offer the opportunity to personalise (e.g. colours, patterns, textures) and add features such as pockets or packs can optimise desirability and instil emotional connections and trust of these devices (Shore, 2019).

Ageing Experience

As we age, functional ability is relied upon and can be a challenge to our autonomy and independence should we experience physical and/or cognitive limitations. Often this decline can be supported through community or local health services (Morris et al., 1996). However, further supports such as assistive technologies and aids can provide liberating support when assessed and prescribed appropriately (World Health Organization, 2011) in turn providing renewed freedom and independence (Gilbert, 2022; Stowe et al., 2010). Furthermore, when not professionally prescribed these devices can in fact lead to increased falls risk (Chen et al., 2011; Gschwind, 2015; Marston et al., 2015). The experience of ageing can be described as successful (Rowe & Kahn, 2015), and satisfying (Shore et al., 2020) or less enjoyable as a result of degenerative conditions (e.g. Dementia) or limitations that impact on QoL (Penninx & Comijs, 2012).

Older Adults and Technology Accessibility

The importance of maintaining independence is a valued characteristic to the experience of ageing, and technology interventions can offset the negative consequences experienced with limitation or disability (Charness & Jastrzembski, 2009; Mitzner et al., 2018). Everyday tasks such as driving can continue to offer choices to journey from A to B, however, age-related conditions may result in no longer enjoying the freedom and autonomy to drive independently (Edwards et al., 2009; Gish et al., 2017; Murray & Musselwhite, 2019). Everyday walking aids such as ski poles have been preferred above 'walkers' or rollators by some older adults who rely on or require mobility assistance. This is perceived as avoiding a sense of devalued identity or vulnerability (McNeill & Coventry, 2015).

Some of the challenges to driving and avoiding fatigue can be offset by forms of gamification (Deterding et al., 2011a/b; Marston & Hall, 2016) such as music trivia quizzes relayed through audio while driving to continue interest and remove boredom of driving (Song et al., 2017).

Technology advancements in driving can potentially offer solutions that equip and support older drivers. These advancements are intended to empower users from all socio-economic areas, however, some older adults may in fact experience inequality through digital poverty resulting in limited access and poor experiences (Marston et al., 2019) and by being digital by default (House of Lords, 2021; Marston et al., 2020). Gerontechnology considerations (Graafmans et al., 1996) and applications that focuses on the interactions and engagement with technology by older adults can provide enhanced user experience of emerging technology devices (Marston & Samuels, 2019). In addition, the involvement of older adults as participants to Co-Design or Participatory design can optimise the opportunity to existing and emerging technology acceptance and adoption (Fisk et al., 2004; Pirkl, 1994; Power et al., 2016).

Chen and Chan (2014) note the importance of high levels of self-efficacy and reduced levels of anxiety as a key factor to technology acceptance and adoption. Barriers to acceptance and low user experience can relate to costs of repairs/maintenance or fears of learning or breaking the technology (Cook & Hussey, 2002). User experience of wearable and interactive technologies can be enhanced by understanding perceptions of trust, security, wearability, and service/device management (Pigliautile et al., 2012).

Research Experiences

Older adult insights and knowledge are beneficial to a UCD process (Shore et al., 2019). Age-related conditions (physical or cognitive) can impact on independence and QoL by older adults in community and care settings (Katz et al., 1963). Ageing in the twenty-first century presents opportunities for technology interventions that can assist with day-to-day tasks and activities, with the reconceptualising of the human ageing body calibrated to remain active and optimised (Katz & Marshall, 2018).

The wearable robotic technology (e.g. smart watches, hearables, head mounted displays, smart clothing) market is forecast to be worth $74.03 billion by 2026 (Research and markets, 2016–2021). The digital divide and digital inequality have previously been commented on as a challenge experienced by older adults as they navigate existing and emerging technology (Shore, 2019; Wang & Wu, 2021;

Wu et al., 2015). It is also noted that older adults today are integrated more than ever in our digital society, the transition, and experiences across the life course and as we age presents opportunity to research, understand, and identify the gaps that can influence use or non-use of technology (Francis et al., 2019).

To gauge understanding and perceptions older adults have to emerging wearable technology, – exoskeletons, Shore (2019) conducted 'in the wild' research observing and spending time with participants in their home environments or accompanying the respective participants as they engaged in day-to-day activities. In the wild approaches facilitate impromptu conversation and observations as well as collective design activity. As a design researcher this approach optimises opportunity to identify unmet needs and discuss these with the participants in order to define solutions throughout the process of design. This research interpreted expressions and experiences shared by the older adult participants related to their life experience, the ageing experiences and speculative perceptions towards robots and robotic assistive devices, including lower limb exoskeletons. There were five main themes that emerged from this fieldwork:

1. Ageing & life stage experiences.
2. Quality of Life.
3. Assistive Technologies.
4. Health Conditions and Care.
5. Products and Service Systems.

The fieldwork findings were a catalyst to innovative outputs and solutions. The empathetic nature of research 'in the wild' generated a volume of codes, categories and themes that were utilised to develop research outputs and design direction. This study generated more than 1300 codes directing new research and design opportunity. One category titled 'Feelings' was generated as a result of 240 codes which documented expression of feelings experienced by the participants as they age, it was so impactful that it motivated the work for this chapter. Fig. 5.1 is an example of the emotional investment and empathy experienced during qualitative research approaches. Grounded Theory supports this journaling and reflective approach as an opportunity to remain focussed on the intention of the research and rely on constant comparison, journaling, and memo writing (Charmaz, 2014).

Perceptions to Emerging Technology

The intense activity of listening back and re-immersing into the research sessions and the life experiences shared by the older adult participants during this fieldwork motivated and inspired this chapter. It shares and offers insights to what it feels like to be old and witness great technology transformation. The experience of spending time 'out in the wild' with participants, added and enhanced knowledge and awareness of the ageing experience and daily interactions by older adults. Documenting these experiences and stories was a challenging undertaking. It was intense and at times generated emotional surges of passion within. This interplay,

> *03.03.2018*
>
> *"Coding makes you realise how emotionally you are invested in your participants and their worlds...*
>
> *I was working today on another section of interview that involved a couple discussing the impact of Alzheimer's – the Husbands brother was living with the condition.*
>
> *Around the time the codes were all around expressions – feelings...*
>
> *Feeling, caring, challenged, fulfilled, intimidated, loved, reassured, pro-active, fear, a burden, a nuisance, etc., etc.,*
>
> *I felt upset – overwhelmed and tears were gently easing from my heart through my head...*
>
> *I love this work; I feel privileged to hear and witness intimate expressions from others...*
>
> *How lucky am I?*
>
> *I stepped away from the desk to take a breath.*

Fig. 5.1.   Direct Reference from Journaling and Memo Writing regarding the Category 'Feelings'. *Source*: Shore (2019, p. 154).

whereby, the researcher is actively responding and working with the data is necessary to the generation of data from the field (Birks & mills, 2015).

Affinity Diagramming (see Figs. 5.2–5.4) is a resourceful design tool that can offer applied and agile responses to developing design direction through recognising the relationships and patterns that emerge from research activity. The practice and application of affinity diagramming, while also building a verbatim database using NVivo software (see Fig. 5.4) and constant comparison methods ensured rigour, discipline, and delivery of rich data. This was a very insightful part of documenting and analysing the participants insights and sharing of their world.

Fieldwork Stories

As stated at the chapter introduction, this chapter began as a result of human interactions and share of the ageing experience in relation to emerging technologies. The author has conducted numerous studies over the years, however, this particular study was exploring and looking retrospectively to the past, while anticipating or considering future life experiences and technology interactions by older adults. In addition, it enquired at times about the relationships that we encounter, build, and sometimes lose during a lifetime. These research sessions presented so much energy, passion, and empathy that the author was mobilised and vividly exposed to the joys and pains that ageing can bring. The summaries below are a small cross section of the expression documented. Each item will begin with the direct quote, followed in brackets by the code.

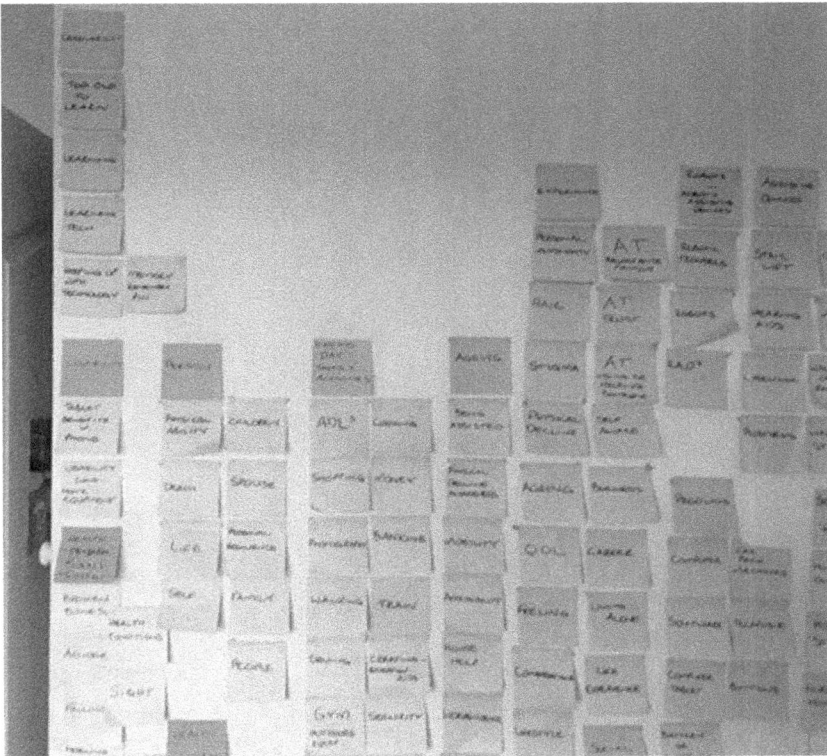

Fig. 5.2.   Examples of Affinity Diagramming to Define Themes. *Source*: Shore (2019).

> Mam or Dad becomes a problem .... [feeling a burden]

This rather poignant statement was expressed on varying levels by several participants who, had a desire not to be a burden, particularly on family members but also to society as a whole. The statement above is a comment internalised but expressed in order to state how it feels sometimes to be old and not capable to conduct tasks independently, relying on others to help or support the effort of that task. From a lifespan perspective, when we are younger, and if we rely on help, we might refer to this support as teamwork or helping each other out? What is it that creates this sense of becoming a burden or an interference to the younger generations time and willingness to help as we get older?

> I find it very, very hard to go to a doctor. [feeling challenged]

The participants shared intimate expression of various challenges experienced on a day-to-day basis, ranging from relationships, to technology, and to services

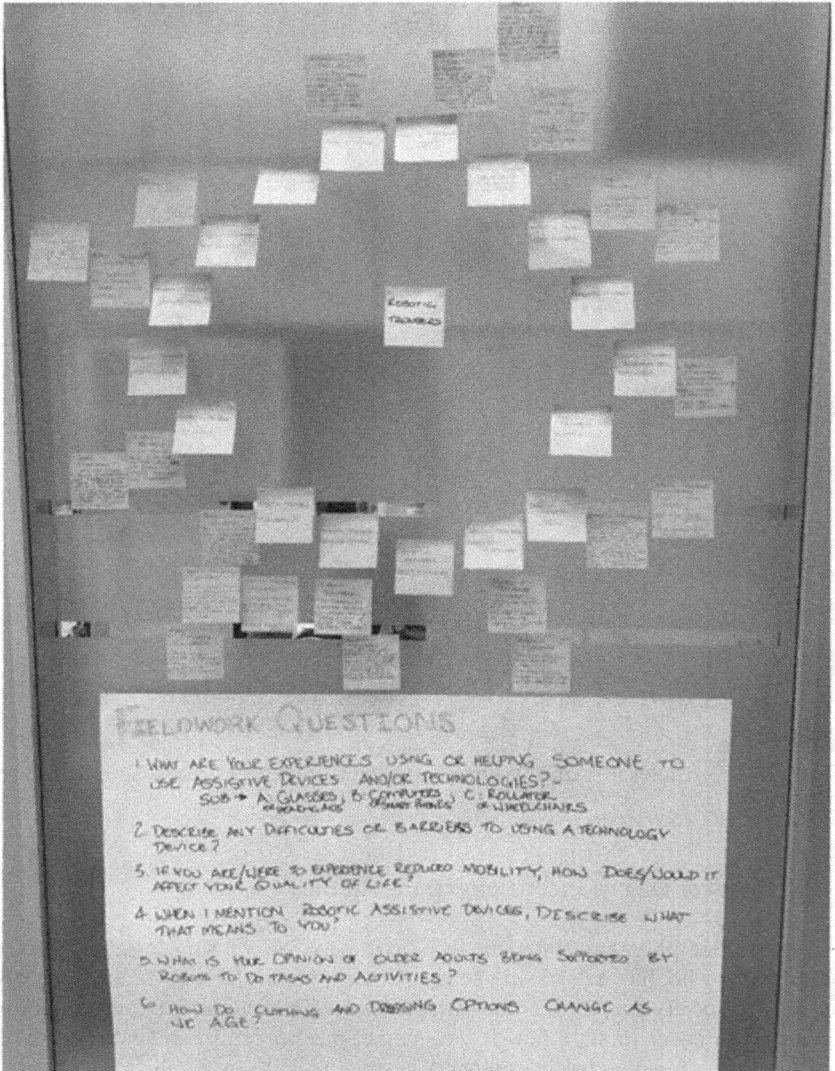

Fig. 5.3. Relating the Research Fieldwork Questions as Part of Affinity Diagramming Focus and Theme Definition. *Source*: Shore (2019).

including healthcare. This was more apparent in larger practices or people who lived in rural areas and needed to arrange transport etc. to access healthcare or GP. The larger practices sometimes were perceived as less personal, and this manifested in a feeling of challenge in case the familiar GP was not available. Furthermore, and layering on to a feeling of becoming a burden, asking for a

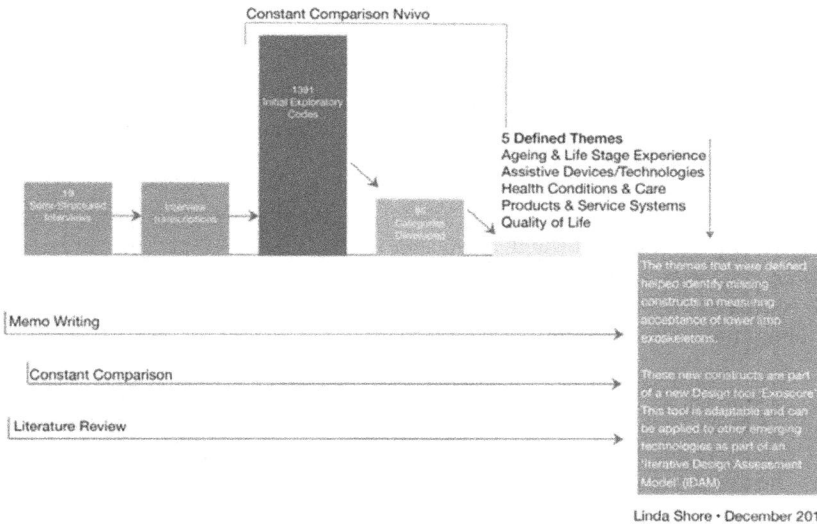

Fig. 5.4. Overview of Research Activity Relying on a Constructivist Grounded Theory Approach. *Source*: Shore (2019).

lift [in a car] could also present challenge that the older adult would not be a nuisance and internally becoming aware of being less capable or independent.

> Sometimes you'd be embarrassed to go to a doctor, sometimes they don't know what's wrong with you. [feeling embarrassed]

Expressions of embarrassment were expressed during the fieldwork sessions more so by female participants who feared or had a reluctance to engage with a male doctor, particularly if the issue was related to intimate tasks such as toileting. In summary, participants might 'eventually' go to the doctor, but were likely to see if the issue would pass beforehand. Lack of trust was manifested through perhaps attending an appointment with symptoms and being told nothing is wrong which could result in a feeling of embarrassment that the doctor's time was wasted.

> Oh I would get clothing that's easier to put on you and shoes you know that's maybe slip on or instead of having to bend down to do laces up the Velcro which is, um and you need, I think as you get older you need warmer clothing …. [feeling cold]

Ageing, and clothing options including wearability and colour were discussed during the fieldwork. Participants were invited to discuss how their younger self dressed, and changes now in their preferences. One constant that was expressed was the aspect of feeling cold, and how in younger days, very few layers of clothing were needed, and yet as ageing progressed, this inability sometimes to stay warm or to feel cold quicker was a consistent expression.

> I was nervous because I didn't want to hurt him. I know I have not got the gentlest of touches and I know he needed to be treated gently. [feeling empathetic]

This expression was documented in relation to a wife who was caring for and supporting her husband through an episode of being unwell. This sense of hurting someone, so important to the woman was expressed with a tone full of empathy and compassion. The ladies' eye glazed as she recalled his illness in greater detail including the story of his recovery.

> I can do – I'm one of these people that whatever it is, whatever I do I think I can climb Mount Everest now and I'm looking at all these people and I think I can do that and I do believe I can do it but I know I can't but I do believe that I could, does that make sense to you? [feeling empowered]

The ability of the mind to stay connected and focussed on activity and being 'able' was prized. The participant spoke about her youth, the various stages of life and her abilities now, despite acknowledging that now, perhaps she might not be as able, she still had a sense of empowerment and owning her world!

> I always loved style but didn't have the same opportunities that I have now, I mean I really love clothes now and I will dress to the best of my ability now at all times and um that's one of my downfalls, I'm always out buying clothes, buying shoes, buying .... [feeling excited]

Some participants were enjoying their retirement years, expressing the various choices and options they had available now compared to their working age selves. They compared the differences and challenge to paying off a mortgage, rearing children and coming then to their retirement with pensions that could provide a QoL that enabled them to remain engaged with society and to select clothing, holidays, or other social activities with excitement.

> Well a robot ... would frighten me. [feeling fear]

During the fieldwork, one of the questions asked was *what did a robot look like* to the participant and *what types of things could a robot do*. The participants varied with their answers, suggesting humanoid types or equipment such as electronic kitchen devices. Some could visualise wearable technology devices with robotic features, however, there was a grouping that expressed challenge or fear when robots were mentioned. Sometimes this related back to working age experience particularly in manufacturing where robotic machinery and systems updated production lines. On occasion this had resulted in redundancies in the place of employment. Others commented or related robotic perceptions to science fiction and movies, again inciting fear at times.

> When, there's two of us (spouse and participant) there, we're fine! [feeling fine]

Death was frequently discussed as a stage considered when we are ageing. There was comfort expressed by those participants in a relationship particularly apparent with those couples who had children and the visits from grandchildren. However, the aftermath and thoughts towards one partner passing away generated reflection to a space of behaviours post-bereavement, and positions expected if you were a widow or a widower – in terms of types of clothing worn, social activities and moving on again with life.

> I had the fright, the shock of it, (participant had a fall at home, broke wrist, lives alone). [feeling a fright]

Awareness of getting old or becoming vulnerable instilled fear in a lot of the participants, particularly when conditions such as dementia were discussed. Falling or becoming frail was expressed poignantly with an ominous outlook. There were stories shared of active older adult participants supporting or helping neighbours and likewise, other participants who had experienced falls, stroke or other ailments that infringed independence and affected QoL.

Technology Acceptance

The ageing experience would imply a life lived that has experienced and witnessed change. In terms of technology, change is happening at such a pace it can present challenges to older adults and their ability to 'keep up' (Wu, Damnée et al., 2015). Emerging wearable technologies such as exosuits are likely to become mainstream devices that assist or augment physical ability in the future (Young & Ferris, 2017). It is critical we ensure optimising acceptance of these technologies to enhance autonomy, and the ageing experience (Shore, 2019). Older adults would like to try newer technologies, for example, touchscreen mobile devices, however they may rely on previously used technology, due to the uncertainty of understanding the new technology (Page, 2014). The intervention of technology-based devices can enhance autonomy (Charness & Jastrzembski 2009), likewise it can also be a source of frustration and ultimately abandoned as a result of shortcomings regarding consumer satisfaction (Cook & Hussey, 2002).

The Technology Acceptance Model (TAM) was introduced by Davis (1985). It has evolved over the years but essentially, TAMs are relied upon to predict user acceptance of a technological application (Venkatesh & Davis, 2000), or as a tool to map influence between a user's intention to use a device and the *actual* use of that device (Heerink, Kröse et al., 2010). The application of TAM involves participants rating statements or 'items' via a Likert scale. However, for several reasons (e.g. self-reported answers, question fatigue) or creative expression for the user to state inventive ways or workaround solutions to the prescribed set of statements (Salovaara & Tamminen, 2009). Wearable technologies may have elements of 'embodiment' with users (Pazzaglia & Molinari, 2016) which requires multi-dimensional understanding and knowledge by design teams (e.g. exosuit control platforms managed on devices such as smartphones or computer tablets). The experience of wearability of an exosuit cannot rely on mainstream application of TAM or usability measures alone during device development. A new hybrid approach – Exoscore, was introduced by Shore et al. (2019) to capture the perceptions, experience, and behaviour intent towards exoskeletons and exosuits. This type of approach could also be adapted to measure acceptance of other emerging technologies and the service design required to optimise acceptance and adoption of wearable technologies.

As discussed earlier, technological applications have evolved at such a pace, that several disciplines beyond Information Communication Technology (ICT) such as health rely on the benefits of TAM to state and define implementation and use of a technology. Holder and Karsh (2010) discuss the need for moderations to TAM in Health settings to include and focus on the end-user reactions – how, and/ or why a particular technology has been introduced rather than the contracted purchase or installation of the technology.

The area of health is just one domain of contemporary society where TAM has been utilised to assess user acceptance. Using various measures to understand the TAM or usability of a system can be found in the iStoppFalls EU project (Chapter 2) whereby, Vaziri and colleagues (2016) used the System Usability Scale (SUS) (Bangor, et al., 2008; Borsci et al., 2009; Brooke, 1996), to measure the usability of the ICT-based system and the Dynamic Acceptance Model for the Re-evaluation of Technologies (DART) (Amberg et al., 2005) to assess user acceptance. At the time, iStoppFalls was the largest international, multi-centred RCT which comprised of over 30 measures (Gschwind, Eichberg, Marston et al., 2014), based on the aims and objectives of the three-year project. Findings showed positive acceptance, usability and the respective participants responded positively to accepting the iStoppFalls ICT-based system into their home(s) (Gschwind, Eichberg, Ejupi et al., 2015).

The onset of the COVID-19 pandemic drove an increase in access and use of digital media. Streaming services witnessed a surge in paid subscriptions, in turn leading to increased digital advertisements that could be opted out depending on which type of service you subscribed to. The experience and acceptance of these technologies was accepted as a basis to offset negative mood and entertain the subscriber (Camilleri and Falzon, 2020). However, the application of 'dark patterns' displays how technology can influence behaviour by people to perform actions (such as sharing information or purchasing premium content) that was unintended when signing up (Yablonski, 2020).

Summary

This chapter discusses and shares some of the rich insights that were expressed during recent fieldwork studies with older adult participants. The experiences shared by older adults as they age generated levels of emotion and empathy that were too powerful to remain unpublished. Researchers and those interested in the fields of gerontology and gerontechnology work towards enhancing QoL experience as we age. We rely on the narrative shared through fieldwork and the empathetic action we utilise in order to define solutions to unmet needs expressed. However, as we approach a time whereby the population will experience change in demographics; and technologies offer supports in ways sometimes not yet realised, *Transgenerational Technology* approaches will offer innovative adaptable solutions that enhance QoL across the life course. While UCD approaches can facilitate and enable interactions and collaborations to research, explore and ideate across the disciplines as we create devices, services and systems that assist, support, and enable those of us with limitation, challenge, and reduced autonomy.

Chapter 6

Digital Inequities and Society

Introduction

Over the last 10–20 years, there has been a growing body of literature and discussion surrounding the use of digital technologies, as discussed in Chapter 2. Greater discussions are occurring surrounding digital poverty, and data poverty which has been exacerbated and brought to the forefront of society via the pandemic. While technology solutions designed for people with disabilities or older adults can sometimes focus on pill reminders and telehealth solutions and less on the 'F' word – 'fun' (Coughlin, 2017). With the advent of the Internet in the 1990s and accessible 24-hour news channels allow citizens access to information, while retrieving information and adapting to a new way of life was afforded through technology. Yet, for many people in society young and old, the same cannot be said. In the following section we explore digital inequities and the notion of digital poverty.

This chapter will explore how digital and societal inequities impact various cohorts and citizens in the twenty-first century. We briefly explore societal and political events of the late twentieth century because we believe such events may impact contemporary experiences to digital inequities, while also advancing experiences. We draw on current narratives and discourse pertaining to digital access, communities, and societal impacts (e.g., education, health, etc.) to comprehend how digital technology and inequities were at the forefront of society from the COVID-19 pandemic perspective. Finally, we explore how digital inequities have been weaponised within society and what the future of digital inequities means for citizens and society.

Digital Divide and Digital Poverty in the Twenty-first Century

The discourse of the digital divide has been an ongoing issue, debate, concern, and topic of exploration for nearly 30 years. For readers who are unfamiliar with the term – digital divide, it refers to the gap(s) between people in our society who do have access to digital devices, and infrastructure (e.g., the Internet)

Transgenerational Technology and Interactions for the 21st Century:
Perspectives and Narratives, 127–156
Copyright © 2022 by Hannah R. Marston, Linda Shore, Laura Stoops, and Robbie S. Turner
Published under exclusive licence by Emerald Publishing Limited
doi:10.1108/978-1-83982-638-220221009

and those people who do not (Hilbert, 2011a; van Dijk, 2020). Research in this area started back in the 1990s with a view to exploring what was termed as the first-level digital divide which primarily sought to understand and reduce the digital divide pertaining to the physical access of computers between 1995 and 2003 (van Dijk, 2020). While the second-level digital divide relates to the space between consumers/users on the Internet and content makers/producers (Schradi, 2011). Scholarship surrounding the digital divide has extended to and continues to understand the inequalities experienced by citizens (DiMaggio et al., 2004; Prensky, 2001a) in society and include the differences between sex (Dixon et al., 2014; Hilbert, 2011b), disability (Dobransky & Hargittai, 2006; Fox, 2011; Roulstone, 2016), and race (Atske & Perrin, 2021; Fairlie, 2014).

Debates surrounding the digital divide have been ongoing for over 20 years (DiMaggio & Hargittai, 2011), including technology use and adoption (Freeman et al., 2020; Loos, 2012; Marston et al., 2019; Ofcom, 2018; Shore et al., 2020) virtual assistant devices (Marston & Samuels, 2019; Yang & Lee, 2019), robots (Anghel et al., 2020; Shamim et al., 2019), social media use (Duggan, 2015), and mobile/smartphone and messaging (Fox & Duggan, 2012; Ofcom, 2018; Smith Pew Research Center, 2015).

Statistics show, across national and international planes greater take-up and use by various societal demographics, and while there is growth of use in digital technologies by older adults, there are still some people who are disconnected. MIT AgeLab is one institute that demonstrate numerous issues and concerns facing our ageing populations, from driving and independence (Gish et al., 2017) to caregiving and well-being, to planning for retirement and financial longevity in later life, and the use of AI to facilitate (potentially) living longer in later life.

While younger cohorts are continuing to be connected through their smartphones, and various online platforms such as Facebook, Snapchat, and Tik Tok, etc. This in turn has led to bridging scholarly areas to move debates forward, such as the extended smart age-friendly framework (Marston & van Hoof, 2019). The COVID-19 pandemic has brought to the forefront the inequalities of digital access, poverty, and data within society. Although there has been an influx of technology use, since the outbreak of COVID-19 on a global scale, the inequalities of citizens surrounding digital technologies has shown there is still a digital divide and digital poverty (Coughlan, 2020; Ed Lounge Ltd, 2020).

For many younger citizens in society, they may not be able to consider what life was like prior to the Internet, mobile/smartphones, tracking data via apps and other devices such as smart watches, or sharing information, uploading videos and photos on to platforms such as Facebook, Snapchat and TikTok. The integration of the Internet within our society has enabled our lives and businesses to be dominated. In so much as, if one does not have the Internet, then access to services such as health, government, banking and more recently education is hindered. Thus, if we think about access to these services now and even more so in the future, the notion of collaborative design approaches can lead to satisfying product and service system experiences for people (Coope et al., 2014).

Over the last 20 years or so, we, as citizens have embraced digital transformation and practices, intersecting across our businesses, educational institutes, and personal lives, whereby we can pay for goods and products via a smart watch or Google Pay on our smartphones. Less than 30 years ago, this notion of digital transformation may have been incomprehensible for many citizens in our society. Conversely, citizens in their late teens and into their twenties could be flummoxed to wonder how we (society) managed 'to get on' with our lives in a pre-Internet era and without Spotify, Facebook, Tik Tok, SnapChat and WhatsApp? Where, we did not 'check-in' on social media, or we were not purchasing goods such as groceries, and music online, and within hours, or a day, our goods would be delivered directly to our front door. These are just some of the benefits we as citizens in the twenty-first century have wholeheartedly embraced.

However, there are challenges and even some people would suggest negatives to digital transformation, including bank fraud, and 'catfishing'. The latter generally experienced through dating apps. If we take the perspective of dating apps, many users can fall victim to fraud, scamming, catfishing and even death (Marston, Niles-Yokum et al., 2020). The pandemic turned society upside down, and with it, various intersectionality's within society such as health and well-being (Marston, Wilson et al., 2020), communities (White et al., 2020) social networks and leisure activities (Marston & Kowert, 2020; Marston & Morgan, 2020a), and celebration of annual festivities (e.g., Christmas) (Marston & Morgan, 2020b) was brought to the forefront of many people minds (Marston et al., 2020).

Although the year 2020 brought tougher than normal circumstances for many people in society, because of government directives associated to lockdowns, which in turn impacted civil liberties, closure of businesses and venues not only affected people on a financial level, but also emotional, mental on social connections, educational achievements, health, and well-being (Ellis & Tucker, 2020). The lockdowns and limitations to social venues familial and friendship connections, coupled with, for some people limited digital access, will have plunged many people, both young and old, into depression and poorer mental health (Gega & Aboujaoude, 2021; Pandya & Lodha, 2021; Sorkin et al., 2021), resulting in a greater feeling of loneliness, and isolation. This 'efficacious outlook' (Bandura, 1994) can influence our abilities to cope with depression, stress reduction and a sense of achievement. Although for some people, owning a smartphone and/or laptop will have assisted them to have some level of connection with friends and family, for many who do not own these devices, let alone who can afford an Internet connection into their home, will have resulted in them being shut off from the world.

Since the first piece of code (06.08.91) was released by Sir Tim Berners-Lee on the alt.hypertext discussion group, and enabling other members to trial it (Ward, 2006), the power of the Internet and its capabilities has grown. Many people through work and/or education can now connect to the Internet to conduct their respective tasks and activities. However, for some people in society, access to and use of the Internet over the years continues to be limited. The Office for National Statistics (ONS) note various changes surrounding Internet use and access across many groups of people including older adults, people with disabilities, sex, age, ethnicity, and region.

From the standpoint of sex, in 2018 (ONS, 2018) both men (51%) and women (38%) aged 75+ years who were 'recent Internet users' were more so than in 2011.

While differences and decreases in sex, show in 2018, men (91%) and women (89%) were using the Internet more so than in 2011, 82% and 77%, respectively. In 2019, of those adults (by sex) who have never accessed the Internet, women (8.7%) were still lagging behind men (6.3%) (ONS, 2019a), while 7.5% of adults reported to have never used the Internet reduced from 8.4% in 2018 (ONS, 2019a). This difference associated to sex, was noticeable in adults aged between 65 and 74 years (ONS, 2019a), specifically 84% of men and 82% of women. Further differences within sex shows 'recent Internet users', aged 75 years and older whereby men (54%) were more recent users than women (41%) (ONS, 2019a). Regarding younger age groups, the gaps are narrowing also in comparison to Internet use in 2011 (Fig. 6.1).

In the context of age, children and young people aged between 11 and 18 years (700,000) reported no Internet access via devices such as a tablet or a computer (Lloyds Bank, 2018; ONS, 2019b). Furthermore, of those young people/children, 60,000 reported to have no Internet access whatsoever, and noted how completion of homework tasks would be difficult. This information suggests for many young people in this situation they are facing inequalities and disadvantages, with their education suffering because of expectations of schools assuming everyone has access to the Internet. Between 2011 and 2018, the number of non-Internet users (not used the Internet within the last 3 months) (ONS, 2019b) is greater in 2018 by older people who are 75+ years, than those people in the same age category in 2011 (ONS, 2019b) (Fig. 6.2).

The relationship between ethnicity and Internet use (Fig. 6.3) in 2011 highlights three ethnicity groups with the highest proportion (over 20.0%) of people who

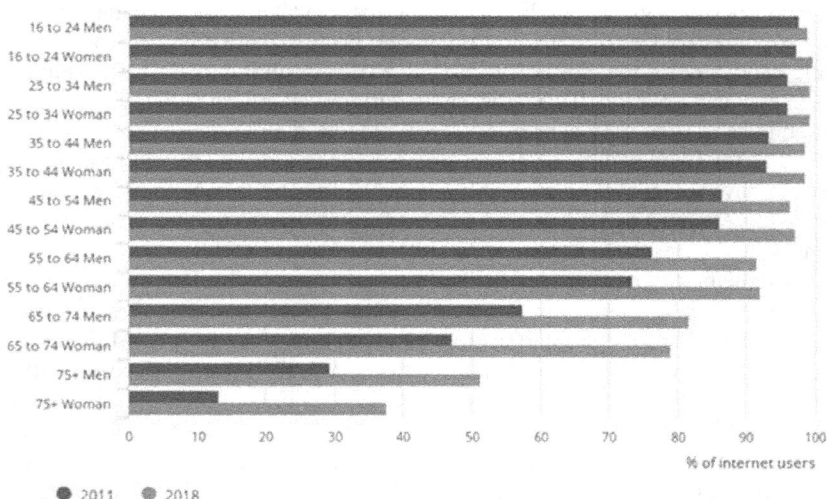

Fig. 6.1.   The Gap Between the Proportion of Internet Users Over the age of 65 Years and Younger Age Groups is Narrowing for Both Men and Women. *Source*: ONS (2019b).

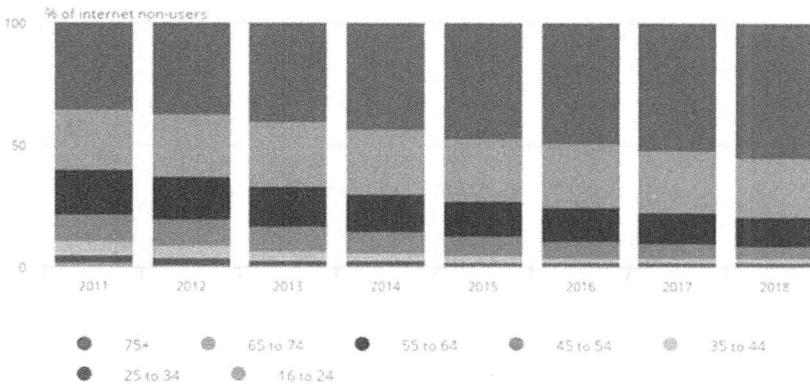

Fig. 6.2. Increasing Proportion of Internet Non-users Over the Age of 65 Years. *Source*: ONS (2019b).

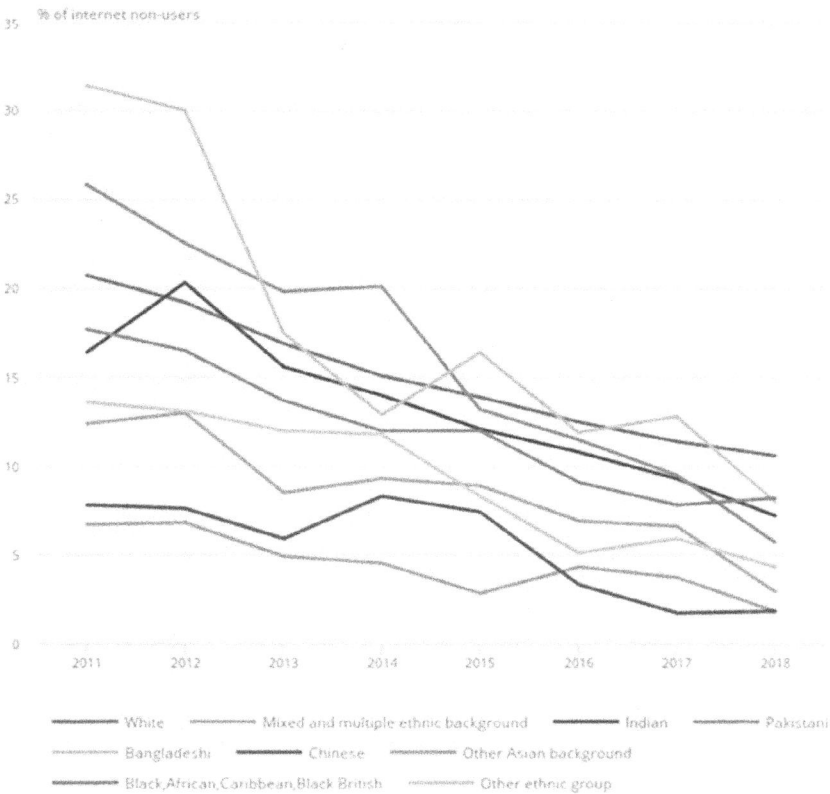

Fig. 6.3. Ethnicity Gap in Internet Usage has Narrowed Over Time as the Proportion of Internet Non-users has Declined. *Source*: ONS (2019b).

were non-users, Bangladeshi (31.4%), Pakistani (25.8%) and White (20.7%) (ONS, 2019b). However, in 2018, although all three ethnicity groups had reduced their proportions, Bangladeshi (8.0%), Pakistani (5.7%), White (10.6%), a fourth ethnicity group was still high (Indian, 7.2%), albeit this too had decreased from 16.4% in 2011. These disparities do not present clarity to understanding why there is a greater lack of Internet use within these respective ethnicity groups. However, assumptions could be made and include language differences, limited/ no digital skills, self-efficacy, understanding/perceiving the benefits and purpose of using the Internet, and/or financial costs.

While people with disabilities (Fig. 6.4) aged between 16 and 24 years and over 75 years are the highest non-users of the Internet at 60.0%. Similarly, people aged between 45 and 54 years (58.0%) and 65–74 years (50.0%) followed, and the least proportion of adults who identified as non-users of the Internet were aged 25 and 34 years (48.0%) (ONS, 2019b).

From a regional perspective, people living in London and the Southeast of England (93.0%) were identified to be recent users of the Internet (ONS, 2019a). While Northern Ireland has the least amount of Internet users (12.2%), followed by Wales (9.3%), and several areas across England, albeit with lesser proportions, West Midlands (9.1%), Northeast (8.7%), East Midlands (8.3%), Northwest (8.2%), Yorkshire and Humber (8.6%), East of England (6.7%). Scotland (8.7%) too has the same proportion of Non-Internet users to that of the Northeast of England (ONS, 2019a). The Southeast and Southwest regions of England reported less than six percent of Non-Internet users. However, the ONS (2019a) reports in the regions of Scotland and Wales, 93% of adults were recent users of the Internet.

We continue this discussion in the following section, exploring digital exclusion across the UK, taking a view of why many people in our society are digitally excluded.

Composition of adult internet non-users by disability and age group, UK, 2017

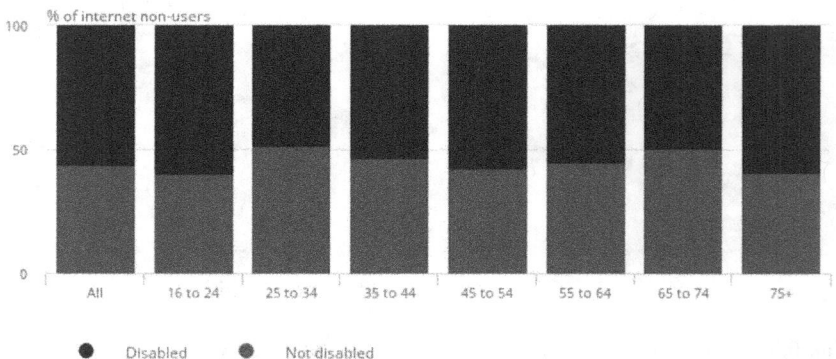

Fig. 6.4.   Disability and Internet Usage. *Source*: ONS (2019b).

Digital Exclusion Across the UK

Household Income and Regions

Digital exclusion can impact low-income households (ONS, 2019b) (Fig. 6.3) with those households who have a range between £0 and £10,000, followed by households with an income ranging between £10,001 and £15,000 being the least likely to have an Internet connection.

There are areas and regions that are experiencing higher levels of exclusion (i.e., Northern Ireland, Yorkshire, East and West Midlands, Wales, Scotland, the North, and the Southwest). New insights (Lloyds Bank 2021 Consumer Digital Index) show the digital exclusion gap is continuing to narrow, with 95% of the UK average being connected, whereas in 2020 this was 92% (Lloyds Bank 2021 Consumer Digital Index). Various regions across the UK have improved and increased their digital access, specifically the Midlands and Yorkshire and the Humber since 2020 (Table 6.1). Wales is showing greater improvement and initiatives are needed, Northern Ireland was not included (the report does not state reasons why) (Lloyds Bank 2021 Consumer Digital Index).

Furthermore, regions across England have shown improvements (Table 6.1) to Internet access. However, some citizens in the Northeast of England (8%) are still not digitally connected and this too relates to having low digital confidence and usage (Lloyds Bank 2021 Consumer Digital Index). Yet, citizens (4%) living in the Northwest of England, are still disconnected, while their confidence (85%) levels are greater, and 13% of people living in Wales reported to have not used

Table 6.1. 'Have you used the Internet in the last 3 months?' Across the UK Regions Between 2020 and 2021 (Lloyds Bank 2021 Consumer Digital Index).

UK Region	2020 (%)	2021 (%)
Scotland	95	96
Northeast	91	92
Northwest	92	96
Yorkshire & the Humber	90	96
West Midlands	89	97
East Midlands	90	94
Wales	85	88
East England	92	92
London	96	97
Southeast	94	96
Southwest	93	92
England	92	95

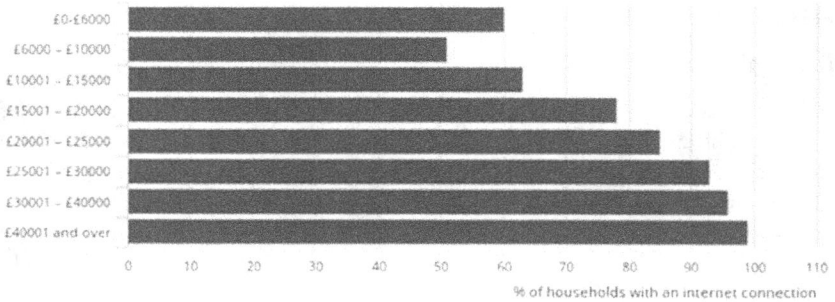

Fig. 6.5. The Percentage of Households with an Internet Connection Increases with Income. *Source*: ONS (2019b).

the Internet within 3-months, 'which is particularly high with the context of lockdowns over the past year' (Lloyds Bank 2021 Consumer Digital Index, p. 18). From the perspective of Scotland, 30% of people have little to low engagement with digital connectivity, while they are ahead of all regions in England except for London when considering digital engagement. Similarly, approaches in respective regions of the UK, seem to have improved digital engagement in comparison to figures from 2018 (Figs. 6.4 – 6.5), yet areas such as Wales and the Northeast of England continue to present the highest level of zero digital skills nationally (Figs. 6.6 – 6.7).

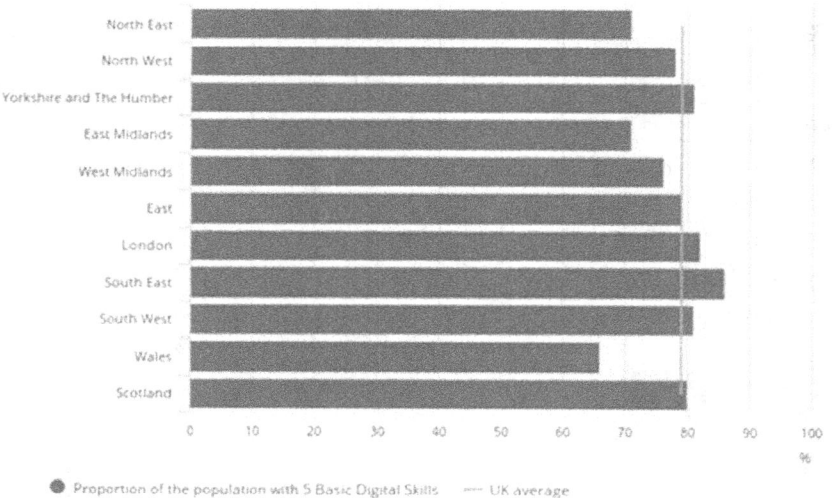

Fig. 6.6. Regional Variation of the Proportion of the Population with the Five Basic Digital Skills. *Source*: ONS (2019b); Lloyds Bank 2018 Consumer Digital Index.

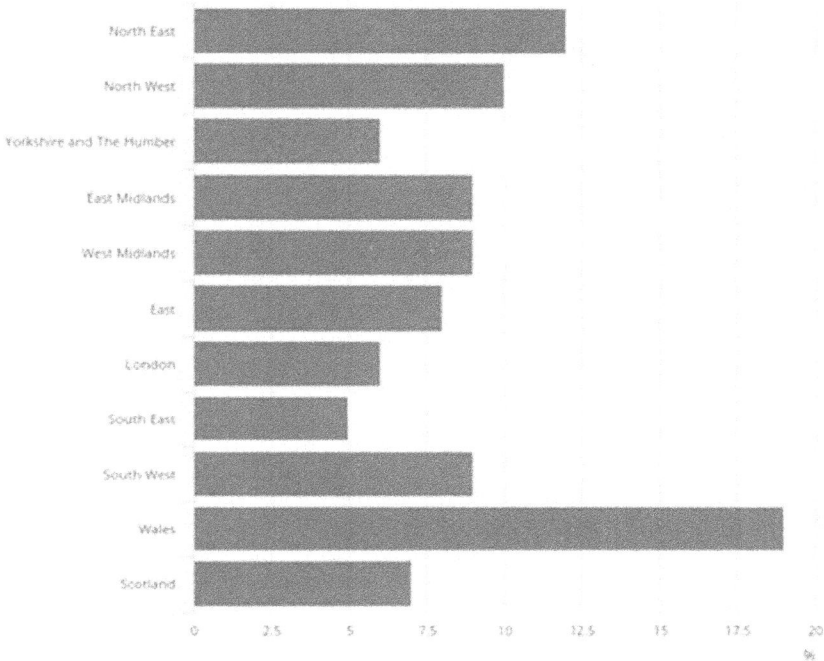

Fig. 6.7.   Regional Variation of the Proportion who do not Have Any Basic Digital Skills. *Source*: ONS (2019b); Lloyds Bank 2018 Consumer Digital Index.

Digital Skills, Internet Access and Purpose

With the rise of technological developments, digital devices and digital transformation greater needs and expectations are placed on citizens at a rate of knots. This too includes keeping up to date with new platforms (e.g., WhatsApp, Zoom etc.) with the unwritten expectations that citizens in both a personal and private capacity can recalibrate their existing mental models (White et al., 2020) by learning new interfaces, and engagement methods. However, citizens in Northern Ireland show the greatest increase in Internet use during the first quarter of 2018 (ONS, 2018) (Figs. 6.4 – 6.5) since 2011. Yet, in comparison to other regions, this specific area continues to have the lowest proportion.

Local and national governments too, are moving or have moved (since the pandemic) their services and associated tasks online (ONS, 2019b). Activities such as sharing information in a newsletter format, engaging with games and hobbies, and supplementing their offline hobbies and leisure pursuits have been reported by citizens who use digital technologies to maintain communication, and share information such as photographs with their friends, children and grandchildren who are geographically displaced (e.g., living across the Country or on another continent) (Freeman et al., 2020; Genoe et al., 2018). Yet, with all this change and expectation, many people are still being left behind, with very little assistance and/or guidance to support them in understanding the importance of gaining basic digital skills or to enhance their existing digital skills.

Within not only regional but also age cohorts do we see this growing digital disparity of citizens and as the years progress, this disparity continues to impact existing older adults, specifically those who are aged 75+ years (ONS, 2019b).

Some of the most common reasons for limited Internet access by older adults is the lack of understanding, the usefulness, or the perception of not needing the Internet (64%), while the lack of digital skills (20%) is rated highly and for some people they would access the Internet elsewhere (12%) (ONS, 2019b) (Fig. 6.7). We also know to access and use services such as the Internet, one needs equipment/ digital devices and this too for many citizens impacts on their choice and use of such services, with 8% of people noting how equipment costs were too expensive. And yet, for many households, there is the requirement of a telephone line/ broadband into the home, and this too is perceived a costly outlay by some (8%). Likewise, concerns surrounding privacy and security fears (7%) (ONS, 2019b) (Fig. 6.8), form additional reasons for low take-up. Similarly, Marston et al. (2019) identified relatable concerns by participants from the *Technology In Later Life (TILL) project* who were living in urban and metropolitan environments.

Further insight in this arena identified in 2018 around 84% of adults aged 60 years and older felt, there was no appropriate solution to assist them with the Internet (ONS, 2019b; Lloyds Bank 2018 Consumer Digital Index). And as Fig. 6.9 shows, by disability which households are least likely to be Internet users, and reasons, with limited online shopping and service habits, with 65% of disabled people primarily preferring to shop in person. Both security/privacy concerns, and the lack of skills were greater concerns by disabled people, than non-disabled people.

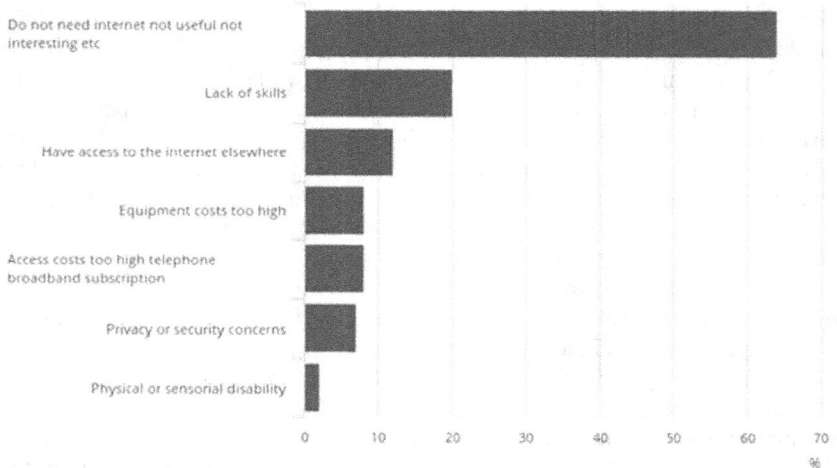

Fig. 6.8.   Percentage of Households by Reason for not Having Household Internet Access. *Source*: ONS (2019b).

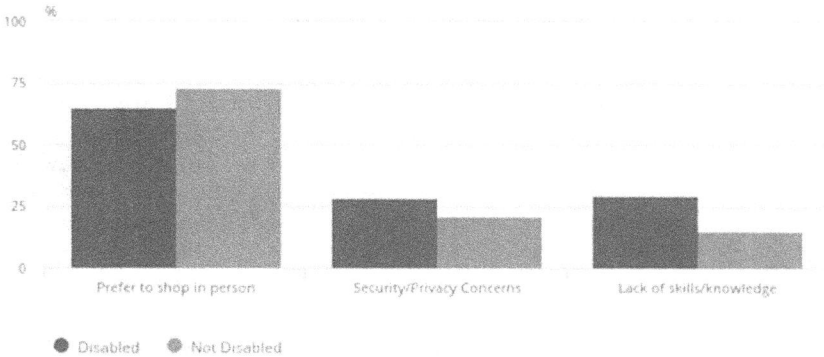

Fig. 6.9. Percentage of Households by Disability for not Having Household Internet Access. *Source*: ONS (2019b).

We continue this discussion in the following section, from the perspectives of community organisations and their abilities to (or not) bring members together online during the pandemic. We also explore the impact inequities surrounding welfare, pensions, and energy bills can and may have on individuals and households who are currently digitally disconnected.

(Digital) Exclusion, Inequities, Community Involvement and the Pandemic

The narrative of digital inequalities was heightened and brought to the forefront of discussion across the education, and health sectors to name but two. News and media channels were reporting on disparities in the homes across the UK, whereby families (Polikoff et al., 2020) or people (across different age groups) did not have a digital device to access online services, or one device had to be shared across multiple children.

Community groups such as the Women's Institute (WI) (n.d.a/b) or the Men's Sheds Association (n.d.a) afford women and men from the age of 18 years the opportunity to come together and share various activities, including arts and crafts (WI, n.d.a/b), practical skills including mending and making objects, woodwork, electronics, metalwork, etc. while some members may assist around towns and villages (WI, n.d.a/b; Men's Sheds Associations, n.d.b/c). In a pre-pandemic society, national organisations afforded their members to come together monthly (the WI) or even more regularly to build and offer social connections to its members who may feel lonely, and/or isolated which in turn can impact on one's health and well-being (Men's Sheds Associations, n.d.b/c).

For many of these organisations, the pandemic will have impacted their regular meetings, for various reasons including, lockdown directives (not being able to meet outside, or indoors), people self-isolating/shielding because of underlying health conditions. However, for some organisations there were opportunities to conduct meetings online, yet, for many of their existing members who do not have broadband and/or own a digital device this would have severed their connection from the outside world. Although some people may own a digital device and have broadband installed, their digital skills are limited. This too imposes another level of hindrance and for many organisations coupled with the decision of what type of platform to use, and ensuring their members knew how to use the chosen platform. Thus, for those members with little to no digital skills, installing and setting up the platform will have proved difficult. Consequently, leaving many members not being able to take part in the online meetings, and becoming isolated.

Case Study #1 – Digital Inclusion and Exclusion Across UK Nations

We explore digital access and use from a regional perspective of Anglesey (Wales), whereby its residents are digitally disconnected, including nearly 12,000 people (20.6%) in this region who have never experienced either using the Internet and/or had not used it within the last three months (Citizens Online, 2017).

From a business perspective in this region of Wales, there are (at the time of the report being published by Citizens Online, 2017) 16% of businesses/premises were unable to receive a download speed greater than 10 Mbit/s, while it is estimated across Wales there is 14.4% of people who have never used the Internet (Citizens Online, 2017). Conversely, this is less so than for residents living in Northern Ireland, whereby it is estimated 18.8% of the population do not use the Internet, with a proportion (32.2%) of residents aged between 16 and 65 years old (over 378,000 people) who have little to no digital skills (Citizens Online, 2017).

The Digital Inclusion Alliance for Wales (DIAW) was created in the autumn of 2020 to reach all citizens across Wales who are digitally disconnected and includes stakeholders such as Digital Communities Wales and Wales Co-operative Centre (Welsh Government, 2021). The DIAW agenda sets out five key areas:

1. Embedding digital inclusion across all sectors,
2. Mainstreaming digital inclusion in health and social care,
3. Addressing data poverty as a key issue,
4. Prioritising digital skills in the post-Covid economy, and
5. Setting a new minimum digital living standard (Welsh Government, 2021).

Digital exclusion and disconnect affects citizens who live in various areas, especially areas which are very remote from public services and outlets, or who need to work multiple jobs to bring a liveable wage into the home, such as forestry, fishing, and quarrying (Citizens Online, 2017). Data highlighted by the ONS, shows older adults in Northern Ireland who are retired, and who are infrequent users of the Internet, are also unlikely to conduct online activities such as banking, and are unlikely to own devices such as tablets, laptops etc. (Citizens Online, 2017).

In the following case studies, we are going to explore and present various scenarios associated to communities that are thriving today and we explore how digital skills may or may not impact the respective lives and how marginalised communities who are not always at the forefront of debate(s) may overcome barriers and challenges.

Education, digital skills, and inequities affects everyone, as we have seen from the statistics presented by the ONS (2018; 2019a/b), in society ranging from one's confidence, knowledge, income, social connections, prospective employment and overall general health and well-being. Many citizens who experience (digital) inequities may have the opportunity to use public venues such as libraries or community centres as well as leisure centres. However, affordability, priorities (e.g., heating, food, etc.) as well as education are key to levelling up the existing inequalities surrounding our communities.

Libraries can offer a range of resources to communities and across the Wakefield district there are 12 libraries offering citizens the opportunity to access online resources including eBooks. With additional provision of free access to computers and Wi-Fi, and during the year 2019–2020 a total of 96,246 hours were logged. Wakefield Council 'runs a subscription-based schools' library service serving local primary schools with classroom resources' (Wakefield Council, 2021, p. 64) enabling 64% of primary school's across this area to subscribe to the service, while in/formal learning experiences are provided by library employees to 13,372 children in libraries and classroom environments (Wakefield Council, 2021).

Conversely, the 'keeping older people connected' initiative is provided by Age UK Wakefield (n.d.). and displays the different library sessions available across the district. While the housing authority through Wakefield District Housing (WDH, 2021) previously created the 'Digital Angels' group comprising of volunteers to provide support to tenants with limited and/or basic digital skills. In 2010, 28% of WDH tenants owned a PC, while 55% of tenants have access to a PC (Wood, 2010), with specially trained employees to teach basic digital skills (Wakefield District Housing, 2021).

A Digital Inclusion Service is available through Age UK Wakefield (Age UK Wakefield, n.d.) which includes a 'Tablet Loan' scheme (for 3 months) for people who have little or no experience with digital devices and is delivered to the recipient's home by a member of the organisation. Informal training is provided to the person, tailored to the needs of the individual, and includes a paper-based guide (which the recipient can keep) to support the recipient with various programmes and apps, including games, online banking, or a telehealth consultation with their GP (Age UK Wakefield, n.d.). Access to the Internet is accessible via the device using 'a data-enabled sim card [...], without having to get any Wi-Fi installed' (Age UK Wakefield, n.d.). This is a positive and realistic approach taken by Age UK Wakefield, and again acknowledges that not everyone has existing Internet access into their home while also reducing the risk of being contracted to a broadband provider and service which they may not end up using in the long-term. Further support is provided by Age UK Wakefield to individuals who wish to purchase their own device (e.g., the loaned tablet) or alternatively seek further assistance on the different devices. Telephone support is available for 'Tablet Loan' recipients and individuals who have chosen to purchase their own device (Age UK Wakefield, n.d.).

In the next case study, we will look at a sub-group of the population, citizens who are AWOC, to understand the role digital technologies may play in their lives, social connections, health, and well-being.

Case Study #2 – Ageing Without Children (AWOC) in the Twenty-first Century

There is a growing body of literature surrounding people ageing without children (AWOC) from the standpoint of (male) childlessness (Dykstra & Hagestad, 2007; Hadley, 2018a, 2019, 2020a/b/c; Kendig et al., 2007; Kendig et al., 2010). However, this area of gerontology which intersects across several societal domains including informal care, social connections, and loneliness has received little to no attention from regional and national policy makers, stakeholder organisations, and the Academy. It was only in August 2020 that the ONS (2020a) published insights into the implications of current and future older populations who are childless. Primary emphasis in this document focuses on the period of the beginning and middle decades of the twentieth century following the birth rates of post-World War 1 (WW1) and WW2. In the 1960s there was a peak of 876,000 births (1964) which in turn has led to greater numbers of older adults currently in their 50s, 70s and 90s (ONS, 2020a).

Looking to the future by 2045, projections suggest there will be 66,000 women aged 80 years because of the 1960s birth rate spike (ONS, 2020a), with a further 23,000 women aged 80 years living in England and Wales, but there are similar proportions for older adults (men and women) who will be reaching 80 years by the late 2020s (Abell et al., 2018).

However, these respective statistics did not acknowledge the impact of AWOC from the standpoint of men, and how childlessness will now and in the future impact their lives. Primarily, informal caring is discussed without consideration to loneliness, isolation, and additional societal facets that may impact this current and future older population(s) (such as people who are Generation X). ONS (2020b) discourse emphasises and posits how care needs will be met in the future for people in these age groups, with many individuals likely to be residing in their own homes. Overall, 3.5% of adults aged 65 years and over, coupled with 15% of adults aged 85 years and older will be living in care homes across England. Those individuals who will require care, children are the 'most common providers of informal care' (2020b) (Fig. 6.10), in addition to extended family networks. Yet, this notion is not always possible for everyone, especially those who are AWOC.

The informal care needs of our current ageing populations are important and should be at the forefront of contemporary discourse to start to identify appropriate solutions. Conversely, what is not acknowledged and is certainly not discussed (presently) is how younger cohorts in society may also be AWOC. Both men and women, who are Generation X, Millennials and Generation Z may have already identified solutions and rationales for AWOC at their respective age/stage in life. Such decisions and circumstances can vary and include precarious employment, financial constraints, the right to choose to not want a family,

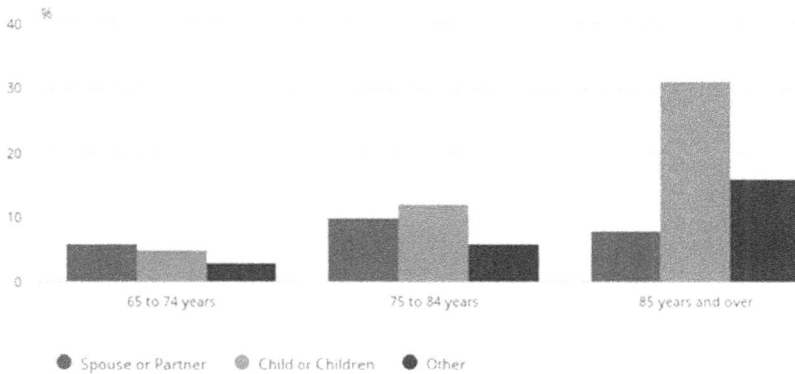

Fig. 6.10.   Displays Adult Children are the Most Common Providers of Informal Care for Those at the Oldest Ages. Percentage of Older People Receiving Informal Care by Age Group and Information Care Provider, England, 2018. *Source*: ONS (2020b).

disability, reproductive loss, and fertility issues. Future generations (Generation X, Millennials and Generation Z) will face similar care needs to that of our current older populations and from the perspective of the pandemic there was little discourse through several actors acknowledging the impact of the pandemic was having on people who are AWOC (across all age cohorts). Thus, for many people who were having to isolate/shield, or who became ill, or who have limited social networks, there is a likelihood their mental health, feelings of loneliness and isolation were exacerbated because of government directives.

The 'Ageing Without Children' organisation (2014) aims to raise awareness to the issues pertaining to people who are AWOC and between the 14th of March and the 19th of April 2021 an online survey was deployed to understand the impact of the pandemic on those people who identify and meet the following definitions of AWOC:

1. 'People who have never been parents either through choice, infertility or circumstance,
2. People who have had children, but those children have either predeceased them or are unable to offer help or support because they live at a great distance, or have care needs of their own,
3. People who have had children, but those children are unwilling to offer help and support because they are estranged or have no contact'. (Ageing without Children, 2021)

Findings showed 213 responses with most respondents being female (82%) with an average age of 62 years (age range of 38–90 years), 13 respondents identified as LGBTQ+, 6 respondents reported to be from Black and Minority

Ethnic (BME) groups, 15% of respondents reported to be a carer, and 15% of respondents reported to have disabilities (e.g., underlying long-term health conditions, and mental health issues (Banerjee, 2020) and who were shielding). A key question focussed on the living circumstances, with 56% of responders stating they lived alone (Ageing without Children, 2021). This is staggering and highlights the critical issues surrounding this sub-population in society. Additional findings highlighted include,

1. Invisibility,
2. Dominance of the family narrative,
3. Loneliness and social isolation,
4. The pandemic as an ageing experience,
5. The role of friendship and alternative social support networks,
6. Views and perceptions of residential care,
7. Being a carer,
8. Practical difficulties, and finally
9. Other issues.

For many people young and old who are AWOC, the pandemic has affected them in various ways, and while technology may be available for many people with or without children there are additional layers and considerations that must be considered for people who are AWOC. Such as, confidence, having the digital skills and knowledge, being able to ask someone/friend for help, whereas for people who do have grand/children who they can ask for assistance or even extended familial networks (Ageing Without Children, 2021). Another factor relating to people who are AWOC is geographic displacement, whereby, for some people who do have children/grandchildren, they may in essence be living in another part of the country or even overseas. And although the pandemic may have afforded these individuals to forge greater meaningful relationships (via social media and communication platforms) this can only be achieved if additional factors are in existence, such as digital confidence/skills, or the financial means to own a device and access to an Internet service provider.

Case Study #3 – Looking Back Through the Lens of the Digital Divide on Historical Events

The following case study is based on a doctoral study by Baker-Green (2013) who explores the impact of digital technologies by residents living in the Grimethorpe community. This former mining village in the county of South Yorkshire is nestled close to the cities of Barnsley, Rotherham, and Sheffield. Baker-Green (2013) sets out several research questions for his doctoral work,

1. 'What is the nature and extent of ICT measures supported by the Objective 1 Programme South Yorkshire in Grimethorpe, and what other ICT related developments are occurring within the same community?

2. How are ICT related measures increasing the social capital within Grimethorpe?
3. How are ICT related measures increasing the ICT skill levels within Grimethorpe, creating an up-skilled workforce that can participate more fully in the information society?
4. How is the rise in mobile technology over the last decade being experienced by families including,

   (a) how they are individuals using new mobile technology,
   (b) is this having an effect on using the mobile technology by other family members therefore helping them to overcome the digital divide?
   (c) is social capital being increased'. (Baker-Green, 2013, p.12).

We will draw on the findings and experiences discussed in this thesis (Baker-Green, 2013) with a view to exploring solutions to moving forward. From the closure of the Grimethorpe colliery, employment, education, and skills were low and resulted in an organic, grassroots creation of the 'Grimethorpe Electronic Village Hall' (GEVH) in the early 1990s, for utilising and innovatively using digital technologies,

> It started off in my front room and the local pub. Five people who knew each other on a personal level through working for British Coal, who all had a really big interest in computers. (Baker-Green, 2013, p. 79)

Initially this computer club formed through friendship and enthusiasts, coupled with assistance of a development worker (Andy Kershaw, the radio presenter and broadcaster) who found provision (a room) at the Acorn Centre which met for 1.5 hours every week. Within two years the computer club was known by many local people as Baker-Green notes *[…] members of the GEVH had passed fifty, they had moved into a permanent room and obtained an Internet connection* (2013, p. 79). Various fundraising activities and donations enabled the club to be digitally connected coupled with 'the kindness of Andy Kershaw' (2013, p. 79). Additionally, a National Lottery grant application and ERDF funding was successful, enabling *the first community owned and managed ICT facilities of its kind in the country and the model on which other initiatives have been based* (2013, p. 79). The aim of the GEVH project was to be community driven, provision of and to develop digital skills with a view to making residents/members more employable to employees. Baker-Green (2013, p. 178) notes,

> In their words, they provided 'a common and easily accessible base for people and organisations connected with the community, to develop further social intercourse and offer specialist advice on how information and communication technology may be relevant to their business or organisation'. (Baker-Green, 2013, p. 80)

Moreover, residents were able to access and study various courses pertaining to computers including 1. *Digital skills*, 2. *Learning how to build your own computer*, and 3. *How to maintain the computer*. Accessibility to the Acorn Centre was available five days per week (Monday–Friday) between the hours of 10.30 am and 4 pm, with drop-in sessions twice a week, one in the afternoon (1–4 pm) and another in the morning (10–1 pm) for people who wish to improve their computer literacy skills. Additional options for learning were created in this area and through the Acorn Centre via Learn direct (see Baker-Green, 2013 for more information) afforded residents (including post-16 education) from within and the surrounding area(s), to receive and gain high quality teaching. At the time the Labour government remit aimed to:

- 'reached those with few or no skills and qualifications who were unlikely to participate in traditional forms of learning;
- equipped people with the skills they need for employability, thereby strengthening the skills of the workforce and increasing productivity;
- was delivered innovatively through the use of new technologies'. (Baker-Green, 2013, p. 80)

The local library was located within the Acorn Centre with access to two broadband connected computers. The Labour government initiative at the time set out in the early 2000s to ensure all public libraries were connected to the Internet by 2003 via the 'The People's Network' and funded via the 'New Opportunities Fund' (Baker-Green, 2013). Thus, access to computers via such environments are usually free, with additional incurred costs resulting from printing, and computer access was usually for a maximum of 2-hours per day.

In Chapter 3, we have seen how residents in Northern Ireland note how they would like to be given formal instruction of digital skills through community spaces. Yet, as noted by Baker-Green (2013) there were differences between the GEVH, Learn direct and the library environments, and include the latter environment having fewer staff to provide direct instruction and support to users. While greater accessibility was available at the GEVH, five days per week, unlike the library whereby accessibility was only available for two days per week – opening at 9.30 am and closing at 5.30, including 1-hour for lunch. Although, this accessibility did increase by 2012 to five full days per week.

However, following a return approximately 10 years later, Baker-Green (2013) states the GEVH had relocated to Wrath-upon-Dearne (Rotherham) and were still providing courses such as website design and hosting, and the library also, had been earmarked for closure in the spring of 2013. Some people including yourselves might wonder why the GEVH located in Grimethorpe was successful? Baker-Green states,

> the GEVHs success was identified as the ability of those that ran it to understand what their community wanted, rather than needed, in terms of access to ICT and the Internet. (Baker-Green, 2013, p. 110)

The main purpose of the GEVH from its inception was to help the people of Grimethorpe initially overcome their fear of computers. It was this according to Gary and Bill, the two key players at the GEVH76 that was viewed as the main barrier in getting people from Grimethorpe involved in the use of ICT and the Internet. The GEVH offered a space outside of the home where individuals could take some time to begin to understand and familiarise themselves with new technological equipment and software. All the residents of Grimethorpe needed was the motivation to take that first step. (Baker-Green, 2013, p. 111)

Similar to the evidence gathered by stakeholders in Wales, and Northern Ireland this notion of service provision and tuition delivered by peers, has the potential to be successful, especially if buy-in is at a grass root level rather than a top-down approach. The GEVH instilled a grassroots approach, including the renovation of the building by members of the community which proved fruitful for its acceptance and usage within the community,

This building we're in now was a shell, a dirty shell, and the people from Grimethorpe, came down here and built all the equipment from scratch. They painted the walls, they put the carpets in, they put the curtains up, cleaned the windows, scrubbed the walls, you name it they did it all. You look at it and it looks a lovely place and it's impressive. I could have gone to PC World and bought that stuff off o' shelf. That ain't the point, that's their baby! It's their baby! (Baker-Green, 2013, p. 112).

Various actors across different sectors and organisation, may find it difficult to comprehend how many people today have limited digital skills, or have a fear of sitting in front of a computer and using a mouse, or interacting with the Internet, and even familiarising themselves with software such as Word – is alien to them. Yet, for discussions and narratives to take a wide leap forward we (collectively) must acknowledge how for many people, old and young there is a genuine fear and apprehension. And this includes the unfamiliarity of digital technologies including basic digital skills. Yet, understanding the purpose, benefits and showing empathy to respective individuals is critical to gaining positive rewards. We must remember that we all learn differently (White et al., 2020) and for some people learning through trial and error and realising if a mistake is made, that it is fine, and there is no long-term damage,

The best way for a lot of people to learn, well a lot of people from here [Grimethorpe], is to tell them to click and play. They learn far more by clicking and playing and finding out the consequences of when they do X, Y and Z. By doing this they realise they can't break the kit and anything they do can be undone! After the

> playing we have two volunteer members of staff who help them
> with basic computer skills. Over the years, we found this was the
> best way to help others overcome their fear and use computers and
> the Internet. (Baker-Green, 2013, p. 113)

With any type of learning it should be fun (Okada & Sheehy, 2020). And learning a new piece of technology, or interacting with a piece of software, or playing a videogame console we must ensure the individual is enjoying themselves (Marston, 2012, 2013 a/b). Understanding and seeing the benefits to learning new digital technologies and devices, even more so if the objective can be relatable to one's existing life can afford a person to persevere and be more motivated (Marston, 2012, 2013a/b).

The type of learning and support provided by GEVH volunteers was primarily aimed at building confidence to those people who had little self-confidence and thus one of the key aims was to ensure learning was conducted in their own time,

> Just turn round and look at that tutor there [points to James]. If
> I'd have said to him three years ago, 'come down here and teach
> these [other students] computers', he would have laughed and
> said, 'the only thing I've ever used right in my life is a seven pound
> hammer'. And that couple that just came in, when they first came
> in they were scared stiff o' computers, they're just building their
> own now. That's taken eighteen months. That's what I'm talking
> about, it's about them doing their own thing in their own time.
> (Baker-Green, 2013, pp. 113–114)

It's not just this case study that we can draw on to illustrate how confidence is integral to the learning of others, but a more recent example is the *Adapt Tech, Accessible Technology* (ATAT) project (2020–2021). The ATAT project included older adults who had little to no digital skills, and who were invited to be co-collaborators alongside the research team. A podcast – *Design for Age – Doing Co-Design Better* (Morgan, 2021) features research team members, co-collaborators and directly illustrates how their inclusion within the project built-up their confidence. Similarly, the following quote refers to the GEVH, and illustrates the importance of building self-confidence prior to undertaking formal learning,

> Initially, we do a lot of hand holding to get them out in the com-
> munity over their fear of computers and get them to understand
> they can't break the machines. They then get their self-confidence,
> that's one of the things we are very good at here, building self-
> confidence, even if this takes a year or eighteen months. Then, and
> only then, perhaps they will be ready for a more formal course.
> (Baker-Green, 2013, p. 114)

Building confidence, sharing knowledge and experience can be conducted in an informal 'environment' of a centre, or even online as the ATAT research team observed, coupled with opportunity to build, and maintain social connections, can be positive too, as well as reducing a feeling of loneliness and social isolation (Wilson et al., 2021). Initiatives such as the GEVH can facilitate such experiences,

> I come here to learn how to use the computer. I know how to use word and excel and I've been on the Internet, but, I mean, it's there [the computers] to be enjoyed as well not only used for work. We have a coffee and a chat; it's more about meeting up with friends than computers. (Baker-Green, 2013, p. 121)

For some residents in the surrounding area of Grimethorpe, they had been using the GEVH because of the lack of facilities in their own village/town. But as time passed by, new initiatives were created. Yet, for existing users of the GEVH they preferred to travel to the centre because of the existing friendships, and the personable feel of the environment offered by staff members,

> They're friendly here. We like to come and Ian [volunteer tutor] is a good laugh, he's a lovely bloke. Basically they did start doing one [at Royston] but we would rather come here, we're happy here, we're with people we know. (Baker-Green, 2013, p. 122)

> There's nothing in Shafton [CTC] so I come all the way here to use the computers here. I could go to Barnsley, but its good here. The staff are very good, they're patient and make you feel like you can do it, you want to do it! They help if you need it and you can just drop-in and not even use the computers if you don't want! (Baker-Green, 2013, p. 122)

Baker-Green's (2013) doctoral work illustrates how 10-20-30 years ago, such initiatives were integral to communities and residents alike who were wishing to up-skill and socially connect at the same time in a less formal space. But more importantly, this initiative and the work posited by Baker-Green (2013) illustrates a greater insight than just the need to up-skill. This thesis demonstrates how a once thriving area, which was ravaged by policy decisions in the 1980s and in turn left many men in later life not only feeling redundant but lost, on the slag heaps, with little to no prospects for the future – hope. Collieries were the heartbeat of communities, residents in areas such as Grimethorpe and across other Northern and Welsh regions had their roots and social connections entrenched in the ground, they were not lonely, nor isolated. Many of the men learnt their skills from working in the pit(s), they worked hard to provide for their families and to keep the country functioning with the coal they mined.

During the interviews with this family, Baker-Green (2013) identified a man and a woman who were 47 and 43 years old, respectively, and their son (one of three children) was aged 20. Their experiences of formal education were not positive, with all of them leaving school with no qualifications. The man was employed as a warehouse operative (for 17 years) and the woman as a part time cleaner. Their household income came to £23,000.00 (Baker-Green, 2013, p. 164).

Yet, as previously mentioned, there are financial implications to installing broadband and for many people this too is a key factor,

> When asked about Sky, <name> pointed out how they had got Sky a few years before and eventually moved their telephone over to Sky and then, on the insistence of their younger son, got broadband. As <name> said *Paul badgered me to death to get broadband* but it wasn't until he found out he could get it for free with the other two services they received that he had agreed to have it. Before this he had told Paul (and his other two children) '*if you want broadband you pay for if*, which of course they never did'. In is defence <name> pointed to the costs associated with buying equipment and then paying for broadband '*if we'd had more money they could've had what they wanted … but we only have an account with the bank, we don't own it*'. (Baker-Green, 2013, p. 169)

This quote illustrates several aspects including the perception of need/ requirement, income and staying up to date with technology, given the son and his mother <name> (to the man's wife) were only able to connect to the Internet via their smartphones (contracted). While the man was unable to do so, because of owning a mobile phone (Baker-Green, 2013) and not a smartphone. What we also do not hear much about is the 'monthly data allowance' that some consumers choose or are limited to because of the package that they have chosen to pay for. This too can be difficult for users, especially if there are various activities such as downloading music, or streaming activities. Data allowance on a smartphone operates in a similar way, and this too can incur additional charges on top of the monthly bill, especially if users have activated the 'roaming' function.

The following quote illustrates how a monthly allowance restricted the son from downloading too much, because he was acutely aware that not only did, he not pay the phone bill (his mother did), but also his father would be displeased too,

> [...] he was *moaned at by his mum if his phone bill was over the monthly charge* because she paid the bill. He was also a keen collector of music, which he downloaded at home or shared with his mates. At home he couldn't download too much because they only had a 2GB monthly Internet allowance and he dare not go over this in case they were charged and his father *would do his nut*. (Baker-Green, 2013, p. 171)

An older man (69 years) came from a family of miners and worked in the Colliery until it closed, before finding new employment (after several years of being unemployed) as working a security guard in Barnsley. Their income was not disclosed to Baker-Green (2013) but he notes how both the older man and his wife (67 years) informed him by stating 'they got "what all pensioners got"'

(p. 166) which at the time of this doctoral work, Baker-Green (2013) notes was approximately £12,000.00 according to Which (Baker-Green, 2013, p. 166). Citizens on fixed incomes may also feel the installation of the Internet is not worth it, or they cannot afford a lavish expense,

> The older man [...] was very keen to make clear was the fact that they only had a pension to live on. He was well aware that new mobile technology existed, particularly the iPad and *mobiles that sing and dance* because he had seen them on TV advertisements. He was also very clear in pointing out just how much they cost and how they *could never afford to buy one of them,* adding *but why would we want one?* (Baker-Green, 2013, p. 173)

A third family formed the final case study of Baker-Green's doctoral work and explored a young family who had moved from Barnsley to Grimethorpe, from rental accommodation to home ownership on one of the new housing developments. A man in his thirties and a woman in her late twenties who had a young family aged 7 and 6, and although there is little milage/distance between Barnsley and Grimethorpe this family were concerned about leaving their friends and family behind for a new home and life away from where they were previously living. They were both employed, as a deputy manager in an electrical store and as a part time receptionist in a school. Their estimated household income was £38,000.00 (Baker-Green, 2013, pp. 167–168). From an educational perspective, they had attained GCSEs in Maths and English (Grade A – <name>) and a Level 3, NVQ in Customer Service and Retail Management, while continuing to work in the store. the man's wife – <name>, also gained GCSEs at grades A and B, and overall, their experiences of education was positive, albeit they both reported to have been 'pleased' to have left. Their experiences and receptiveness to digital technologies and the Internet was positive, having owned various devices (e.g., iPhone, iPad etc.) and were using a reconditioned laptop, desktop computer and their Internet was provided via their Sky package (Baker-Green, 2013, p. 168).

The closure of the colliers did not just throw the men onto the slag heaps, it also told younger generations that future employment opportunities were going to be limited and sought alternative employment regardless of whether they wanted to move away or even travel outside of their familiar area. Thus, becoming geographically displaced, having to forge new social connections, and risking the feeling of loneliness. However, for some people, new housing developments formed on former colliery sites afforded young families such as the man and his wife to put down roots albeit a few miles away from their existing networks, they were able to afford to buy their semi-detached house. The man and his wife note their initial experiences of taking this move and displacement a few miles up the road,

> When they first moved in they were a little apprehensive at leaving their friends and families but over the last three years they have come to call Grimethorpe home. They like the village and have found most people they have met to be extremely friendly and

helpful, particularly their immediate neighbours who they are on good terms with. (Baker-Green, 2013, p. 167)

This quote demonstrates the importance of community support/spirit, friendly neighbours, social connections, while affording opportunities to build self-confidence with technologies and recognising that people learn differently. In the following case study, we explore how military personnel who are leaving the armed forces contend with the changes from a regular routine to the civilian landscape.

Case Study #4 – From Military Personnel to Civilian, Impact(s) of Leaving the Armed Forces

An ever-growing societal problem are the high numbers of former soldiers (not officers) who leave (veterans) the British Army and other military forces (e.g., Navy, Air Force, and the Royal Marines) and struggle to adjust back into civilian life culminating in approximately 6% of all the UK homeless population being veterans (Office of Veterans' affairs, 2020).

Many veterans are located within and across the regions of the UK (Map of Need), and in some instances, these areas are in former industrial areas, which have low deprivation, and precarious/variable employment opportunities – as noted in Case Study 1. Much of the financial hardship experienced by veterans residing in the Northeast are primarily located in and around the City of Newcastle, South Shields, Sunderland, Redcar and Hartlepool (The Map of Need, 2019a). Similarly, the Yorkshire and the Humber region, financial hardship experienced by veterans are residing in the areas of Grimsby, Hull, Doncaster, Darlington/Richmond border (The Map of Need, 2019b) which are previous industrial areas. Although there are some heavy populous of veterans located in Thirsk, Harrogate, and York – which are not necessarily perceived as areas of deprivation but are near Catterick Garrison – the largest British Army garrison in the world (Military Wikia, n.d.).

The cause of this anomaly is an area of ongoing debate, but one could argue that there are two key 'catalysts'. The first being the most populous recruited demographic, of young working and non-working class white males coming directly from high school level education with little to no life skills. This leads the Army and other military forces to have the responsibility of managing the new recruit's military life which in turn leads to the under development of their life skills. Military personnel are provided with accommodation and includes all their utilities (water, fuel), clothing (uniform and associated equipment), and dining facilities which for many young soldiers they don't care about because everything is provided to them within their (military) social bubble. It is common that many individuals live on a hand to mouth basis, which is comically referred to as being a weekend millionaire following pay day, a soldier can live without any actual funds quite happily as everything is provided for.

There are cultural elements that are synonymous with the Army and military life such as the drinking culture. Much of the army life is punctuated by social events involving a culture of drinking, and these events are perceived to be positive and good for moral and afford a form of motivating and continuing bonding amongst the personnel (Alcohol Concern, 2012; Jones & Fear, 2011). However, this can result in greater issues and concerns such as over consumption and/or lead onto dependency and in some instances 'doctors believed that alcohol gave a degree of protection against various lethal disease and was safer to drink than water' (Kiernan et al., 2018, p. 725).

This perceived beneficial approach to developing positive moral can lead onto greater risks. For example, individuals who exit the military before the 10 year point in their career, who have been and are fully trained to be the consummate professional soldier are also ill equipped for life in the civilian world, in comparison to those individuals who chose not to have a military career. There is a paucity of understanding why veterans are reluctant to and find it difficult to engage with treatment for alcohol consumption, but Kiernan and colleagues (2018) identified how many veterans normalised their behaviour. This leads on to either delaying or not engaging with appropriate treatment programs. Given the nature of military life experienced by many veterans, bonding with friends and colleagues, for those individuals who wish to seek out and engage with treatment programs, peer-support models may afford individuals the opportunity to limit opportunities to disconnect and withdrawal (Kiernan et al., 2018, p. 725).

The second catalyst is the significant ramping up of military operations in recent years and decades. The Falkland's War in 1982 was the most recent active campaign until the first Gulf War (Operation Desert Shield, 1991). This campaign itself saw limited action and there was very little combat or war fighting campaigns involving the British Army. From 1992 onwards the most notable engagements were peace keeping in Sierra Leone, Bosnia, and Kosovo. These engagements which had their challenges for a limited number of personnel but on the most part was benign. The operational profile of the British forces through several operations under the authority of either NATO or the United Nations was supporting in the establishment of stability, security, law, and order in post conflict zones. This profile changed however with the advent of offensive action in Gulf War 2 (2003–2011) and resulted in initially allied forces facing very limited resistance. However, overtime due to a persistent presence in Iraq an enduring insurgency developed creating a real insidious threat to life. This was manifested in vehicle born suicide attacks, individual suicide attacks and roadside bombs on alliance personnel and infrastructure.

Iraq was paralleled by the Afghanistan (2001–2021) campaign and was truly a harrowing experience for the individual soldier. The perception of the individual was that it was not a single war but multiple wars as many had to return again and again and engage in brutal conflict. In this campaign a much higher proportion of actual war fighting was required, with troops engaging a very capable Taliban insurgency on the ground, often room to room in extremely hard conditions. The psychological impact and toll of these experiences from both the Iraq and Afghanistan conflicts, is now only being appreciated, assessed, and addressed albeit in what is widely agreed as being an inadequate response.

The outcome(s) for these two factors result in a disproportionate number of individuals struggling to function in society, resulting in identifying suitable housing to facilitate limb loss (Wilson et al., 2020), homelessness, drug and alcohol abuse (Kiernan et al., 2018, p. 725), family breakdowns, imprisonment, appropriate rehabilitation for physical, psychological, and social well-being (McGill et al., 2020) and destitution. That is the reality for many veterans living as a civilian in our communities and society at large. In 2016, the numbers of veterans across the UK are estimated to be 2.50 million (SSAFA, 2014–2019), with an increase of veterans of working age set to increase from 37% in 2016 to 44% by 2028. To date there is a paucity of literature and understanding surrounding the provisions across the different regions of the UK to support veterans and their families, respectively (The Map of Need, n.d.). Statistics present one in eight armed forces personnel were seen in military healthcare for a mental health related reason. With many military personnel (2 in 1000), being diagnosed with Post-Traumatic Stress Disorder (PTSD) (Forbes et al., 2019) but many cases are thought to go undiagnosed or treated (Ministry of Defence, 2020a) as noted below,

> Rates of PTSD were higher in those who had previously deployed to Iraq and/or Afghanistan than those not deployed there. In 2019/20, there was an increased risk of 90% for PTSD for Service personnel previously deployed to Iraq and/or Afghanistan. (Ministry of Defence, 2020a, p. 14)

Access to mental health services varies across the UK, England, and the Northeast and areas such as Sunderland, South Shields and Newcastle upon Tyne seem to have greater access to mental health services than other areas in this region (The Map of Need, 2019a). Moreover, across the areas of Scarborough, Keighley, Bradford, and Hull there is a large populous of veterans accessing treatment (The Map of Need, 2019b). Mental health can be exacerbated more so in these areas through a myriad of triggers including low or little employment opportunities, resulting in financial hardship(s) coupled with alcohol abuse and the experiences of military life.

What these figures (The Map of Need, 2019a/b) show, are many veterans in certain pockets of the Northeast, Yorkshire, Humber regions and elsewhere across the UK are accessing mental health services in a bid to improve their day-to-day living for themselves and that of their family members. Yet, across many of these areas and regions there is deprivation (of all forms). For many veterans, they may choose to reside in the area that they are originally from, to be closer to family members, existing social networks, and familiarity and while they may have had a positive experience during their military careers, this change in circumstance(s) may enhance one's mental health.

Since the pandemic openly discussing mental health concerns is more widely accepted in society, endorsed by many TV personalities. However, for many serving personnel and veterans alike across the life course, we as civilians hear little about the impact(s) of campaigns on their lives and the lives of their families and wider social networks. And despite focussed initiatives by the Ministry of Defence (2017), individuals continue to struggle to seek help. Especially if an individual is faced with no support or mainstream support and they often choose no support due to social stigma(s) or their perception of what seeking that support means. As a result, bespoke specialist support for this community has a much better uptake and can include,

- Launch of anti-stigma campaign 'Don't Bottle It Up' and 'Time to Change',
- Establishment of the Stress and Resilience Training Centre at the Defence Academy of the UK, providing resilience training to Regular, Reserve and MOD Civil Service personnel and authority for TRiM training,
- Launch of bespoke resilience initiatives: START Taking Control by the Stress and Resilience Training Centre, Royal Navy Op REGAIN, Army OP SMART and Royal Air Force SPEAR. (Ministry of Defence, 2017, p. 19)

The armed forces are not the only area across the UK whereby mental health (King's College London, 2020) has become a focus point, but this focus has become integral within UK policing and blue light services (Marston et al., 2020). Similarly, the UK MoD launched a mental fitness platform – HeadFIT for Life (Ministry of Defence, 2020b) which aims to provide self-help tools for personnel wishing to improve their drive, mood, and confidence. While virtual reality technology (Morgan, 2019) using a treadmill, exposure trauma, and other aspects to facilitate veterans with 'treatment-resistant PTSD' (Jones et al., 2020).

The app 'Headspace' is available to British Army personnel for an annual subscription of £50.00, and via the British Army website, findings from the App state,

- '96% of Headspace users reported significant improvements in stress
- 91.5% reported significant improvements in helping with sleep with Headspace
- 98.2% of Army employees recommend Headspace'. (British Army, 2021)

The 'Headspace' app is available for serving members of the British Army there is an app available for veterans (Ministry of Defence, 2014). And while there seems to be positive movements in app development for military personnel aimed at managing and tackling mental health issues, this does not afford solutions for military personnel who decide to leave the armed forces with little life skills. As previously noted, many recruits are young, from working class backgrounds and are regimented into a routine from the moment they start basic training and continues throughout their career (regardless of the length of service). Life skills such as cooking, cleaning, seeking employment outside of the military, preparing for and attending a job interview(s), continuing education (formal) or learning a trade are important for positive day-to-day living and reducing the risks of mental health, alcohol, and drug abuse. While continuing and/or starting relationships (e.g., family, partners/spouse, grand/children) and reducing the risk of experiencing loneliness and feeling lonely are important factors associated to positive mental health and resilience.

Thus, given the digital transformation within our society and even more so since the pandemic, which has in turn facilitated the move of many services and communications onto various platforms, the need for basic digital skills (e.g., using Zoom, and/or Microsoft office packages) or guidance on how to write personal statements and CVs for job applications is crucial. Many individuals who choose to leave the armed forces have opportunities to transfer their skills and take-up an array of opportunities, via charities such as the 'Blu-digital' (2022) who facilitate veterans in seeking employment as well as employers seeking veterans.

There are many Armed Forces charities which can provide veterans, and families with support. As well as providing researchers and policy makers with current findings and data surrounding the health and financial issues experienced by veterans. This information is crucial for now and in the future as a means of ensuring respective individuals can access and improve their (mental) health, well-being, and day-to-day-living.

Summary

The global COVID-19 outbreak has shone a spotlight on the continual digital and social inequities experienced and lived by people across all age groups in the UK. Prior to the UK lockdown commencing 23 March 2020, Marston et al. (2020) posited how technology and social media (Marston & Morgan, 2020a) may play a role within one's life and offer support for mental well-being. At the time, it was unclear how long and how quickly the pandemic would unravel. Yet, at the time of writing this (August 2021), many citizens are still working from home, and it is possible that certain aspects of our lives will remain changed forever. Changes to school examinations were implemented and in addition, home schooling, working from home, and possibly annual booster vaccinations. These different factors all impacted on our lives respectively, and as some media outlets reported, the digital divide highlighted how homes (including families with children) had limited or no digital access. We presented in Case Study 1 how digital technologies are used and accessed in different communities. The narrative provides examplars of how communities are trying to bridge the digital divide with residents who have limited access to technology devices and services. All the while, many families and individuals are continuing to use whatever technologies they can, to complete educational and work tasks, stay connected with organisations and assist friends, neighbours, and older family members with digital queries. Therefore, will more young people suffer in the future because of the changes to their schooling in response to the pandemic?

Although, 2020 highlighted the importance of technology/digital access, greater strides are required to ensure in a post-pandemic society, everyone (who chooses to) still has access. Through government directives, we are aware of citizens who were categorised as being vulnerable because of health status (Earle & Blackburn, 2021) and/or age (British Society of Gerontology, 2020) and who were directed to self-isolate/shield, to reduce the risk of them becoming ill and/or even dying. While the voice of carers has featured seldom in both discourse and research-related activities (Astbury et al., 2021) and instead, we hear the voices and narrative purported by stakeholders (Astbury et al., 2021). Is it therefore discourse, and future research agendas aim to emphasise the actual voices of carers with a view to making positive and real impact?

Previously in Chapter 4 we highlighted one of the action points (Action 2) posited in the release of the *research framework for the United Nations Decade of Healthy Ageing (2021–2030)* (World Health Organization, 2020–2030). In this framework there are additional action points for researchers and policy makers alike to consider and include,

- Action 3. 'Deliver person-centered, integrated care and primary health services responsive to older people' (World Health Organization, 2020–2030, p. 12),
- Action 4. 'Provide access to long-term care for older people who need it' (World Health Organization, 2020–2030, p. 14).

The actions above highlight the need for appropriate solutions and actions towards long-term care (LTC) provision, acknowledging the current provision is unstainable (relying on families) which is usually left to women to carry out. However, what is disappointing is the paucity of acknowledgment surrounding future LTC implications for men and for people who are AWOC. Why are these sub-groups not considered? Surely, if we are truly expecting to make great strides with 'Healthy Ageing' over the coming decade (World Health Organization, 2021–2030), then boundaries need to be pushed and explored?

Furthermore, the 'Smart Homes and Independent Living' Commission (Gilbert, 2022; Policy Connect, 2021), are seeking solutions in social care policies and practices, including the delivery of (assistive) technology for health and social care needs by incorporating co-produced products and services for disabled and older adults. Implementing and reframing our societal approaches across different sectors by employing a *Transgenerational Technology* approach, we believe is an appropriate method for the next decade(s). We can learn from existing frameworks such as the DIAW roadmap,

1. Embedding digital inclusion across all sectors,
2. Mainstreaming digital inclusion in health and social care,
3. Addressing data poverty as a key issue,
4. Prioritising digital skills in the post-Covid economy, and
5. Setting a new minimum digital living standard (Welsh Government, 2021).

Addressing and embedding the points above across each region has the potential to be viewed as a blueprint for local and national governments and actors. We must listen to the voices within our communities and as many citizens in Northern Ireland suggest, greater assistance is required when it comes to understanding and learning about new technologies. Drop-ins, or 'cafes' offering informal classes can support people of all age groups to enhance their digital skills. Case study 3 and Baker-Green (2013) doctoral thesis demonstrates this, while acknowledging the informal nature, coupled with empathy is key (Citizens Online, 2017). Future innovations, and provisions would have to identify and ensure appropriate sustainability for classes to continue within communities, coupled with existing stakeholders and organisations, considering collaborative partnerships to reach all citizens (Citizens Online, 2017).

Employing a *Transgenerational Technology* approach to future initiatives, research agendas, health, social care and caring delivery is critical because we cannot keep continuing to reinvent the wheel (for every new cohort), and listen to the same, status quo, and tokenistic discourse (van Hoof et al., 2021). Action rather echo chambers is needed if change really is what is wanted. Data (including Chapter 3) and the four case studies presented here demonstrate an array of circumstances and interconnected issues concerning citizens living within our society today. It is evident that support is required for digital skills, and technology, and for many individuals who are not only affected by the pandemic but who were struggling in a pre-pandemic society, accessing relevant support is key to ensure 'Healthy Ageing' is experienced for them – regardless of age.

The need to facilitate people with digital skills is critical if we are to reduce the digital inequities and improve self-confidence. From the standpoint of veterans, greater understanding is needed relating to digital skills, and practices as a means of ensuring that this community in society are not left behind. We believe there is a continuum for digital skills in various communities and sectors across the UK to serve those individuals who feel they lack the basic skills, confidence, and knowledge to lead a positive, healthy, and successful life. The notion and suggestion of ' "[...] resilient" digital inclusion ecosystem' (Citizens Online, 2017, p. 13) could afford identifying and collaborating partnerships across multiple organisations, and actors – while marginalised communities (Marston, Wilson et al., 2020) should be considered in a post-pandemic society (Marston, Morgan et al., 2021).

Chapter 7

The Research Environment

Introduction

Conducting research is part and parcel of working in academe, be-it as a graduate student, post-doctoral fellow or as an early career research (ECR). Within many projects there are various responsibilities relating to project management, personnel, numerous research studies, personal circumstances (e.g., caring responsibilities for dependents), and health issues all the while attempting to manage a work life balance.

The purpose of this Chapter is to provide an insight into the different aspects of research. We share insights from the third sector, social enterprise and industry relating to career and the environment as a researcher. We explore the challenges, positives, and facilitators of conducting research drawing on the perspectives of the authors, selected projects that they have been involved in, and their experiences, in a bid to share insights to working in a collegiate and positive collaborative environment and practice. Initially, we explore the area of interdisciplinary research (IDR), and what this means from the standpoint of the primary UK funder, UKRI.

Interdisciplinary Research (IDR)

In the last 10–20 years, there has been a shift in the academy to conduct research together with stakeholders and (prospective) target audiences and recipients of this research. This approach is known as co-production (Newbury-Birch & Allan, 2019) and affords many research teams the opportunity to ensure research has meaningful impact, and purpose specifically for the target audience.

For many scholars who conduct research, it is usually within their respective discipline(s) with a purpose of specifically understanding health and well-being (e.g., loneliness, fall prevention, technological concern (e.g., user experience, privacy, and data sharing)), or social issue (e.g., sexuality, social connections). Some scholars choose to stay in the confines of their discipline, for many others, there are opportunities and positives to conducting IDR.

Transgenerational Technology and Interactions for the 21st Century:
Perspectives and Narratives, 157–172
Copyright © 2022 by Hannah R. Marston, Linda Shore, Laura Stoops, and Robbie S. Turner
Published under exclusive licence by Emerald Publishing Limited
doi:10.1108/978-1-83982-638-220221010

Universities and strategic leaders define IDR and the current landscape in the context of the UK as:

> [...] IDR is not an end in itself – but a means to an end such as impact or new knowledge – and that IDR should not be incentivised at the expense of good quality monodisciplinary research. (Technopolis, 2016, p. 7)

IDR is a growing area of research which enables researchers (across careers) to collaborate across various disciplines. The notion of IDR may stem from doctoral studies for many scholars who choose to lean towards IDR (UKRI, n.d.a). Whether a researcher chooses to be interdisciplinary or not, conducting research affords individuals the opportunity to collaborate with various stakeholders, businesses/small-medium enterprises (SMEs), charities, social enterprises, HEIs and specific target audience(s). Building external collaborations does not happen overnight and this can be said also for academic collaborations. For many relationships to successfully work, the foundations of trust, integrity, and respect are essential. In addition to meeting deadlines, attending meetings (and on time), conducting appropriate communication (e.g., not ignoring emails), and overall making valuable contributions are key to successful collaborations.

Surrounding the precarity of (IDR) the British Academy (2016) provides an overview into the barriers, challenges and enablers for scholars entering this process, while detailing how IDR provides scholars the opportunity to learn new methods from outside of their discipline. For example,

1. Explore collaborations with colleagues and external partners from different fields but who have common or similar interests,
2. IDR enables scholars to identify new innovative approaches to problem solving,
3. Meet new challenges, through new or existing collaborations and disciplines,
4. Conduct research in emerging disciplines enabling scholars to crossover their interests, share experiences and expertise,
5. Facilitate scholars who are perceived as already conducting IDR to address societal questions and challenges. (British Academy, 2016)

It is not the purpose of this chapter to discuss funding avenues surrounding research. However, it should be noted that there are a handful of funding streams via respective UKRI funding councils (UKRI, n.d.b). Within UKRI there are various programmes of funding enabling scholars the opportunity to apply (via the Je-S system) and is reviewed by external reviewers (experts from different fields) and discussed at a panel (varies at time, dependent of the call). Feedback is usually provided which can (not always) assist in reworking the grant for re-submission. In some instances, institutions facilitate seed corn funding to enable scholars to conduct pilot work, with a view to scaling up and applying for larger research grants at a national level. In the following section we will explore the barriers and enablers to conducing IDR, based on published reports from governing bodies.

Barriers and Enablers to Conducting IDR

In 2016, the *Landscape Review of Interdisciplinary Research in the UK* report (Technopolis, 2016) published insights into the perceptions, incentives, and barriers of IDR across the UK (Table 7.1).

In the following section we briefly highlight and explore aspects and considerations which may for some researchers be barriers, challenges, and enablers for a life in research.

Research Experiences

In this section there are two areas of focus, 1. *Researcher experiences*, and 2. *Examples of different types of research* (e.g., online data collection, international collaboration etc.).

Conducting a programme of study (e.g., PhD) is not for the faint-hearted, and for many individuals, this journey is the start of their academic, industry, or stakeholder career. Given the current precarity of the research environment, researchers are now experiencing continuous fixed term contracts, and in some instances having to commute various hours from their home, while others choose to move to a different location within a country or even move to a different country. However, moving locations whether it is in the same country or abroad is not (in some instances) feasible for everyone. For example, for some people they have caring responsibilities (Ferrant et al., 2014) for older parents and/or adult children. Financial implications can impact on the decision to move, especially if there is the possibility of long-term opportunities (e.g., contract extensions) or, even starting a tenure-track position (Academic Positions, 2019; Phinney, 2009; University of Berkley, n.d.) will not outweigh the financial implications. Similarly, health and dental insurance should be considered, and be explored, especially if there are pre-existing health conditions. It is not uncommon if residing in another country to 'file taxes' and if you find yourself having to do this, seeking out expertise with an accountant is the most appropriate way of ensuring one is keeping within the law. Being culturally aware of the environment that you are working in is important, and for some environments/countries, there is a greater expectation and rule of

Table 7.1.   Barriers and Facilitators to Interdisciplinary Research in the Context of the UK (Technopolis, 2016).

Barriers	Facilitators
Collaboration	Pursuit of knowledge
Discipline-oriented cultures	Academic quality
Career-related barriers	Impact
Evaluation of research outcomes	Funding
Funding for IDR	

Source: More information about the points above can be found via HEFCE & RCUK (2016) and Technopolis (2016)

formality (e.g., addressing a line manager – Mr/Dr/Ms), whereas in other countries there is a more informal approach (e.g., using first names).

Taking a perspective of managing one's health and well-being, specifically relating to *imposter syndrome* (McMillan, 2016) – which for many people in academia is not uncommon. The feelings of impostor syndrome can impact not only our feelings during our working day but also seep into our evenings and weekends, to ensure we are meeting the expectations as well as aiming to meet our respective objectives and progress (Dickerson, 2019). Overcoming this feeling can be achieved by conducting meditation exercises, to enable a person to become 'less preoccupied by the progress of others and better able to focus on what I want to bring to the table' (Dickerson, 2019). Conversely, there is a growing body of research surrounding classism within academia (Binns, 2019). Types of discrimination (Crew, 2021) and unbiased classism can relate to regional accents, for example,

> For many years, I have felt that my background, upbringing and identification as 'working-class' has been something of a hindrance to my development and progression ... I have a strong regional accent ... I did not attend an independent school or even a nice state school located in some leafy home county .... (Binns, 2019, p. 67)

> [...] and I just didn't think I was good enough really and I always used to get the piss taken out of me because of my voice, right, because I'm from XXX [city] ... and to be fair people do it here, but I don't take it as much of an offence now cos I've actually got a my PhD so I feel like I don't mind that, but I think at that time ... I felt like, sort of you know the Northerner who's come down South sort of thing. (Binns, 2019, p. 67)

Conversely, working with colleagues from different disciplines can lead to learning new *Language (interdisciplinary awareness)*. Communications between team members is crucial to developing rapport, understanding the approaches that can complement the efforts of a project or writing collaboration. The initial development of collaborations relies on these communications being effective and utilised as opportunities to learn, observe, and share our expertise and contribution. Terminology of tasks/work applied in one discipline, for example, coding (design, social sciences) can vary to indicate something different in another (Computer Science) however, essentially coding is language and relied on as a communication tool/application to develop research or concepts. Equally being *Self-aware and*, taking the time to acknowledge our efforts is important, and being aware of time, self, and a balance to facilitate social activities and pursuits encourages a sense of autonomy and contribution. In addition, stepping away from the core work for momentary distractions can enhance productivity (Leszczynski et al., 2017) and foster a sense of contribution.

In the following section we provide exemplars of research projects which have different approaches to study design, participant recruitment, and national and international perspectives. The purpose of these exemplars is to demonstrate how various multi-and inter-disciplinary research studies can be conducted across different disciplines, sensitive topics, and research lens.

Examples of Research Projects and Approaches

Case 1 – Conducting Sensitive Research (Topics)

As we will explore in this section planning and undertaking sensitive research is not so straight forward and may create concerns pertaining to methods and technical execution for the individual research and/or research team (McCosker et al., 2001). Conducting sensitive research with vulnerable and/or marginalised audiences is the norm for some researchers and can be very rewarding. In this example we explore three different projects, while drawing on existing literature to illustrate how researchers consider participant recruitment, project materials (e.g., information study) and personal conduct when undertaking sensitive research, such as sexuality, death, sex work/prostitution (Cowles, 1988; McCosker et al., 2001).

The *COVID-19: Vulnerable Young People Living with Life-Limiting/Life-Threatening Conditions and their Families* (Health and Wellbeing SRA, 2020b) project aimed to understand the impact of the first UK lockdown on young people (18+> years) who have life-limiting/threatening health conditions (LLTCs) (Earle & Blackburn, 2021) and their families. Utilising existing project partners/co-researcher networks from the *Talking About … Sex and Relationships: Young People Speak Out* (Health and Wellbeing SRA, 2017–2019) project in conjunction with social media posts, resulted in 40 face-to-face interviews being conducted.

This qualitative research project included a co-produced topic guide and included topics relating to LLTCs (e.g., congenital heart condition, cancer, hypermobility, neuro degenerative muscle weakness, muscular dystrophy, etc.). Additionally, the topic guide explored the living environment, type of employment (if any), when the young person received their government letter stating that they were 'at risk' and needed to shield, advance care planning and digital technology use. Whether it is a young person, or a family member being interviewed, discussing advanced care planning, which may include a 'do not attempt resuscitate' (DNAR) order is in place, can be difficult. For the interviewers, this too can be distressing, and as an interviewer, if the interviewee chooses not to talk about this topic (even though it is part of the topic guide), it is their choice not to answer the question. Researchers should keep in mind when conducting sensitive research, data analysis may cause distress and heightened emotions.

Since its conception in the late 1990s, the Internet has facilitated citizens to conduct various online day-to-day activities. In this second example, we turn our attention to the field of research surrounding sex work and technology, which can facilitate sex workers (independents), 'escort agencies' or massage parlours who advertise/market the sex workers or themselves, via photograph(s), varying in the quality of the image and may include tasteful to hardcore pornography alongside corresponding information including, pricing, the type of services offered, contact information (usually an email address) (Sharp & Earle, 2003).

Previously, there was little scholarly work in this area during the mid-to-late nineties (Chapkis, 1997; Scambler & Scambler, 1997) because it,

> [...] remains among the most discreditable and potentially stig-matising of activities in which a man can engage. (Sharp & Earle, 2003, p. 42)

Research conducted by Sharp and Earle (2003) nearly 20 years ago explored online reviews by men who solicit sex work, also known as a 'punter' and is defined as,

> [...] punting has been a lonely activity. The considerable stigma attached to paying for sex has traditionally meant that men who do are reluctant to reveal their activities to even their closest friends. The risks of being discredited as a man who pays for sex are considerable and multifaceted. (Sharp & Earle, 2003, p. 38)

Given the nature and difficulty of recruiting men who solicit sex work Sharp and Earle (2003) explored reviews left by men on the website 'Punternet'. Analysis of the reviews included the identity of primary and secondary themes including 1. *the preference of location and how discreet it is*, 2. *the notion of giving pleasure to the sex worker*, and 3. *the experience of 'girlfriend sex'*. Specifically, this research did not require Sharp and Earle (2003) to recruit or interview the men who pay for sex but was primarily desk-based data collection. However, given the nature of the work conducted, accessing, and reading the reviews may, for some people be distressing and against their own cultural views and beliefs.

Continuing this discussion, we draw on contemporary literature by Redmiles (2020) who focus on sex workers situated in specific cities across two European countries Switzerland (Basel, Lugano, and Zurich) and Germany (Berlin, Saarbruchen, and Hamburg). Planning the study design and participant recruitment Redmiles (2020) describes how the documentation undertook several iterations including specific contact information (e.g., email addresses, telephone numbers) and/or online contact information for the brothels, and the 'sex worker organisations and unions'.

Flyer distribution was conducted after making initial contact with the brothel owners, and the flyers included information detailing University ethical approval and contact details. Although, it is usually standard practice to include university logos on recruitment material, Redmiles (2020) notes

> We quickly found that being affiliated with a university – provid-ing the implication of authority – did not help us build trust but rather raised suspicion, inspired immediate fear, and led to curt responses. (2020, p. 107)

As university logos and other authoritative information were visible on the participant recruitment documentation, this did not build an initial level of trust. The initial responses from the first evening of recruitment, led to Redmiles reworking the flyers to include an extended explanation of the study (e.g., what exactly was intended, risk to the interviewee), and remuneration for taking part in the study (examples of the flyers can be found on pages 108–109 of Redmiles, 2020). Redmiles (2020) describes how a researcher, must think 'out of the box', and take into consideration how the information may be perceived by prospective participants. This example illustrates how certain information (e.g., University Logo(s)) were omitted from the flyers – because they were deemed too authoritarian and off putting to the target audience. Gaining ethical approval from any institution usually includes a question relating to 'risk', risk to the participants as well as the risk to the participant/research team. In this case, Redmiles describes her perspective of distributing flyers throughout the red-light areas,

> […] I lived on one of the red-light-district streets, I distributed a few flyers on my street every night as I came home from work – a perk of working late, as most brothels in Zurich open around 7 pm. I was only comfortable distributing flyers on my street as I came home from work, as it was in the center of Zurich and well populated enough that I could easily ask for help if needed. I always brought someone with me when recruiting in other red-light districts, as at times I was followed by clients who thought I might be working. (Redmiles, 2020, p. 110)

Whether it is research such as this, or research being conducted 'in the wild' (see example 4 below for more information) the risk and safety of a researcher is also important and should be considered during the study design. Further 'risks' were considered including how Redmiles would dress, and she chose to dress in her 'usual work clothes' (including a rucksack, for carrying the flyers) rather than trying to 'fit in' (Redmiles, 2020, p. 111).

Similarly, in the previous Chapter [6] Case Study 3 Baker-Green (2013) describes how education was (for many residents) not the primary focus and for many people who left school, they ended up securing employment in the Colliery. However, there was an embedded culture within the GEVH to ensure everyone felt comfortable and this also included dressing accordingly, and instead of dressing in a professional manner (similar to how teachers may dress), members of staff 'were careful to dress very casually' (Baker-Green, 2013, pp. 114–115). Further, the following quote supports the notion and approach of 'dressing casually',

> It's like tutors wearing a suit. Nobody comes in a suit here, as such. So, we're actually mixing with people, by us being dressed the same, casually, it's automatically taking a barrier away from ordinary people coming through the doors. You put them at ease because when they're coming to learn something they get very 'et up'. (Baker-Green, 2013, p. 115)

Similarly, having an 'accent' can also lend itself (positively) to a project and participant recruitment. In some instances, it can be perceived negatively because people from other regions may make assumptions of one's education, financial status, and suitability for a job. Having an accent, and especially if you're conducting research with participants who may have a similar accent to yourself may likely ingratiate yourself to them.

In the following Case [2] we provide examples of different international research projects, conducted in both a pre-pandemic and during pandemic society. The purpose of showcasing these examples is to highlight to researchers who are keen to be involved in international research the different processes and considerations.

Case 2 – Conducting International Research

International research can be very engaging, fun, and culturally rich. Two different examples of international research projects are presented in this section, with the first example focussing on the *iStoppFalls* (2011–2014) research project, funded through the European Commission – Framework 7.

The study design aimed to execute a randomised control trial (RCT) in the latter part of the study period, and it was believed at the time, to be the largest RCT to have been conducted, across three sites (Germany, Spain, and Australia). With any type of research project, regular meetings are crucial to ensure milestones are going to be met on time, and to share any (potential) concerns and issues arising. Except for the Australian partner, the iStoppFalls Consortium were all on the same time zone, and as a team we accommodated the two different time zones, and at times, required meetings to be held early in the morning (e.g., 8am CET). Ethical approvals were required for the RCT phase and were approved by the respective sites/members (Gschwind et al., 2015; Marston et al., 2016 ; Marston, Woodbury, et al., 2015). However, research ethics committees do vary by institutions within countries and externally researchers who are part of an international project should be mindful of the variances in expectations, required documentation, and the time it may take for approval to be granted. The iStoppFalls Consortium constituted inter-and-multidisciplinary partners who brought together their knowledge, expertise, strengths, and existing external partnerships with stakeholders to the project. Such a project can facilitate junior researchers and post-graduate students the opportunity to engage and learn (from mid-and-senior level scientists) how an EU project is executed. There were strict deadlines agreed with the European Commission for the submission of reports and with this, internal deadlines and quality control mechanisms were set in place. This too showcases the level of organisation and planning required for this type of project. The project Consortium has published an array of publications (Gschwind et al., 2014, 2015; Marston et al., 2016a, 2016b; Vaziri et al., 2016) providing insights into the study protocol, findings, technical, and social science developments.

A second example focusses on the *COVID-19: Technology, Social Connections, Loneliness and Leisure Activities* project (April 2020). This project organically grew into an international project with multiple sites and languages. A study protocol (Marston et al., 2020) details the recruitment of the consortium partners including how 'This is a cooperative project that responds to the need of urgent information during the unexpected COVID-19 pandemic' (p. 10). Each site lead worked directly with the PI pertaining to the translation of documents, refinement, survey deployment on the Qualtrics software and ethical approval. As researchers, we are not always aware of the laws of different countries.

Usually, large consortiums such as this have additional assistance in the form of administration built in via the funding grant. However, there was no external funding attached to this project and administration support was limited. Given the purpose and time sensitive nature of this project meticulous organisation and administration was needed to ensure survey deployments and closures for each site was met. Ethical approval and accompanying documentation were shared with the partners for them to gain approval, while updates and sharing of this approval was submitted to the lead institution's ethics committee.

In contemporary years, gerontological research is now taking and implementing a life course perspective (Green, 2017) and theory (Elder, 1985) to capture the voices and narratives of all research participants. Employing a life course perspective facilitates all actors within society the opportunity to explore solutions through the lens of those people who are being targeted, their personal experiences and/or historical events, affording a 'personal biography' (Elder, 1985). In the following section we explore a scenario relating to a project focussing on Millennials, because while gerontological research solely focusses on older adults, this field should start to explore younger generations of society because they too will be older adults in the future, with different expectations and needs to current older adults.

Case 3 – Conducting Co-Production Research

The *Adapt Tech, Accessible Technology* (ATAT) project (2020–2021) aims to understand the type of technology adjustments needed by older adults with limited digital skills and literacy. This multi-and-inter-disciplinary (gerontologists, gerontechnologists, health, well-being and social sciences, and computer scientists) research team included Digital VOICE Newcastle and Digital Communities in Wales as project partners, who facilitated participant recruitment.

Utilising the positive rapport built-up during the workshops, additional interviews with recruited participants, members of the research team, and stakeholders were conducted to understand everyone's experiences of working together. From the perspective of the stakeholders, these interviews enabled their voices to be heard and shared as an active member, while the voices of the recruited participants enabled them to share how their thoughts of being involved from the beginning, and describing their experiences of being involved in the research projects, which in turn facilitated the development and content for a podcast (Morgan, 2021), an Icon booklet, and a prototype of a launcher app.

Several online workshops were executed with co-collaborators using the Zoom platform and by employing this approach with participants located across different areas of Wales, and England it facilitated everyone to attend the scheduled workshops and contribute meaningful information and insights to achieving the objectives.

Case 4 – Conducting Intergenerational and 'in the wild' Research

Research is not limited to laboratory settings, and rich insights can be generated regarding peoples' interactions and use of technology in the home or community settings (Carroll & Rosson, 2013). The term 'in the wild' has been utilised as a research term for HCI (human computer interaction) researchers who work with participants as a means to understand experiences and develop concepts/prototypes from that understanding (Crabtree et al., 2013). In essence it is a qualitative approach not dissimilar to ethnographic approaches that aim to understand user behaviour in the home or native settings (Blomberg et al., 2009). Design research of emerging technologies, may rely on exploring and understanding current technologies, enquiring or asking participants to speculate about future technologies in order to understand their perceptions towards these (Shore, 2019).

Constructivist Grounded Theory approach (Charmaz, 2014) affords the curious and speculative nature of a design research study that explores the perceptions expressed by older adults to different technologies, such as lower limb exoskeleton (Shore et al., 2019). In this context and drawing on the work by Shore et al. (2019) the older adult participants who, alongside the researcher, expressed and shared their experiences relating to assistive technologies, ageing experience and how a future may look with robots and robotic assistive technologies available as supports to enhance quality of life and independence. Taking this approach facilitated the researcher to understand the complexities of the work being conducted within the participants' own environment instead of a laboratory. This too identified where 'pinch points', may occur within the respective environments which may not have been ascertained in a different environment.

Following on from this example, we explore the nature of conducting 'intergenerational relationship' research in the second example, whereby we focus on intergenerational research between students and participants. It has been demonstrated successfully, how undergraduate students working with older adults, and researchers can present design and innovation opportunities (Shore et al., 2018). The ageing experience does not necessarily have a start or an end date, for example, chronological age. Across the various scenarios above we have showcased a variety of research projects. However, with many research projects there are project partners/stakeholders and in the following sections we will explore the positives, enablers, challenges, and barriers to conducting research from the perspectives of stakeholders and industry.

In the following sections we provide an overview of research related activities through the lens of stakeholders and industry. Engaging with stakeholders and partners within the project life cycle, from conception to dissemination and pathways to impact can be a rewarding process for all team members. Because it can ensure everyone's voice(s) are being heard, while fostering positive relationships with a view to supporting large-scale projects, dissemination, and recommendations, implemented within communities and organisations where needed. Age NI describe the benefits and challenges of being involved in research projects.

Age NI Stakeholder

Age NI strives for a co-design approach in its engagement work. Co-design does not simply involve presenting a group of older people with options and asking them for their views (Bate & Robert, 2007). Co-design involves older people being recognised as 'lived experience experts' who work alongside professionals, decision-makers in public bodies to engage meaningfully in discussion about the shape or content of a future service, policy, or strategy.

The process followed in Age NI is a research proposal is received and shared with the entire Consultative Forum (CF) membership along with any other Age NI service users or network groups who may have an interest. As outlined in Chapter 3, the CF aims to identify the needs and concerns of older people. Individuals who express an interest in the research project then form a working group (WG) who guide and shape the project going forward. Typically, this would involve between 6 and 10 people depending on the requirements of the project. The decision by Age NI to take part in research is guided by the interests of older people involved and informed by organisational priorities.

In the Spring of 2020, in response to views expressed by older people that their voices were not being heard by decision-makers during the emergency response to the pandemic, Age NI brought together their concerns, and fears, as well as their hopes for a safer future in a report called, *Lived Experience – Voices of older people on the COVID-19 pandemic 2020,* The report sets out a range of immediate and longer-term actions urging decision-makers to act, plan and prepare for life during and after the pandemic, and to learn from older people's shared experiences.

The role of the stakeholders was to share their views and insights around their lived experience. Evidence was collected by staff through engagement with the CF, the wider age sector, along with regular feedback from people receiving Age NI services. Age NI CF involves a group of older people with the aim of identifying the needs and concerns of older people in relation to issues such as poverty, health, equality, technology, and many other issues. This required Age NI staff time to communicate with older people across the organisation, older people's groups, and networks, arranging and facilitating conversations to collect the insights.

To gain a deeper understanding of the experiences and issues that matter the most to older people during COVID-19, a Lived Experience survey of older people was then carried out in 2021. The survey invited older people to rank the issues identified in the first Lived Experience report (2020) in order of importance. As part of the co-design model, an older persons' WG was developed which met regularly on Zoom to influence the survey concept and design, inform plans on the distribution of the survey, provide input into the report on survey findings and discuss next steps. This co-design model required staff time and resources to organise and facilitate each session, to take minutes and circulate them as well as to implement agreed changes.

Given the context of COVID-19, the Lived Experience survey required a lot of promotion in the form of reaching out on social media and via age sector networks and groups across Northern Ireland. Initially, it was decided to promote the survey through social media as it was not possible to visit older people's services and there were concerns at the time around transmission through paper surfaces. Age NI did, however, offer to print off and send hard copies to individuals and groups on request. Despite these constraints, the survey received 752 responses from across Northern Ireland.

Age NI was keen to share the findings of the survey with older people, key influencers, and decision-makers. The WG was involved in the development and delivery of two events, one which was solely an online event and the other which was a hybrid event and offered involvement in person or online.

The first event, which only took place online through Zoom, launched the Lived Experience 2021 report, shared findings with older people, gathered their feedback through smaller discussion groups and, using an online poll, identified priorities participants wished to be discussed at the second event which was a Pensioner's Parliament, where older people asked government Ministers questions based on the priorities identified by older people included in the Lived Experience 2021 report.

The Pensioners' Parliament was planned with the Northern Ireland Assembly engagement team and was the first engagement event that had taken place in Parliament Buildings since the start of the pandemic. Everyone had their own level of comfort around attending in-person events and as such, some older people opted to pose their questions virtually, while others wished to participate by attending the event in the Senate Chamber. The use of technology enabled Age NI to meet the needs and preferences of both those who wished to participate in the event in person and those who preferred to make their contribution virtually.

Involving stakeholders in research projects at various stages provides an opportunity for meaningful engagement. Services and support can be shaped to meet the needs of the older cohort more accurately through involving them throughout the project lifecycle. Stakeholders share that they feel valued, listened to and respected when they are given the opportunity to contribute to research projects. In addition, the experience of involvement in research often provides the benefit of social contact with others which we know can impact mental well-being.

Target Audiences and Co-Researchers

Age NI believe involving older people as co-researchers can provide a rich insight and ensure that any research materials developed are appropriate for the target audience. At Age NI a group of older people volunteer as peer facilitators. This role involves supporting any research of interest being conducted both internally and externally. An example of this, prior to COVID-19, was work being conducted by the PHA (Public Health Agency) in Northern Ireland which aimed to better understand the experiences of people living in care homes. The method of data collection involved completion of an interview style questionnaire. The group of Age NI peer facilitators were involved in testing the questionnaire and offering suggested improvements. Following this, peer facilitators then visited care homes and sat with older people to complete the questionnaire.

Feedback received suggested that many older people felt they could relate more easily to peer facilitators who were similar in age to themselves and, therefore, may have a greater understanding of their experiences. From the perspective of the peer facilitators, they were involved in valued work, which ensured the views of older people in care homes were heard. Valuable co-researcher experiences continued during the global pandemic through utilisation of technology. An example of this is the WG of older people involved in generating content for Chapter 3 of this book as well as guiding the general older person narrative. All engagement relating to the development of this book took place on Zoom and started with participation in a series of focus groups on topics such as, feelings towards technology, inequalities relating to technology, and technology in the context of COVID-19.

Following the completion of the focus groups, the role of the older person WG shifted more to that of co-researchers as they helped develop a survey to collect a wider array of views on technology. Co-researcher involvement in the design of the survey was extremely valuable as it highlighted any issues with wording of questions, use of generational language and ensuring any answer options would be relatable to the older cohort. Additionally, some of the co-researchers had previous experience in education and/or academia and therefore offered valuable guidance on general grammar, writing style, survey techniques, etc.

Analysis of the survey findings were conducted in collaboration with the co-researcher group. Initial findings were generated by an Age NI staff member and a Zoom meeting took place with the co-researchers whereby they offered feedback on the findings and on how the findings were presented (e.g., graph style, level of decimal point etc.). This insight was valuable as it provided a fresh perspective for the analyst and ensured that the survey data ultimately was accessible to the reader.

Challenges and Benefits to Co-Production

Some of the challenges around engaging co-researchers can be the time and resources needed to effectively engage the group regularly throughout a project. Arranging meeting times, developing materials for review ahead of meetings, writing and sharing meeting minutes and providing regular project updates all require considerable resource. Depending on the research being conducted there can be limitations to the level of involvement co-researchers can have and therefore being clear about their role and managing expectations of the group appropriately is key.

There are many benefits to involving co-researchers in a piece of work that involves areas of interest to them, or which may have an impact on them. A key benefit is that you can test any research materials with the intended target audience. This often provides the opportunity to identify potential issues before distributing to a wider audience. From the point of view of the co-researchers themselves they report feeling valued and gaining a social, connection element to being involved in the research. This in turn helped improve many of the co-researchers' mental well-being during the uncertain and challenging time of a global pandemic.

Social Enterprises

A trend is forming and growing within large organisations who require research and study activities related to technology orientated topics to utilise social enterprises and not-for-profit (NFP) organisations. Previously, the rational for these studies and research tasks would historically have been the norm to seek out industry as the foremost experts, but it has since been identified by asking the technology manufacturer which technology is the most effective or which will be the next innovation, they very seldom provide objective and independent guidance. It is only natural a commercial organisation will assume the technology they are manufacturing or developing is the best on the market, and therefore it would be a very strange circumstance indeed for them to propose a competitor's solution.

It is considered a progressive approach or initiative to engage specialist NFP entities with technical associations and academic institutions for study and research support. However, this mindset seems to be gaining popularity, for example, the creation of framework agreements with qualifying entities in this new more agile and competitive format and arena is currently being pioneered by organisations such as the NATO (North Atlantic Treaty Organization) Communications and Information Agency (NCIA, n.d.). Currently, NATO is considering and planning a similar framework approach in conjunction with their UN division, EU institutions and at national government levels. Taking this agile and progressive approach will facilitate NATO to gain independent insight and guidance relating to their objectives.

A fringe benefit of this activity is the potential opportunity to inject revenue into these supporting entities and as a result will facilitate NFP entities to financially support and conduct more of their own research activities. Such activities will also align with national and global societal benefits (e.g., UN Sustainable Development Goals[1]) who without an agenda can share their findings with broader audiences, such as policy makers without the need to profit from them.

Industry

Large international organisations such as the UN (United Nations) and NATO have their own mature and established research capabilities spanning a wide range of subjects and disciplines. In many cases the application of the research is used for policy, research and development processes, and operational efficiencies.

Entities such as the Science and Technology Organisation[2] situated within NATO continuously conduct research with the aim of the findings to be utilised by all and for the benefit of 28 NATO nations. The UN have several comprehensive research organisations, whilst many of them are focussed on social and economic topics they still have technology driven research activities[3]. These examples for

---

[1]https://sdgs.un.org/goals
[2]https://www.sto.nato.int/Pages/activitieslisting.aspx
[3]https://www.un.org/technologybank/content/current-activities

NATO and the UN are not isolated, and similar organisations both at government and international organisation levels have open source and accessible research outputs easily available to any party who wishes to take advantage of these great resources.

Researchers who are completing post-graduate research programmes (e.g., Masters or PhD) acquire a range of transferable skills that can be utilised by industry, NFPs, and social enterprises. Regardless of the discipline, transferable skills (e.g., report writing, presentations, data analytics, project management, teamwork, etc.) are essential attributes within these sectors.

Summary

The purpose of this chapter was fourfold:

1. We present an overview of different items that can impact being a researcher, coupled with different elements that may have to be considered when starting out on a career in research,
2. We present different cases of research studies to afford insight and alternative approaches, thoughts and considerations when planning and conducting research,
3. We provide insight from a stakeholder perspective with the aim of illustrating how co-production research is perceived from their standpoint and more importantly the peer-researchers within the network of Age NI,
4. We provide industry and social enterprise insights, to demonstrate how industry is utilising agile approaches in a bid to gain independent knowledge.

Being a researcher is and can be fun, all the while juggling various personal and professional pressures. Seeking out opportunities to accept a position abroad can afford different opportunities to experience another culture, and a different work environment. If possible, gaining advice and guidance from peers who may have undergone similar experiences as well as exploring Internet forums associated to the country that you are moving to can be a good starting point.

There are several cases demonstrating various (not all) methods, or processes and factors that need to be considered by researchers when conducting their respective research studies. We hope these examples provide insight into how scholars tackled their challenges and enablers.

Hearing the positive benefits of co-production activities from Age NI demonstrates and highlights the importance of initiating and building a relationship with stakeholders and their co-researchers. Stakeholders such as Age NI have their own processes before they can agree to be part of a research project, and, we have demonstrated here how Age NI, do enjoy being part of projects. In addition, the data presented in Chapter 3 of this book, was conducted with co-researchers and what we as researchers should remember is, co-researchers do have value and being able to work alongside them affords everyone involved the opportunity to learn from one another and to inform practice.

Conversely, from the industry standpoint, we have described how agile practices are being utilised in organisations such as NATO, to deliver their objectives across the 28 member states. Employing such techniques can facilitate greater agile responses by industry and individuals, while maintaining the remit of delivering pathways to impact activity across respective industries, drawing on expertise and transferable skills.

Chapter 8

Not a Conclusion – But a Manifesto!

The latter part of the twentieth century, and to date in the twenty-first century, we have witnessed a growing and phenomenal amount of research and innovation in new technology development. The realm of research that we explored (e.g. digital games, design, technology, digital health, age-friendly cities, inequalities, and communities) published previously has revealed continuing and disregarded problems that despite being stated, remain unanswered.

Technology has, and continues to offer potential and critical benefits to the lives and experiences of citizens and society. However, technology products and service systems use, and experience can also be a source of pain and frustration. At times this can result in abandonment and an inability for the person to perceive and experience the intended benefits and usefulness to support day-to-day tasks and activities. The variety of discussion in this book collates decades of discussions, numerous insights, and application of research methods and deliverables. This knowledge activated frustrations that we collectively were witnessing through our research and industry practice – twenty-first century technology interactions at times was not assisting or enhancing quality of life and autonomy across the life course.

Industry is relied on to manufacture and deliver the products, services, and digital technologies realised through socially conscious research which is often generated from consumer demand. Products and services created as a result of this activity, for example, medical devices, communications and digital devices can enhance quality of life, experiences, and interactions across the generations. Therefore, it is vital that industry participates and contributes to the promotion of *Transgenerational Technology* awareness.

The agenda for this needs to include small to medium size companies and entrepreneurs that can be mobilised, inspired, or incentivised to innovate in these areas. Growing old is a privilege that is not experienced by everyone. It is clear that longevity and the lived experience improves with each generation. Industry can provide support and become active partners to our life journey as we interact with technologies.

At the front and centre, this book has been composed with humanity and how we as humans navigate the twenty-first century interacting with technologies,

Transgenerational Technology and Interactions for the 21st Century:
Perspectives and Narratives, 173–176
Copyright © 2022 by Hannah R. Marston, Linda Shore, Laura Stoops, and Robbie S. Turner
Published under exclusive licence by Emerald Publishing Limited
doi:10.1108/978-1-83982-638-220221011

including those that are intended to support and enhance our experiences across the lifespan. It has demonstrated knowledge and creative courage across our disciplines. We have mobilised and collaborated to design a tangible artefact in the format of a manifesto that is intended to assist and empower the creative and innovative process when developing technology-based products and service systems for people across generations and abilities.

Given the nature of research and the multi-faceted processes that are needed to move debate and discourse forward, we present a 12-point manifesto titled *'Transgenerational Technology: Well-being & Innovation Opportunity for the 21st Century'* as a collective statement and an actionable tool. This manifesto pinpoints succinctly the critical considerations to assist and avoid compromising the person intended to benefit from a technology intervention.

Fig. 8.1 is presented as a declaration of the aims that we as a group have developed with passion and empathy. Our creativity and humanity expressed in this book comes as a result of the very nature of our differences – professionally and personally. It is these collective differences that materialised a common aim and conversation towards the potential for *Transgenerational Technology*.

Our individual and collaborative contributions throughout this book offer strategic, collective, and multi-faceted awareness to bring a new perspective. This new perspective will, in our opinion assist the identification of user needs and requirements, whilst remaining focussed on user autonomy. It will offer prospect to clearly state innovation opportunity that can be recognised through and by design, and the creative collaborations that interdisciplinary research presents.

As we digest the conclusion of this book and the collaborative effort of the journey, it is worth reflecting on the position and direction that generated our manifesto. The various chapters were strategically positioned to share experience, expertise and creative activity that culminates to this manifesto. The perspectives and narratives shared will undoubtedly contribute to positive *Transgenerational Technology* interactions for the twenty-first century. We do not view this as the conclusion of the book, but – a new beginning, and a shared optimism.

Chapter 2 – *The Current State of Technology and Digital Games* presented an in-depth review, and commentary to the current state of the art positioning of gerontechnology, and interactions with technology across the lifespan. It informed and presented motivation to the importance of interdisciplinary research and action to innovate and development of technologies and digital games.

Chapter 3 – *Adoption, Benefits and Challenges of Technology: Insights from Citizens in Northern Ireland* introduced and presented direct insights documented and recorded by Age NI researchers. This mixed methods study adds value to our collective understanding of the ageing experience throughout the pandemic and the digital interventions relied on to assist day-to-day tasks, experiences, and activities.

Chapter 4 – *Technology in the Role of Stakeholders, Social Enterprise, Industry and Smart Age-friendly Ecosystems in the 21st Century* explored and offered speculative commentary regarding age-friendly cities in the current format and how they may evolve through the twenty-first century. It expands on this by discussing further

Transgenerational Technology:
Well-Being & Innovation Opportunity
for the 21st Century
- A Manifesto

We are an interdisciplinary team that share a common focus – the value and quality of peoples' interactions and experiences with technologies should be enhanced, supported and unhindered. Commercial gain, hurried assumptions or lack of enquiry to human concern should remain secondary to the primary intent and value of defining the user needs requirements identified during research. Empathic and purposeful design approaches offers inclusive and human centred focus defining the 'how' and positive augmentation of abilities, experience and activity of not just the person & context of use, but also of their network of stakeholders.

1) We believe that chronological age should not determine vulnerability, for we are aware, vulnerability and age/longevity is not always mutually exclusive.

2) People should not be discriminated upon because of their beliefs, who they are, identify as, or what role they partake in society, and their voices should be expressed freely and listened to.

3) As a follow to Point 2, the expressive commentary voiced and expressed freely should not harm or hurt others by malicious criticism or attack.

4) Research and recruitment of participants who are perceived to be and/or are marginalized in society should not result in discrimination or biased research outputs.

5) We believe that a citizen continues to learn and gain life experiences and can offer contribution to society across their lifespan.

6) Innovation and research practices must consider democratised voices and user experiences as valuable catalysts to creativity and technology well-being for all.

7) Interdisciplinary research must be recognised across all disciplines as a vital contributor to societal growth and documented interactions

8) Inter & multi-disciplinary and unique language and terminology is recognised across disciplines through collaborative research providing a rich embrace and appreciation as we co-design, innovative research approaches and create new technologies, services and systems that benefit all.

9) We believe cognitive and physical limitations can be supported, and dignity is always offered and placed central to the person.

10) To reflect on digital legacies, emerging and future technologies should not harm or injure and should obey the instruction as directed by the human.

11) At all times the intervention of future technologies should not place any person in a position of feeling stigmatised or excluded by society.

12) The data that effectively is created and stored by actors (e.g., stakeholders) will be done collectively and offers the person (including guardian, next of kin) autonomy in voicing their agreement or dissatisfaction to this activity.

Signed.......Hannah R. Marston, Linda Shore, Laura Stoops, Robbie S. Turner | 2022 ©

Fig. 8.1.   Transgenerational Technology (TT) a call to action Manifesto!

empirical enquiry to understand the differences if any that are as a result of the location of communities, for example, rural, coastal or furthermore the citizen types that occupy these ecosystems, for example, dementia, and inclusivity.

Chapter 5 – *'The older you get, people get less active, and then they feel the cold'* documented ageing experiences and perceptions towards emerging technologies and user-centred design approaches to share the valuable expression recorded during fieldwork. Similar to the opinions and voices shared in Chapter 3, this chapter presents important insights that demonstrate how a novel approach relying on *Transgenerational Technology* consideration may offer innovation opportunity that once developed enhances quality of life and experience.

Chapter 6 – *Digital Inequities and Society* discussed how poorly considered digital technologies and practice can impede and negatively impact people who are socially disadvantaged or from different cultural and societal backgrounds. There was narrative offered which supports again our position to mobilise and present our manifesto in order to positively impact future technology experience and interactions in health, well-being, and digital autonomy.

Chapter 7 – *The Research Environment* discussed the barriers, challenges and implications of interdisciplinary research, the various stakeholders including policy makers and how the process and language of research can offer optimal benefits when we consider the values and expertise of our colleagues within and out-with our professions and disciplines.

Chapter 8 – *Not a Conclusion – But a Manifesto!* collates the journey of this book and the values that the authors positioned as a new beginning and presented as a tangible tool. Our manifesto titled: *'Transgenerational Technology: Well-being & Innovation Opportunity for the 21st Century'* presents 12-points as a 'call to action' for researchers, practitioners, policy makers and stakeholders. This manifesto is intended to position narratives and interdisciplinary research agendas forward into the twenty-first century and define technology innovation.

Chapter 9 – *The Journey: Author Biographies and Trajectories* offers our individual biographies, including a question and answer section to share as individuals, our present (Pandemic experience) passions that motivate and have helped form our career directions, and a future or speculative vision.

We invite others to consider these points, join in the discourse and to start working towards implementing them in practice. Although living in the moment is important, we must look to the future, and by this we mean 30-40-50 years from now, not just the next decade. New terminology is being used as a smoke screen for reinventing the wheel, previous research is being overlooked, resulting in lessons and recommendations being discounted. Learning from the past can afford the research, industry, and stakeholder communities to look to the future, and we must start to consider younger generations in this planning. Without doing so, when other generations reach 'later life' we anticipate little advancement in knowledge around the needs of this cohort. Therefore, by starting now to understand the needs, expectations, and behaviours there will be a body of work to build on.

Chapter 9

The Journey: Author Biographies and Trajectories

We read many books, journal papers and articles in our respective fields, but do we ever really know the author(s) behind the literature?

Forming part of the proposal for this book, all authors agreed that there should be a chapter dedicated to author biographies, including a question-and-answer section. In some academic books we do see a brief overview of respective authors and/or contributors. However, what we never read about are the journeys and trajectories that they have experienced, and which led to their current situations.

We hope the stories and journeys in the following pages will provide readers with inspiration as they travel on their pathways in what is currently a precarious environment, but an environment that can be very fulfilling and rewarding.

Hannah R. Marston

Hannah is an interdisciplinary researcher, and her interests lie in the fields of videogames, digital (health) technology, technology adoption, gamification, health, well-being, digital ex/inclusion, age friendly cities and communities, ageing, gender and user experience (UX).

Currently, Hannah is involved in a wide range of research projects and is the principal investigator for the *COVID-19: Technology, Social connections, Loneliness and Leisure Activities* international, multi-site project. Consortium partners are in Austria, Canada, Germany, India, Portugal, Romania, Singapore, Spain, Turkey, and USA. Additionally, she is part of the *Adapt Tech, Accessible Technology* (ATAT) research team working alongside colleagues from Swansea University, Northumbria University, Digital VOICE Newcastle, Digital Communities in Wales, Age NI, and end-users.

Hannah holds a PhD (2010) in Virtual Reality and Gerontology from Teesside University, UK. Previously, she worked as a research assistant at the Centre for Innovative Ageing – Swansea University, and in August 2010 she relocated to Canada to take-up a one-year post-doctoral fellowship in the David R. Cheriton School of Computer Science at the University of Waterloo. Upon completion

Transgenerational Technology and Interactions for the 21st Century:
Perspectives and Narratives, 177–194
Copyright © 2022 by Hannah R. Marston, Linda Shore, Laura Stoops, and Robbie S. Turner
Published under exclusive licence by Emerald Publishing Limited
doi:10.1108/978-1-83982-638-220221012

Fig. 9.1.   Dr Hannah R. Marston.

Hannah relocated to Germany to commence a position at the German Sport University Cologne (DSHS) as a research scientist on the iStoppFalls EU project (2011–2014); which aimed to design, develop, and evaluate a purpose-built ICT system to assess fall risk, and to provide tailored exergames incorporating strength and balance exercises. Currently, Hannah is a research fellow in the Health and Wellbeing Strategic Research Area (H&W SRA) at The Open University. The H&W SRA is a pan-University initiative which supports colleagues from across the four faculties with networking opportunities with both internal and external academics, stakeholders, and industry.

Over the last 12-years Hannah has published over 40 peer-reviewed journal papers, 9+ book chapters, led and co-guest edited special issues and has presented her research at both national and international conferences. In 2018, Hannah gave a keynote presentation at the *'International Child and Information Safety Congress "Digital Games"* conference held in Ankara, Turkey. In conjunction with colleagues, Hannah has submitted evidence to different UK government Committees including the *Science and Technology Ageing: Science, Technology and Healthy Living* Committee' and more recently to the UK government, COVID-19 committees. One piece of evidence was cited in the report *Beyond Digital: Planning for a Hybrid World*. In the Spring of 2021 Hannah was invited to attend a round table discussion as part of the Assistive Technology All-Party Parliamentary Group (@AT_APPG) and she is also a member of the Smart Homes Commission.

Questions and Answers:

What Inspired You to Work in the Field(s) of Your Choice?

I accidentally fell into my PhD – it wasn't something that I had planned to do or even had crossed my mind. In my childhood in the late 1980s I was a gamer, playing Mario Bros and Duck Hunt on the Nintendo NES console. During my teenage years and early 20s I did not game as much, and only got back to it when starting my PhD. I spent several days and weeks playing *REZ* on the Dreamcast and having completed all four levels, I opened a secret level [5] which even my supervisor at the time didn't know about.

In the early 1990s I learned within my family about the disease – Alzheimer's Dementia through the diagnosis of my maternal grandmother. As a young person, I witnessed the emotional impact this diagnosis had on my mother, grandfather, and wider family members. My grandmother's diagnosis was recognised by my grandfather's sisters who, holidaying with my grandparents, started to notice 'things' that my grandmother was doing. They were asked to keep a diary by the doctor, and this was the pathway to knowing about her condition. As a young person, aged 11–13 years old, I witnessed the deterioration, which was painful, in addition to the supplementary long-lasting impact(s) within the family because of my grandmother's death.

Conversely, it was not until the latter part of my Master's degree and while I was attending my graduation ceremony, that the thought of undertaking a PhD became a reality. After the graduation ceremony, my parents telephoned me stating that if I wanted to do a PhD, then I should use the time that I had left (visiting Teesside) to seek out appropriate information. This is when I found out about a possible project commencing in January 2005 and I spoke with the PI of the project, which in turn resulted in my going back home to Pontefract, in West Yorkshire to hand my notice in at Dorothy Perkins (at the time I was working part time in retail), and then I started to make plans to move back to Teesside, to start as a research assistant and to commence a part-time PhD from January 2005.

I have my parents to thank for giving me their blessing and supporting me with my education. Without them, I wouldn't be where I am today. With the exception of the first 18-months of my PhD, I was self-funded, and I was a teaching assistant within the School at Teesside, which enabled my fees to be paid by the school. I had to work part time to support myself and this included retail jobs, administration, and independent research contracts. It took me 4.5 years to complete and submit my thesis, and then a further six months to wait until my viva (January 2010). I initially spent 10 years living in Teesside (2000–10), and more recently I moved back to the area and overall, it's great to be back and reconnecting with old friends. Teesside is a gritty place and not everyone who visits will enjoy it, but it has everything, such as the beach at Saltburn and Redcar, the North York Moors, train links to Scotland, the South, and an airport. An industrial area, Teesside was primarily steelworks and docklands, many of which are now long gone, but the landscape is still there, coupled with a thriving digital tech community located in the BOHO.

What Impact has the Pandemic had on You?

From a professional perspective, the pandemic allowed me to conduct specific COVID-19 research and as a result, I'm leading two projects. One project is UK centric, and the second project is an international study comprising of colleagues from several countries. Setting up the second project gave me the opportunity to keep busy as well as contribute (potentially) to future findings on this historic event in our lifetime. The data generated from these two projects is vast, and it will take some time to analyse, write up and publish. But what has also been positive is that through these projects, new collaborations and networks have come to fruition and that too is one of the positive elements I enjoy about my job – the ability to bring individuals together.

From a personal perspective, throughout the initial months of the pandemic until June 2021, I lived in the south of England, with very few social networks and no family close by. Based on this experience, I decided in early 2021 to move back to the North, where I would be closer to the people I knew. So far, I have not regretted this decision, and it is great to be back in the North of England, where I am able to see friends and family more frequently than I was previously.

Name 1–3 Things that You Enjoy about the Work that You Do?

Throughout the last 16 years there have been many aspects of my work that I have enjoyed and still do. The first is working with colleagues and forming new collaborations with colleagues and peers who are from a different discipline and yet through conversation (organically) concepts and ideas come to fruition. Inspiration can come from anywhere: some people find a common inspiration from art or through outdoor activity – this too can inspire my creative and innovative thought processes. Although if I'm struggling with concepts or feeling fidgety, I usually find cooking or baking is a good way to ease and process my thoughts. However, just having a conversation with a friend can spark something off, and over the years, this has occurred at all times of the day and night, and it can only be a couple of words – and boom there's another concept! I enjoy and feel privileged to be invited to join a team, or write with colleagues, or to be an invited keynote speaker at a conference or giving a presentation to industry, such as in 2019 when I was invited to talk with industry professionals at Massive Entertainment – Ubisoft in Malmo (2018). I have to say I do have a problem with saying no.

I've been very fortunate to have experienced different working environments since completing my doctoral studies and this in turn has enabled me to grow not only as a person but also as a researcher. Moving to a new country to take-up a post where you don't have any friends, and your family are left back at home, you're on a different time zone, coupled with the challenges of a new position etc., certainly tests your emotional, mental, and physical abilities.

But each new experience brings with it new challenges and capabilities, be it language, the physical environment and climate conditions, or working on large projects, which in turn affords you the opportunity to learn from more senior colleagues as well as colleagues from different disciplines. Moreover, learning to understand the bureaucracy of a different country to ensure you are being a good citizen when it comes to taxation, filing taxes, maintaining personal health etc., as well as starting over again building friendships, and navigating the rules of the education institute that you're working in, are also character building. Although it should be noted, it was not until the summer of 2020 that I became a permanent member of staff at my current institution. Up until this point, I had been on fixed term contracts, which also facilitated me to move around to different countries, and for 11 months in 2016 I was in receipt of state welfare, living back at home with my parents, applying and interviewing for many academic positions in the UK and internationally – this all added to my character building, while it was also emotionally stressful. Although a very difficult time, it was very interesting and insightful to witness the various standards and approaches to interviews within academe and in other sectors.

Interviewing participants, data collection and analysis, have always fascinated me. I've conducted an array of workshops and interviews over the years, be it on a one-to-one level or as a team. Reading transcripts conducted by colleagues or transcribing them yourself; not only allows you to immerse yourself within the words for data analysis, but in some ways it's a privilege. By privilege I mean that I am hearing about many people who are opening up and talking (possibly) about sensitive and painful discussions and experiences. This I believe is an honour.

Since I have both dyslexia and dyspraxia which were only diagnosed 7 months into my graduate studies, some people may think numbers and statistics are not my favourite part of data analysis, but I do enjoy statistical analysis. I do believe mixed methods combine and complement one another very well, especially if/when the quantitative data is showing some odd patterns, the qualitative data may assist in unpacking any anomalies and help to tell the narrative.

Share a Vision You have to the Future?

My vision for the future looks towards the use of implantable devices as we discussed in Chapter 2 of this book. If we fast forward 40-50-60 years from now, I truly believe people will be implanting 'wearables' into their bodies and similarly wearing tattoos for tracking, recording, and sharing data. While the technology is here and is improving and being refined, the thought for many people of having a small 'micro-chip' or some kind of wearable tattoo placed within or on their body may not be for them. However, I think as future generations become more accustomed to the innovative developments of technology, these fears and apprehensions may subside.

For the future, it would be great if different elements in our society inter-connected better and by this, I mean research, policy, end-users, etc. We continue to see throughout our work how language plays an integral role within interdisciplinary research and two different words can mean the same thing. While there are many researchers who do (now) take an interdisciplinary approach, I would like to see more of this in the future, and for peers in the Academy to recognise the importance and positive contributions that individuals who do use interdisciplinary methods can bring to a study.

Linda Shore

Linda is a UX (User eXperience) Designer/Researcher with specific research interests in the ageing experience and gerontechnology/emerging technologies. She is currently a researcher as part of the DHI (Digital Health & Care Innovation Centre) at Glasgow School of Art, Scotland. Previously she was the Programme Leader for the BSc UX Design at Edinburgh Napier University, and is a member of several research groups including creative and social informatics. Her current research areas include the adoption of emerging wearable technologies by older adults, the impact of amputation/age-related conditions on Quality of Life (QoL) as we age, and a focus on areas of Trust, QoL and Perceptions to future applications taking a User-Centred Design approach. Additional areas of research interest include cryptography, service blueprint development for healthcare, transgenerational technology that adapts to users' needs and the impact of service systems on the user experience.

Linda has presented her research at a number of international conferences. She has published and reviewed various articles in peer-reviewed journals. Her previous research includes exploring and developing the concept of Shared Usability in Product Design for older adults.

Her PhD research titled 'Development of a design tool to optimise acceptance of an exoskeleton by older adults' was by publication from the University of Limerick, Ireland. Linda was a team member of the Design Factors group at the University of Limerick who were part of 'XoSoft' a Horizon 2020 (EU funded) soft robotic exoskeleton project with multiple academic and industry partners across Europe. The team at Design Factors, University of Limerick were responsible for the User-Centred Design (UCD) work packages to this major project.

Linda has a career that includes industry experience in Design, Financial Services, and Sales. This broad experience has enhanced her skills of enquiry, empathy, and observation to articulate and define unmet needs creatively, while placing people as central to solutions optimisation. Linda is excited about the possibilities of technologies for the future and how these can enhance the worlds, lives, and experiences as we age.

Fig. 9.2.   Dr Linda Shore.

Sometimes the research experience reminds you to pause momentarily and reflect on where you are in relation to the project development. This awareness lends itself well to Linda's personal pursuits which include drawing, walking, running, swimming, and paddling. Often during the chaos and ambiguity of research and design, Linda can be found baking cakes or outdoor pursuits as she relies on her creativity incubation time to process the work to hand.

Questions and Answers:

What Inspired You to Work in the Field(s) of Your Choice?

Growing up as a creative introvert, I often found it hard to express or state my ambitions or motivations to assist people. My family life growing up consisted of creativity, adventure, and humanity. I spent many happy hours in the company of my grandparents as a child, fascinated by the tales they could share such as the observation of my grandmother making pastry and deftly rubbing flour and butter through her fingers as she produced a most lovely array of bakes for the visitors and family members that would drop by.

My maternal grandparents facilitated my love of nature and animals, including my creativity and adaptation of my grandmother's used cigarette packets into caterpillar homes on the sideboard – which often not robust enough to contain the number of caterpillars I had gathered from the cabbage plants in the garden! My parents, my grandparents, my siblings, my children and my grandson: these are the people I love, and I cherish their contribution and stories which have influenced my creativity and curiosity to explore a world from a reflective past, an aware present and an intrigued sensitivity to our future!

What Impact has the Pandemic had on You?

The pandemic has been a time of transition for me: I had finished my PhD and was open to the future career activities that would open up. I was actively looking and applying for new roles when everything stopped! ... abruptly, in March 2020. It was initially a time of isolation, communicating in digital spaces instead of the formerly 'taken for granted' face-to-face times. It was also a time when I was so annoyed at the term 'Cocooning'! The older adults I was familiar with through my research over the previous numbers of years, in my opinion, were being encouraged to become sedentary, non-social, and isolated from activity. I was so relieved when the summer opened, we could engage or briefly meet people outdoors. The summer of 2020 for me was spent swimming or kayaking in the river, having socially distanced coffee outdoor catch ups, and climbing mountains that I could access within the COVID limitations. As autumn drew in, I opened up to where was I needing to be? This presented a new opportunity: I now live in Scotland, having moved from Ireland in January 2021 to undertake a new career adventure, and build new research and academic opportunities!

Name 1–3 Things that You Enjoy about the Work that You Do?

1. **People** – the space to be curious, creative, discuss and act to build new ideas, create new outputs and interact with colleagues, participants who have other perspectives and viewpoints.
2. **Collaborative opportunities** – As a UX Designer there is great potential to work with people from numerous backgrounds in turn this presents new research opportunity and projects – I love the interdisciplinary approach as we work out new ideas to explore and deliver creative solutions.
3. **Creative expression** – the ability to express and release my creative introvert. I do more than ever now with a confidence that life experience and education have provided me in such a surprising and unplanned way.

Share a Vision You have to the Future?

I anticipate that the future may become quite responsive and iterative to the environmental needs to ensure the planet's stability. In addition, there is a real human concern: we will have more older adults than working age adults, so how does this impact humanity, relationships, access to resources and QoL? I see a future whereby UX Design and User-Centred Design solutions include harnessing and resolving environmental concerns, economy-led innovations regarding income and work life balance, and humanity-based solutions that enhance the lived experience for all.

Laura Stoops

Laura is the Impact and Evaluation Manager at Age NI, a charity that supports older people in Northern Ireland. Age NI is the leading charity in Northern Ireland dedicated to helping everyone make the most of later life. Age NI believes that people should be supported to love later life, to know and understand their rights, to remain as independent as possible and connected to their communities. Age NI provides care, well-being and advice services to thousands of older people, their families, and carers across Northern Ireland.

Laura's professional interests are using technology-based solutions to support older people or those with a disability and assessing the impact and evaluation.

Fig. 9.3. Dr Laura Stoops.

She has a keen interest in using research skills to support the voluntary sector and to share this knowledge widely. This is demonstrated through her employment endeavours which include supporting Parkinson's UK (as a data analyst) with their 'Get it on time' campaign which focussed on the importance of patients with Parkinson's disease receiving their medication on time when in hospital for issues unrelated to the disease. Previously, Laura worked for Mencap NI, a charity that supports people with a learning disability. She was for 5 years in a role which focussed on impact and evaluation.

Laura holds a PhD (2011) in Computer-Based Assessment and Diagnosis of Parkinson's Disease from the University of Ulster, Northern Ireland. Laura combined her computer science knowledge and research skills to develop two computer-based software tools with the capability to assess/monitor and diagnose Parkinson's disease in a more objective manner than the process in use at the time. The prototype software tools aimed to reduce hospital/GP visits for people with Parkinson's disease by offering the opportunity for assessment/monitoring to take place in the comfort of their own homes.

The interest in using computer-based tools to assist those who were older and/ or disabled began for Laura during her BSc (Hons) in Interactive Multimedia Design (2006), where her final project saw her develop an interactive smart home for older and/or disabled people.

As part of her PhD work, Laura has written and published 5 journal papers including a paper entitled *Assessment of Bradykinesia, Akinesia and Rigidity Using a Home-Based Assessment Tool* which was published in the International Journal of Assistive Robotics and Systems (2009). She has also written and presented papers at 5 conferences and had 3 posters/abstracts accepted.

Questions and Answers:

What Inspired You to Work in the Field(s) of Your Choice?

Growing up I developed a strong sense of motivation and determination coupled with a sense of curiosity and a desire to be challenged. Largely, these qualities emerged due to being born with a rare physical condition called Arthrogryposis. This meant that in order to gain any level of independence, I needed to learn unique and innovative ways to do things others can naturally do, such as, hold a pen, write, feed myself and much more. Spending much of my childhood learning to do things for myself despite the physical obstacles I was born with, ignited a side of me that strived to challenge the 'impossible'. This nature I had moulded meant that as I began to reach a stage of personal development where I felt I was as independent as possible, I began to seek out other challenges.

Research by its very nature involves being curious, innovative, and challenging in order to seek new information or improve/create new ways of thinking or working. This really spoke to me and felt like a natural step following the completion of my own personal journey. As I began to carry out research, first as an assignment in my undergraduate degree and then as part of my PhD, I realised that my curious, logical, and innovative mind would mean research was an area of work I could thrive in. Although my PhD contained a strong element of research, it was embedded in computer science which was the main focus of my undergraduate degree. Like research, computer science also involves being curious, innovative, logical, and determined in order to identify and solve any issues in the code. Throughout the three years spent completing my PhD I swayed between being drawn to a career in computer science and one in research.

As my PhD drew to a close, I realised that whilst I loved the challenge of computer science, it was quite a solitary role with no real interaction with others. This didn't feel like the best fit for me as my personality is such that I enjoy interacting with others. In fact, the element of my PhD that motivated me the most and that I gained most enjoyment from was the randomised control trial (RCT) whereby I recruited volunteers with Parkinson's to participate in focus groups and to test out the prototype computer programs I had developed. This experience was extremely enriching and rewarding.

Looking back again to my childhood I can see that I was always drawn to others and felt attuned to their emotions. During my years at boarding school from the age of 4 to 17, I focussed on helping other children manage their emotions around being away from home. This desire to help others is a theme that has remained throughout my life. It was this part of me that guided me towards the decision to combine all of my strongest drives and skills to work in a role that utilised my research skills but also had a strong element of engaging with and helping others. I took up my first role in the voluntary sector over 8 years ago and I still work in it to this day. The role in impact and evaluation requires regular use of my research skills combined with my sense of empathy and care towards others. As part of the role, I regularly carry out focus groups and interviews with people who require extra help or adaptations to have their views and voices heard by decision makers and this is combined with the more academic side of data analysis and writing reports. The role provides, challenge, fulfilment and joy and is one I hope to continue for many years to come.

What Impact has the Pandemic had on You?

Like others, the onset of the global pandemic came as a surprise and initially brought with it lots of fear, uncertainty, and loss. In an instant the way of life and work I had grown accustomed to changed. Work shifted from being in the office with colleagues and spending time with the older people we support in our day centres, to working remotely from home. Simultaneously, my personal life changed from going out with friends, having family over, and going out on adventures with my husband, to remaining in the house and socially distancing from others. In these early days of the pandemic and the lockdown it brought with it, I experienced an increase and acceleration of work to ensure we offered much needed support to older people in an extremely isolating and challenging time. In many ways this increased workload and focus on work proved to be a welcome distraction from what was unfolding across the world.

I can honestly say that in the initial weeks of the pandemic I did experience worry and periods of panic. However, as time went on, I started to reframe the experience and consider any other aspects to the pandemic apart from the loss and pain it was generating for many. I found that, for me, the pandemic served as a pause or slow down button for my life. I no longer felt that sense of urgency and need to rush that I often felt prior to the pandemic. There was no longer a need to commute to work, which often brought with it many frustrations. Instead, I found that I had more time in the mornings and decided to take the opportunity to incorporate more self-care into my life. As a result, I now carry out regular mindfulness activities and feel more fit and healthy than I ever have, thanks to having the ability to exercise in my garden on lunch break and adopting a more balanced diet.

Aside from improving my mental and physical well-being I found that the pandemic offered a nudge towards exploring a future career in counselling. I signed up to complete a part-time degree in counselling in June 2020 and I started my journey in September 2021. This is something that I have always felt I would both enjoy and would fit my nature and skillset well. Without the pandemic I am not sure that I would have taken that leap as it provided time to reflect and consider my future. My work with Age NI still remains my priority and the degree furthers the sense of fulfilment I already experience through my work.

On a professional level, the pandemic has enabled me to become more productive and manage my time more effectively. Working remotely from home means that I have silence and can continue working until a task is complete without the need to leave when buildings are closing or when others are leaving. As a result, a large project focussed on streamlining Age NI data collection and reporting has progressed much more quickly than initially anticipated prior to the pandemic. In part, I feel this is due to the move to using Teams as our collaboration and communication platform. Colleagues were suddenly much more readily available and there was no longer a need to book venues and plan travel for meetings. In addition, I supported the development and provision of a new Age NI service (Check in and Chat) that was set up in response to the extreme isolation and loneliness being experienced by older people as a result of the pandemic. This service has proven to be a lifeline for many and may never have been developed if not for the pandemic.

On balance, the pandemic changed my life significantly in both positive and negative ways, but I do feel that I have emerged a healthier, happier, and more professionally and personally fulfilled person.

Name 1–3 Things that You Enjoy about the Work that You Do?

I feel lucky to be in the position to say that I love the work that I do. There are three areas that stand out as being the aspects of work that I enjoy most:

1. Interacting and engaging with older people,
2. Generating and maintaining an impact culture,
3. Team spirit.

I will talk more about each of the areas of work that I enjoy most below.

1.   Interacting and engaging with older people
The work that I do at Age NI often involves carrying out interviews, focus groups or facilitating working groups with older people. With each story or insight an older person shares, I feel privileged that they have chosen to share it with me. I always learn something new from each person I engage with and always come away from it feeling a sense of connection. It always amazes me how the older people I engage with are so willing to share some of the struggles they may be facing in life in a bid to help others who may be in a similar situation. There is generally always a spirit of fun and light heartedness with the engagements I carry out with older people, and I often come away with a smile on my face and warm heart. I take pride in the fact that the small part I play in promoting the voices of older people may help move us a step closer to a society where older people are full, active, and valued members.

2.   Generating and maintaining an impact culture
I am a strong believer that generating an impact culture in an organisation is beneficial both in relation to showcasing the work of the organisation, and for providing recognition and motivation to staff. Teams within any organisation are naturally focussed on the work that they do and rarely take the time to step back and really absorb the impact of what they do. I thrive on coming up with new ways to engage all staff in the organisation in the impact cycle. One way that I currently do this is by producing a monthly snapshot infographic which showcases the work of each team across the organisation, along with the impact their work has made on the lives of older people. The infographics are designed to be both accessible and attractive and the content of which has been developed through working directly with staff teams to determine what matters most to them and the people they support. As the infographics are branded with Age NI's bright colour palette and information on it can be quickly and easily digested, staff across the organisation have gained a greater sense of the value of focussing on impact and on the importance of their role within it. Witnessing the shift towards an impact culture is certainly one of the aspects of the work I do that I truly enjoy.

3.   Team spirit
The final element of the work I do that shines through as one I enjoy most is the strong team spirit within the organisation. It is clear to see that each member of staff has a passion for doing the best they can for older people and will offer support to fellow staff members to ensure older people receive the best possible care and support. It is really satisfying and rewarding to know that the organisation you work for has an open and supportive culture where the focus is 100% on the people we support.

Share a Vision You have to the Future?

I envisage a future where the concept of intergenerational interaction is a commonplace, where younger and older people live together offering mutual learning and/or support. Initiatives such as those currently seen in Belgium and France where students find a room with an older person experiencing loneliness, will be seen across the world. I feel this would help shape generations who respect and admire older people, learning from their experience, better maintaining their legacy, and reducing loneliness.

Optimistically, I hope that technology will be enriching the lives of those experiencing loneliness and/or cognitive difficulties. I envisage this in the form of advanced robotics incorporating chat bot technology resulting in a more conversational and human element. An example I foresee would be a robot that a person living alone with cognitive difficulties could have which reinforces their routine (e.g., time for dinner, time to take medication, etc.). It could also be used as an advancement of the fall alarm pendants where the inconvenience of wearing something around your neck at all times would be replaced by voice commands. I would also like to see advancements in the robotic pets' arena whereby they are much more lifelike and offer the companionship and interaction actual pets do without the responsibilities around caring for them, which many people cannot manage.

The final technology focussed vision I have for the future is for improved use of technological advancements to allow for effective remote monitoring of health. This field has progressed over the past decade with the ability to monitor health vitals using devices such as smart watches. However, I envisage the next step being taken which links this remote health data to the health professionals who can oversee individuals' health and intervene when necessary.

Alongside the technological advancements, I envisage Age Friendly initiatives developing more 'age friendly cities' across the world. The age friendly cities will have considered the needs of older people when designing public spaces, such as parks, and will have the necessary facilities for older people to engage in their community easily. This future will also have more community spaces for older people to informally come together for a chat, walk or cup of tea and where they can easily access any information or support, they may need. This is the future I both hope for and envisage.

Robbie S. Turner

Robbie is a partner and founder of Spektrum-Group, a Barcelona based management consultancy which operates in the Defence, Humanitarian and Aerospace markets.

Robbie resisted education and the value of it wasn't quite made clear during his early years, so as a result when leaving high school, he was left with two choices: the military or working in a factory. After a few months of 12-hour shifts in a drinks factory near his hometown of Castleford West Yorkshire, the British Army just felt right.

When joining the British Forces, in Robbie's case the Army, within the regiment of the Royal Corps of Signals, an IQ test was taken, and a long list of trades or jobs were presented to him. At this point educational grades were checked and 95% of the list was taken away again, so he started his career as a Royal Signals Driver Lineman, a trade and brotherhood/sisterhood Robbie is immensely proud to have been part of.

Fig. 9.4.   Mr Robbie S. Turner.

After a short training period split between technical training in Dorset and driver training in East Yorkshire, at the age of 17 Robbie was sent to his first working unit in Germany, a small NATO camp in a forest close to Krefeld. This was his first time overseas and his first time on an aeroplane while beginning a life of travel and ever broadening experiences.

Working in the military was very much like working in any other job, except that it's like a hybrid between working on a university campus, with its own enforced laws and deep traditions, whilst being part of a special club with a strong sense of belonging. The club includes free gym membership with compulsory regular visits. However, the day-to-day routine is like any other job.

When describing his life in the Army there are several myths Robbie is always keen to dispel based on his experience, such as: you are not shouted at a lot, bullying and intimidation are not a way of life nor are racism or sexism.

Several peacekeeping deployments to Bosnia were Robbie's first experience of a 'war zone', albeit in 1997 after the war had ended. The people and the place still very much showed the signs of recent conflict. His first tour of duty was Sarajevo, and he recalls how striking it was to see bullet holes and artillery damage in every inch of the city's beautiful buildings. His last tour of military duty was in Kosovo, arriving in the second wave of personnel. He first lived in a tent in Pristina and then moved to be part of a three-man British team assigned to be with the German contingent in the city of Prizren in the south of Kosovo. To sum up this chapter of his military life, although challenging and often arduous, Robbie feels these experiences are a large part of who he is and constitute much of what could be described as the positive attributes he now possesses. When Robbie reminisces, he recalls laughing a lot between 1996 and 2001 whilst forging lifelong friendships and gaining unique experiences to be truly thankful for.

When Robbie left the military in 2001 at the height of the telecoms boom in the UK, it was an extremely good time to be an ex-military communications engineer even at the low end of the technical hierarchy which is where Robbie was at that time. After being approached by several leading communications companies it became apparent that there was a gap in the recruitment market. This was the genesis of 4-Exmilitary, the very first dedicated recruitment company created to connect employers looking for ex-military personnel and ex-military personnel looking for employment. This was Robbie's first business and to give credit where credit is due, the actual concept was the brainchild of his business partner Stephen Wildridge, also a former Lineman in the Royal Corps of Signals.

With no general business experience or experience in recruitment, the learning curve was steep. Initially, both Robbie and Stephen had to work nights driving HGV trucks for an agency whilst trying to build the business during the day. They had to learn skills such as web design as this was, unlike today, before clever easy to use web design tools were readily available. It became clear very quickly that recruitment is pretty much 90% business development and sales. Apart from a couple of minor detours, this would become the theme of Robbie's career going forward.

A great milestone was getting the business to a place where the second job wasn't required, and a meagre living was possible. Much of what was done was done the hard way as the easy way had yet to be learned.

The next significant event was the Iraq war and a new policy in the use of private military companies to provide support for government operations. Overnight thousands of ex-military personnel were needed to fill roles in Iraq as contractors for everything from engineers to bodyguards.

4-Exmilitary, albeit for a very low fee, began providing personnel for Iraq. During this process they recognised that many of the personnel would need additional training for this environment and set out to remedy this. Robbie incognito attended a specialist course in America to assess if they would be a good partner, only revealing they were being scouted at the end of the course. Before his real intentions were known, Robbie achieved the award of best student and was informed he had a real vocation for this kind for work!

This planted a seed if there were jobs in Iraq as a security consultant for over £8,000 per month, this would be enough to take a salary and invest much needed capital back into the company. So, the decision was made. Three weeks later Robbie was in Baghdad as a bodyguard for British Diplomats of the Foreign and the Commonwealth Office, working for the most prestigious security company in that theatre. His teammates were all either elite soldiers such as the Royal Marines, the Parachute Regiment or Special forces from the Special Air Service, so his presence and capability were initially a point of 'discussion' and his life expectancy in such an environment was questionable in some others' opinions. However, his performance under fire and in the most difficult of circumstances soon gave him an excellent reputation and he became a trusted and valued colleague. A temporary engagement turned into three and a half years. Despite the dangerous nature of the environment, Robbie very much loved this type of work and only when his wife became pregnant with their son Ethan, did it feel like the right time to return to a less hazardous means of making a living.

Robbie returned to a now rebranded 4-Exforces which still had many of the same challenges. With his new experience Robbie was then approached for a role as a business development manager, leading a company that provided covert communication solutions to police counter terror units, UK security services and Special Forces units. This learning experience within a large well-established company was another important jigsaw piece in a much bigger puzzle and under the mentorship of the formidable sales director, Robbie gained invaluable experience. His entrepreneurial spirit surfaced again, and he decided to create his own company, but attempting this at the height of the financial crisis was not his best conceived plan and the company failed, taking with it much of his savings and confidence in business.

Eventually, after a divorce, some sobering hardship and a couple of enjoyable business development roles, Robbie started work back in Kosovo with a Norwegian communications company that would later be absorbed by Airbus Defence and Space. Although looking for a change and accepting an engineering role, he was soon identified for his business skills and offered a role in the sales team in Macedonia. This is where he met his current business partner at Spektrum Consulting. Together they became a formidable team at Airbus, heading up much of the business towards NATO and UN and growing a modest office of 4 people in the Macedonian capital in upwards of 30.

The 11-years at Airbus were the place when everything came together for Robbie, constantly being challenged, solving problems, and developing broader and broader skills due to necessity. Demonstrating a work ethic and determination is only possible when you love your work. Through this position Robbie became a recognised and respected individual in the industry, whilst in parallel he realised that the knowledge and experience gained is a valued commodity. This would be the principle on which Spektrum-Group would be created.

Spektrum is located in Barcelona due to the appeal of the city and the non-geographic nature of the business. It has gone from strength to strength, validating the concept and providing a genuinely valuable service to its clients. The learning and the journey continue.

LinkedIn: https://www.linkedin.com/in/robbie-turner-04252b30/

Questions and Answers:

What Inspired You to Work in the Field(s) of Your Choice?

Working in my field was more from circumstance than a conscious choice. Choosing initially to join the military was for the lack of better options but choosing to learn a technical type of job set me on my present trajectory. I will take ownership of that. If I described my field, it would now be government and international organisation procurement and business development. This is an area of business I love, I think of it as a continuous game of chess and a place where wins and losses are as fair as they can be.

What Impact has the Pandemic had on You?

Professionally the pandemic happened in a period where I needed time to plan and reflect. Working remotely enabled me to do this whilst at the same time the drop in tempo was also beneficial. At the height of the pandemic I was based in

Macedonia, whereby, the government implemented strict curfews which meant people had to stay indoors between certain hours of the day which also varied depending on whether it was a weekday or weekend. Additonally, facemasks were also mandatory in public places such as going to supermarkets – apart from working from home, much of the time I was unscathed.

The defence market was also largely unhindered by the pandemic and seemed to only have a slight dip in activity whilst recognising the reality of the situation. Personally, with travel being restricted and being located overseas, seeing friends and family, and most importantly my son, was not possible. Luckily my son is at an age where he understood the situation and the reason for my absence. For me this was the main negative impact on a personal level. Also, I do not personally know of anyone to date who has had a severely bad experience with the disease.

If there is a lasting negativity in my mind regarding the pandemic, it is the way in which important topics such as the vaccine have been handled. I very much believe in freedom of choice, and this seems to have been severely eroded by the way of intimidation and bullying to meet the vaccine agenda.

Name 1–3 Things that You Enjoy about the Work that You Do?

1. The work feels important. I genuinely get the sense that while I am involved in some topics or projects that I am skirting around the fringes of history. Walking the halls of power at NATO as I often have felt in the middle of some large events.
2. This sounds like a cliché, but the work is challenging, but comes with new dynamic problems to solve each day, together with the freedom to think and act fast. The nature of this type of business or the support we provide to our clients, is often a case of directly pitting your wits, competence, and capability against someone trying to achieve the same aim for their own business. There are always wins and losses. When you lose, you reflect on what you could have been done better and when you win, you reflect on what you could have improved on (but just in a better mood).
3. As a business owner, my thinking is very much aligned with my business partner. We can implement policies and initiatives that are positive and indeed we have several projects we are developing that will be a force for good in our market. Only with the freedom afforded by running your own business, can these ambitious undertakings be developed in line with how you envision them.

Share a Vision you have to the Future?

I am always optimistic for the future and aware that every generation's perception is that they are living in an age of unparalleled and important change. This in many ways is both true and false, as many generations before lived in important periods of change that were their present experience, but they too faced an unknown future. The point I am making is the present which you are experiencing, always seems to be more significant and momentous than the past, due to its importance or the lack of it still being assessed.

Technology will become more and more prevalent, dually improving, and diminishing the experience of people who interact with it as against the people who make it. The gaps of understanding will become less and less as today's generation are in many ways fluent in the language of the digital age of technology, even though they may speak it less and less as they get older. However, this will be counteracted by improvement in how we interact with technology, such as developments in AI and voice recognition. This combination, to allow a device to truly contextualise and comprehend human to machine communication, will be revolutionary.

Currently, the most important areas of research are efficient power storage and sustainable generation. It seems only cracking this combination will take the world off its currently inevitable path towards smashing through global warming targets and potentially experiencing first-hand the very first runaway greenhouse effect caused by human behaviour.

I close my thoughts with sobering news: it is a mathematical certainty every 100 million years or so, an object from space will impact the earth, causing an extensional level event. Several of these will occur on earth before our sun runs out of fuel and ruins the party anyway.

References

AARP. (2019a). *Gaming among Adults in their 50's, 60's, and 70's*. Retrieved March 15, 2021, from https://doi.org/10.26419/res.00328.006 .

AARP. (2019b). *Gaming motivators*. Retrieved March 15, 2021, from https://doi.org/10.26419/res.00328.007.

AARP. (2019c). *Gaming – more than just entertainment: African Americans and gaming*. Retrieved March 15, 2021, from https://doi.org/10.26419/res.00328.003.

AARP. (2019d). *Gaming gains: Hispanics and gaming*. Retrieved March 15, 2021, from https://doi.org/10.26419/res.00328.004.

AARP. (2019e). *Gaming after 50*. Retrieved March 15, 2021, from https://doi.org/10.26419/res.00328.005.

Abdi, S., Witte, L. D., & Hawley, M. (2021). Exploring the potential of emerging technologies to meet the care and support needs of older people: A Delphi survey. *Geriatrics (Basel), 6*(1), 19. https://doi.org/10.3390/geriatrics6010019.

Abell, J., Amin-Smith, N., Banks, J., Batty, G. D., Breeden, J., Buffel, T., Cadar, D., Crawford, R., Daemakakos, P., de Oliveira, C., Hussey, D., Lassale, C., Matthews, K., Nazroo, J., Norton, M., Oldfield, Z., Oskala, A., Prattley, J., Steptoe, A., & Zaninotto, P. (2018). *The dynamics of ageing. Evidence from the English longitudinal study of ageing, 2002–16 (Wave 8)*. Retrieved September 1, 2021, from https://www.ucl.ac.uk/drupal/site_iehc/sites/iehc/files/elsa_-_wave_8_report.pdf.

Academic Positions. (2019). *What is the tenure track? Career advice*. Accessed August 3, 2021, from https://career.berkeley.edu/PhDs/PhDtransition.

Adams, R. (2020). 'Digital poverty' could lead to lost generation of university students, vice-chancellors say. *The Guardian*, January 18, 2021. Retrieved February 19, 2021, from https://www.theguardian.com/education/2021/jan/17/digital-poverty-lost-generation-university-students-vice-chancellors.

Adapt Tech, Accessible Technology (2020-2021). *Project website*. Retrieved 21st June 2022 from https://www.open.ac.uk/health-wellbeing/projects/adjust-tech-accessible-technology-atat.

Adeney, M., & Lloyd, J. (1988). *The miners' strike 1984–5: Loss without limited* (p. 169). Routledge & Kegan Paul.

Age NI. (2020). *Lived experienced: Voices of older people on the COVID-19 pandemic 2020*. Retrieved March 1, 2022, from https://www.ageuk.org.uk/globalassets/age-ni/documents/policy/lived-experiences-brochure-final.pdf.

Age NI. (2021a, October 13). *Senior management team*. Retrieved December 29, 2021, from https://www.ageuk.org.uk/northern-ireland/about-us/senior-management/.

Age NI. (2021b, December 7). *Board of trustees*. Retrieved December 29, 2021, from https://www.ageuk.org.uk/northern-ireland/about-us/board-of-trustees/.

Age NI. (2021c, November 9). *Policy and engagement*. Retrieved December 29, 2021, from https://www.ageuk.org.uk/northern-ireland/about-us/policy-engagement/.

Age UK Wakefield. (n.d.). Age UK Wakefield district digital inclusion service. Retrieved August 27, 2021, from https://www.ageuk.org.uk/wakefielddistrict/activities-and-events/keeping-older-people-connected/#.

Ageing Without Children (AWOC). (2014). Retrieved October 18, 2021, from https://www.awwoc.org/.

Ageing Without Children. (2021, July 30). *"A lonely place to be" ageing without children and the impact of the Covid-19 pandemic*. Retrieved August 24, 2021, from https://www. awwoc.org/_files/ugd/10277e_65a0b33f5561481d8f9878e6eaa3586b.pdf.

Aguilar-Martinez, A., Sole-Sedeno, J. M., Mancebo-Moreno, G., Medina, F. X., Carreras-Collado, R., & Saigi-Rubio, F. (2014). Use of mobile phones as a tool for weight loss: A systematic review. *Journal of Telemedicine and Telecare, 20*, 339–349. doi:10.1177/1357633X14537777.

Alcohol Concern. (2012). *On the front line: Alcohol concern Cymru briefing*. Alcohol Concern. Retrieved January 15, 2022, from https://s3.eu-west-2.amazonaws.com/files.alcohol-change.org.uk/documents/On_the_front_line_Final.pdf?mtime=20181218131024.

Ali, M. (1986). The coal war: Women's struggle during the miners' strike. In R. Ridd & H. Callaway (Eds), *Caught up in conflict. Women in society* (pp. 84–105). Palgrave. https://doi.org/10.1007/978-1-349-18380-7_5.

Altman, I., Lawton, M. P., & Wohlwill, J. (Eds). (1984). *Human behaviour and the environment: The elderly and the physical; environment*. Plenum.

Alzheimer's Research UK. (2017, September 14). *A walk through dementia – at home*. Retrieved August 23, 2021, from https://www.xrportal.io/mental-health/a-walk-through-dementia-at-home-2/.

Andersen, P. B. (1997). *A theory of computer semiotics*. Cambridge University Press.

Anderson, M. (2015, November 10). *Key takeaways on mobile apps and privacy*. Pew Research Center. Retrieved May 4, 2021, from https://www.pewresearch.org/fact-tank/2015/11/10/key-takeaways-mobile-apps/.

Anderson, M., & Perrin, A. (2017). *Tech adoption climbs among older adults*. Pew Research Center. Retrieved July 1, 2020 from https://www.pewresearch.org/internet/2017/05/17/tech-adoption-climbs-among-older-adults/.

Anghel, I., Cioara, T., Moldovan, D., Antal, M., Pop, C. D., Salomie, I., Pop, C. P., & Chifu, V. R. (2020). Smart environments and social robots for age-friendly integrated care services. *International Journal of Environmental Research & Public Health, 17*, 3801.

Apperley, T. H. (2006). Genre and game studies: Toward a critical approach to video game genres. *Simulation & Gaming, 37*(1), 6–23. doi:10.1177/1046878105282278.

Aronson, S. H. (1977). The Lancet on the telephone 1876–1975. *Medical History, 21*(1), 69–87. https://doi.org/10.1017/s0025727300037182.

Astbury, J., Drake, P., Price, D., Allen, N., Herron, D., Runacres, J., Dalgarno, E., & Harrison, A. (2021). Research with family carers of people living with dementia: Recruiting during the pandemic. *Ageing Issues*, November 13. Retrieved January 13, 2022, from https://ageingissues.wordpress.com/2021/11/13/research-with-family-carers-of-people-living-with-dementia-recruiting-during-the-pandemic/.

Astell A., Alm, N., Dye, R., Gowans, G., Vaughan, P., & Ellis, M. (2014). Digital video games for older adults with cognitive impairment. In K. Miesenberger, D. Fels, D. Archambault, P. Peňáz, & W. Zagler (Eds), *Computers helping people with special needs. ICCHP 2014*. Lecture Notes in Computer Science, Vol. 8547. Springer. https://doi.org/10.1007/978-3-319-08596-8_42.

Atkinson, R. (1995). *Crusade: The untold story of the Persian Gulf War*. Houghton Mifflin.

Atske, S., & Perrin, A. (2021, July 16). *Home broadband adoption, computer ownership vary by race, ethnicity in the US*. Pew Research Center. Retrieved October 13, 2021, from https://www.pewresearch.org/fact-tank/2021/07/16/home-broadband-adoption-computer-ownership-vary-by-race-ethnicity-in-the-u-s/.

Atterton, J. (2006, September 7). *Ageing and coastal communities*. Final Report for the Coastal Actional Zone Partnership. Centre for Rural Economy, University of Newcastle Upon Tyne. Retrieved February 14, 2022, from https://www.coastal communities.co.uk/wp-content/uploads/2015/07/Ageing_Communities_Report.pdf.

Auditor General for Scotland. (2011). *A review of telehealth in Scotland*. Retrieved October 22, 2021, from https://www.audit-scotland.gov.uk/docs/health/2011/nr_111013_telehealth.pdf.

Baker-Green, K. (2013, July 30). *Community regeneration: The information society in deprived areas of South Yorkshire*. Ph.D. thesis, Sheffield Hallam University. Retrieved September 29, 2021, from https://shura.shu.ac.uk/19307/1/10694188.pdf.

Bandura, A. (1994). Self-efficacy. In V. S. Ramachaudran (Ed.), *Encyclopedia of human behavior* (Vol. 4, pp. 71–81). Academic Press.

Banerjee, D. (2020). The impact of Covid-19 pandemic on elderly mental health. *International Journal of Geriatric Psychiatry*, *35*, 1466–1467.

Bannock, C. (2015). 'Miners' strike 30 years on: 'I fought not just for my pit' but for the community'. *The Guardian*, March 5. Retrieved August 30, 2020, from https://www.theguardian.com/politics/guardianwitness-blog/2015/mar/05/miners-strike-30-years-on-i-fought-not-just-for-my-pit-but-for-the-community.

Bardus, M., van Beurden, S. B., Smith, J. R., & Abraham, C. (2016, March 10). A review and content analysis of engagement, functionality, aesthetics, information quality, and change techniques in the most popular commercial apps for weight management. *International Journal of Behavioral Nutrition and Physical Activity*, *13*, 35. doi:10.1186/s12966-016-0359-9.

Barnsley Metropolitan Borough Council (BMBC). (2019, September). *Poverty in Barnsley – Preliminary findings, business improvement and intelligence team*. Retrieved September 29, 2021, from https://www.barnsley.gov.uk/media/15794/imd2019.pdf.

Bate, P., & Robert, G. (2007). Toward more user-centric OD: Lessons from the field of experience-based design and a case study. *The Journal of Applied Behavioral Science*, *43*(1), 41–66. https://doi.org/10.1177/0021886306297014.

Bayut. (2021). *Pedestrian safety in Dubai*. Retrieved October 19, 2021, from https://www.bayut.com/mybayut/pedestrian-safety-dubai/.

BBC Home. (1983, March 28). *1983: Macgregor named as coal boss. On This Day*. Retrieved August 30, 2020, from http://news.bbc.co.uk/onthisday/hi/dates/stories/march/28/newsid_2531000/2531033.stm.

BBC News. (2019, November 5). Fall of Berlin Wall: How 1989 reshaped the modern world. *BBC News Europe*. Retrieved August 13, 2021, from https://www.bbc.co.uk/news/world-europe-50013048.

BBC News. (2010, August 25). *Profile: Arthur Scargill*. Retrieved August 30, 2020, from https://www.bbc.co.uk/news/uk-politics-11090551.

BBC News. (2020b, December 23). *Christmas rules 2020: What are the new rules on mixing?* Retrieved February 19, 2021, from https://www.bbc.co.uk/news/explainers-55056375.

BBC News. (2020c, October 28). Covid-19: I'll be hosting my Christmas over Zoom. *BBC News*. Retrieved November 1, 2020, from https://www.bbc.co.uk/news/uk-54674883.

BBC Newsbeat. (2017). This man had the chip from his travel card implanted under his skin. *BBC*, June 28. Retrieved January 15, 2022, from https://www.bbc.co.uk/news/newsbeat-40429477.

BCS. (2020, September 22). *Digital poverty and digital capital*. Retrieved February 19, 2021, from https://www.bcs.org/content-hub/digital-poverty-and-digital-capital/.

Bean, A. M. (2018). *Working with video gamers and game in therapy: A Clinician's guide*. Routledge.

Beaumont, M. (2017, April 20). Why GoldenEye 007 is still one of the greatest video games ever. *NME*. Retrieved August 31, 2020, from https://www.nme.com/blogs/nme-blogs/goldeneye-007-n64-greatest-video-games-2055196.

Beckers, J. J., Schmidt, H. G., & Wicherts, J. (2008). Computer anxiety in daily life: Old history? In E. Loos, E. Mante-Meijer, & L. Haddon (Eds), *The social dynamics of information and communication technology* (pp. 13–23). Ashgate.

Benedetti, W. (2014). Xbox leak reveals Kinect 2, augmented reality glasses. *NBC News*. Retrieved October 27, 2020, from https://www.nbcnews.com/tech/tech-news/xbox-leak-reveals-kinect-2-augmented-reality-glasses-flna833583.

Binns, C. (2019). *Experiences of academics from a working-class heritage.* Cambridge Scholars Publishing.

Blackman, T., Hobbs, B., Fencott, C., Martyr, A., Robinson, J., & Schaik, P. (2006). *A VR-based method for evaluating outdoor environments with people with dementia.* Retrieved October 20, 2021, from http://itc.scix.net/paper/3108.

Blackman, T., Mitchell, L., Burton, E., Jenks, M., Parsons, M., Raman, S., & Williams, K. (2003). The accessibility of public spaces for people with dementia: A new priority for the 'open city'. *Disability & Society, 18,* 357–371. https://doi.org/10.1080/09687 59032000052914.

Bleakley, C.M., Charles, D., Porter-Armstong, A., McNeill, M.D.J., McDonough, & S.M., McCormack, B. (2015). Gaming for health: A systematic review of the physical and cognitive effects of interactive computer games in older adults. *Journal of Applied Gerontology, 34,* NP166-NP189. .

Blomberg, J., Giacomi, J., Mosher, A., & Swenton-Wall, P. (2009). Ethnographic field methods and their relation to design. In *Participatory design* (pp. 123–155). CRC Press.

Bloom, D. E. (2020). Population 2020. *Finance & Development, 57*(1), 4–9.

Blu-digital. (2022). *Digital skills for army veterans.* Retrieved January 4, 2022, from https://www.blu-digital.co.uk/blog/digital-skills-for-army-veterans.

Boot, W. R., Kramer, A. F., Simons, D. J., Fabiani, M., & Gratton, G. (2008). The effects of video game playing on attention, memory, and executive control. *Acta Psychologica, 129*(3), 387–398. doi:10.1016/j.actpsy.2008.09.005.

Booth, R. (2020, September 14). UK care home residents facing fresh restrictions as Covid infections rise. *The Guardian.* Retrieved August 10, 2021, https://www.theguardian.com/world/2020/sep/14/uk-care-home-residents-facing-fresh-restrictions-as-infections-rise.

Booth, R., & Blackall, M. (2021). 'She just wanted to hug me': tears of joy as in-person visits return to English care homes. *The Guardian,* 8th March 2021. Retrieved 15th June 2022 from https://www.theguardian.com/society/2021/mar/08/id-love-to-hold-his-hand-english-care-homes-weigh-up-risk-of-reopening.

Bort, J. (2014). 8 People who implanted tech gadgets directly into their bodies. *Business Insider,* August 8. Retrieved January 15, 2022, https://www.businessinsider.com/cyborg-people-who-implanted-tech-2014-8?r=US&IR=T.

Bouma, H. (2012). Foundations and goals of gerontechnology. *Gerontechnology, 11*(1), 1–4.

Bowerman, M. (2017). Wisconsin company to install rice-sized microchips in employees. *CNBC,* July 24. Retrieved January 15, 2022, from https://www.cnbc.com/2017/07/24/wisconsin-company-to-install-rice-sized-microchips-in-employees.html.

Bozionelos, N. (2004). Socio-economic background and computer use: The role of computer anxiety and computer experience in their relationship. *International Journal of Human–Computer Studies, 61,* 725–746.

Brandão, J., Ferreira, T., & Carvalho, V. (2012). An overview on the use of serious games in the military industry and health. In M. M. Cruz-Cunha (Ed.), *Handbook of research on serious games as educational, business and research tools* (pp. 182–201). IGI Global. http://doi:10.4018/978-1-4666-0149-9.ch009.

Britannica. (n.d.a). *Afghanistan war.* Retrieved August 14, 2021, from https://www.britannica.com/event/Afghanistan-War.

Britannica. (n.d.b). *Iraq war.* Retrieved August 14, 2021, from https://www.britannica.com/event/Iraq-War.

Britannica. (n.d.c). *M*A*S*H.* Retrieved January 20, 2022, from https://www.britannica.com/topic/M-A-S-H.

British Academy. (2016). *Crossing paths: Interdisciplinary institutions, careers, education and applications.* Retrieved January 19, 2021, from https://www.thebritishacademy.ac.uk/documents/213/crossing-paths.pdf.

British Army. (2021, October 8). *Free headspace for army personnel.* Retrieved January 4, 2022, from https://www.army.mod.uk/news-and-events/news/2021/10/free-headspace-for-army-personnel/.

British Society of Gerontology. (2020). *BSG Statement on COVID-19: 20 March 2020.* Retrieved August 31, 2020, from https://www.britishgerontology.org/publications/bsg-statements-on-covid-19/statement-one.

Brown, H. M., Bucher, T., Collins, C. E., & Rollo, M. E. (2019). A review of pregnancy iPhone apps assessing their quality, inclusion of behaviour change techniques, and nutrition information. *Maternal & Child Nutrition, 15*(3), e12768. doi:10.1111/mcn.12768.

Brown, J. A. (2017). Digital gaming perceptions among older adult non-gamers. In J. Zhou & G. Salvendy (Eds), *Human aspects of IT for the aged population. Applications, services and contexts. ITAP 2017.* Lecture Notes in Computer Science, Vol. 10298. Springer.

Brown, J. A. (2019). An exploration of virtual reality use and application among older adult populations. *Gerontology and Geriatric Medicine.* doi:10.1177/2333721419885287.

Brown, J. A., & De Schutter, B. (2016a). Game design for older adults: Lessons from a life course perspective. *International Journal of Gaming and Computer-mediated Simulations, 8*(1), 1–12. doi:10.4018/IJGCMS.2016010101.

Brown, J. A., & Marston, H. R. (2018). Gen X and digital games: Looking back to look forward. In J. Zhou & G. Salvendy (Eds), *Human aspects of IT for the aged population. Applications in health, assistance, and entertainment.* Lecture Notes in Computer Science, Vol. 10927. Springer. doi:10.1007/978-3-319-92037-5_34.

Buffel, T., Handler, S., & Phillipson, C. (Eds). (2019). *A global perspective, age-friendly cities and communities.* Policy Press.

Burholt, V., & Dobbs, C. (2012). Research on rural ageing: Where have we got to and where are we going in Europe? *Journal of Rural Studies, 28*(4), 432–446. https://doi.org/10.1016/j.jrurstud.2012.01.009.

Burholt, V., Foscarini-Craggs, P., & Winter, B. (2018). *Rural ageing and equality* (pp. 311–328). Routledge.

Burholt, V., Scharf, T., & Walsh, K. (2013). Imagery and imaginary of islander identity: Older people and migration in Irish small-island communities. *Journal of Rural Studies, 31*, 1–12. https://doi.org/10.1016/j.jrurstud.2013.01.007.

Bussolo, M., Koettl, J., & Sinnott, E. (2015). *Golden aging: Prospects for healthy, active, and prosperous aging in Europe and Central Asia.* World Bank Publications.

Camara, C., Peris-Lopez, P., & Tapiador, J. E. (2015). Security and privacy issues in implantable medical devices. *Journal of Biomedical Informatics, 55*, 272–289. https://doi.org/10.1016/j.jbi.2015.04.007.

Campbell-Kelly, M. (1987, July–September/October–November). Data communications at the National Physical Laboratory (1965–1975). In *Annals of the history of computing* (Vol. 9, 3/4, pp. 221–247). doi:10.1109/MAHC.

Care Quality Commission. (2015). *Thinking about using a hidden camera or other equipment to monitor someone's care?* Retrieved January 30, 2022, from https://www.cqc.org.uk/contact-us/report-concern/using-cameras-or-other-recording-equipment-check-somebodys-care.

Carers UK. (2013, September 10). *Potential for change: Transforming public awareness and demand for health and care technology.* Retrieved November 11, 2021, from https://www.carersuk.org/for-professionals/policy/policy-library/potential-for-change-transforming-public-awareness-and-demand-for-health-and-care-technology.

Carers UK. (2014a). *Why we are here.* Retrieved November 11, 2021, from https://www.carersuk.org/about-us/why-we-re-here.

Carers UK. (2014b). *What we do.* Retrieved November 11, 2021, from https://www.carersuk.org/about-us/what-we-do.

Carers UK. (n.d.a). Retrieved November 11, 2021, from https://www.carersuk.org/.

Carroll, J. M., & Rosson, M. B. (2013). Wild at home: The neighborhood as a living laboratory for HCI. *ACM Transactions on Computer–Human Interaction, 20*(3), 1–28. https://doi.org/10.1145/2491500.2491504.

Cassell, J., & Jenkins, H. (2000). *From Barbie to Mortal Kombat: Gender and computer games*. MIT Press.

Cavendish, H. (2011). *The Scientific Papers of the Honourable Henry Cavendish, F.R.S:* Volume 1.

Centers for Disease Control and Prevention (CDC). (2013). *Healthy places – Healthy places terminology*. Retrieved August 11, 2021, from https://www.cdc.gov/healthyplaces/terminology.htm.

Centre for Ageing Better. (n.d.). *UK network of age-friendly communities*. Retrieved October 22, 2021, from https://www.ageing-better.org.uk/uk-network-age-friendly-communities.

Chandler, D. (2017). *Semiotics: The basics*. Routledge.

Chao, Y. Y., Scherer, Y. K., & Montgomery, C. A. (2015). Effects of using Nintendo Wii™ Exergames in older adults: A review of the literature. *Journal of Aging and Health, 27*(3), 379–402. https://doi.org/10.1177/0898264314551171.

Chapkis, W. (1997). *Live sex acts: Women performing erotic labour*. Cassell.

Charmaz, K. (2014). *Constructing grounded theory* (2nd ed.). Sage.

Charness, N., & Jastrzembski, T. S. (2009). Gerontechnology. In P. Saariluoma & H. Isomäki (Eds), *Future interaction design II* (pp. 1–29). Springer. https://doi.org/10.1007/978-1-84800-385-9_1.

Chaudhury, H., & Oswald, F. (2019). Advancing understanding of person–environment interaction in later life: One step further. *Journal of Aging Studies, 51*, 100821. 10.1016/j.jaging.2019.100821.

Chen, K., & Chan, A. H. S. (2014). Gerontechnology acceptance by elderly Hong Kong Chinese: A senior technology acceptance model (STAM). *Ergonomics, 57*(5). https://doi.org/10.1080/00140139.2014.895855.

Chen, W.-Y., Jang, Y., Wang, J.-D., Huang, W.-N., Chang, C.-C., Mao, H.-F., & Wang, Y.-H. (2011). Wheelchair-related accidents: Relationship with wheelchair-using behavior in active community wheelchair users. *Archives of Physical Medicine and Rehabilitation, 92*(6), 892–898. https://doi.org/10.1016/j.apmr.2011.01.008.

Cheng, T. Y., Liu, L., & Woo, B. K. (2019). Analyzing Twitter as a platform for alzheimer-related dementia awareness: Thematic analyses of tweets. *JMIR Aging, 1*, e11542.

Chivers, S. (2021). "With Friends Like These": Unpacking panicked metaphors for population ageing. *Societies, 11*(3), 69. http://dx.doi.org/10.3390/soc11030069.

Chowdhury, S. A., Arshad, H., Parhizkar, B., Obeidy, W. K. (2013). Handheld Augmented Reality Interaction Technique. In: H. B. Zaman, P. Robinson, P. Olivier, T. K. Shih, S. Velastin (Eds.), *Advances in Visual Informatics. IVIC 2013: Lecture Notes in Computer Science* (Vol. 8237). Cham: Springer. https://doi.org/10.1007/978-3-319-02958-0_38.

Chu, C.-Y., & Patterson, R. M. (2018). Soft robotic devices for hand rehabilitation and assistance: A narrative review. *Journal of Neuroengineering and Rehabilitation, 15*(1), 9–9. https://doi.org/10.1186/s12984-018-0350-6.

Citizens Online. (2017). *Switch Report, A baseline evaluation of digital inclusion in your area*. Retrieved October 19, 2021, from https://www.citizensonline.org.uk/wp-content/uploads/2017/12/Citizens-Online-Switch-sample-report-v2.0.pdf.

Cocker, G. (2007, January 24). Q&A: Every extend extra's Tetsuya Mizuguchi. *Gamespot*. Retrieved December 13, 2021, from https://www.gamespot.com/articles/qanda-every-extend-extras-tetsuya-mizuguchi/1100-6164638/.

Cook, A. M., & Hussey, S. M. (2002). *Assistive technologies* (2nd ed.). Mosby.

Cooper, A., Reimann, R., Cronin, D., & Noessel, C. (2014). *About face: The essentials of interaction design*. John Wiley & Sons.

Copeland, B. J. (2000). *The modern history of computing*. Stanford Encyclopedia of Philosophy. Metaphysics Research Lab, Stanford University. Retrieved January 6, 2022, from https://plato.stanford.edu/entries/computing-history/.

CoronaDiaries Research Project. (2021). Swansea University. Retrieved January 22, 2021, from https://www.swansea.ac.uk/press-office/news-events/news/2020/04/how-your-coronadiary-could-help-us-understand-more-about-living-through-a-pandemic.php.

Cote, A. C. (2020). *Gaming sexism*. New York, NY: New York University.

Cotten, S. R., Anderson, W. A., & McCullough, B. M. (2013). Impact of Internet use on loneliness and contact with others among older adults: Cross-sectional analysis. *Journal of Medical Internet Research, 15*, e39. doi:10.2196/jmir.2306.

Cotton, S. R., Anderson, W., & Tufekci, Z. (2009). Old wine in a new technology or a different type of digital divide? *New Media & Society, 11*, 1163–1186. doi:10.1177/1461444809342056.

Coughlan, S. (2020, April 24). 'Digital poverty' in schools where few have laptops. *BBC News*. Retrieved August 14, 2021, from https://www.bbc.co.uk/news/education-52399589.

Coughlin, J. F. (2017). *The longevity economy: Unlocking the world's fastest-growing, most misunderstood market*. Public Affairs.

Couldry, N. (2012). *Media, society, world: Social theory and digital media practice* (p. 2). Polity Press.

Cowles, K. (1988). Issues in qualitative research on sensitive topics. *Western Journal of Nursing Research, 10*, 163–170.

Crabtree, A., Chamberlain, A., Grinter, R. E., Jones, M., Rodden, T., & Rogers, Y. (2013). Introduction to the special issue of "The Turn to The Wild". *ACM Transactions on Computer–Human Interaction, 20*(3), 1–4. https://doi.org/10.1145/2491500.2491501.

Crew, T. (2021). Why is addressing class in higher education important? *Transforming Society*. Retrieved October 1, 2021, from https://www.transformingsociety.co.uk/2021/08/19/why-is-addressing-class-in-higher-education-important/.

Crum, P. (2019). Hearables: Here come the: Technology tucked inside your ears will augment your daily life. *IEEE Spectrum, 56*(5), 38–43. https://doi.org/10.1109/MSPEC.2019.8701198.

Currys, PC World. (n.d.). *IROBOT Roomba I7158 Robot vacuum cleaner – black*. Retrieved May 3, 2021, from https://www.currys.co.uk/gbuk/home-appliances/floorcare/vacuum-cleaners/irobot-roomba-i7158-robot-vacuum-cleaner-black-10194642-pdt.html.

Da Silva Júnior, J. L. A., Biduski, D., Bellei, E. A., Becker, O. H. C., Daroit, L., Pasqualotti, A., Tourinho Filho, H., & De Marchi, A. C. B. (2021). A bowling exergame to improve functional capacity in older adults: Co-design, development, and testing to compare the progress of playing alone versus playing with peers. *JMIR Serious Games, 9*(1). https://doi.org/10.2196/23423.

Davalbhakta, S., Advani, S., Kumar, S., Agarwal, V., Bhoyar, S., Fedirko, E., Misra, D. P., Goel, A., & Agarwal, V. (2020). A systematic review of smartphone applications available for Corona virus disease 2019 (COVID19) and the assessment of their quality using the Mobile Application Rating Scale (MARS). *Journal of Medical Systems, 44*(9), 164. https://doi.org/10.1007/s10916-020-01633-3.

Davey, J., Nana, G., de Joux, V., & Arcus, M. (2004). *Accommodation options for older people in Aotearoa/New Zealand*. Wellington: NZ Institute for Research on Ageing/Business & Economic Research Ltd, for Centre for Housing Research Aotearoa/New Zealand.

De la Hera, T., Loos, E., Simons M, & Blom, J. (2017). Benefits and factors influencing the design of intergenerational digital games: A systematic literature review. *Societies, 7*(3), 18. https://doi.org/10.3390/soc7030018.

De Schutter, B. (2011). Never too old to play: The appeal of digital games to an older audience. *Games and Culture, 6*(2), 155–170. https://doi.org/10.1177/1555412010364978.

De Schutter, B., & Brown, J. A. (2016). Digital games as a source of enjoyment in later life. *Games and Culture, 11*(1–2), 28–52. https://doi.org/10.1177/1555412015594273.

De Schutter, B., & Vanden Abeele, V. (2010). Designing meaningful play within the psychosocial context of older adults. In *Proceedings of the 3rd International Conference on fun and games—Fun and games'10* (pp. 84–93). https://doi.org/10.1145/1823818. 1823827.

De Schutter, B., Brown, J. A., & Vanden Abeele, V. (2015). The domestication of digital games in the lives of older adults. *New Media and Society, 17*(7), 1170–1186. doi:1461444814522945.

Delahunty, S. (2021, January 11). *Just giving profits more than double to £9.4m after switch to voluntary donation model*. Third Sector. Retrieved January 23, 2022, from https://www.thirdsector.co.uk/justgiving-profits-double-94m-switch-voluntary-donation-model/fundraising/article/1704195.

DeMello, M. (1993). The convict body: Tattooing among male American prisoners. *Anthropology Today, 9*(6), 10–13.

DeMello, M. (1995). "Not just for Bikers Anymore": Popular representations of American tattooing. *The Journal of Popular Culture, 29*(3), 37–52. https://doi.org/10.1111/j.0022-3840.1995.00037.x.

Department of Health and Social Care. (2019). *Assistive technology research development work: 2017–2018*. Retrieved October 12, 2021, https://www.gov.uk/government/publications/assistive-technology-research-and-development-work-2017-to-2018.

Department of Health Northern Ireland. (2021). *COVID-19: Guidance for nursing and residential care homes in Northern Ireland*. Retrieved November 11, 2021, https://www.health-ni.gov.uk/publications/covid-19-guidance-nursing-and-residential-care-homes-northern-ireland.

Department of Health. (2020, August 14). 250,000 Downloads of StopCOVID NI App. Northern Irish Government. Retrieved May 4, 2021, from https://www.health-ni.gov.uk/news/250000-downloads-stopcovid-ni-app.

Deterding, S., Dixon, D., Khaled, R., & Nacke, L. (2011a). From game design elements to gamefulness: Defining "gamification". *Proceedings of the 15th International Academic MindTrek Conference: Envisioning Future Media Environments*. ACM.

Deterding, S., Sicart, M., Nacke, L., O'Hara, K., & Dixon, D. (2011b, May). Gamification. Using game-design elements in non-gaming contexts. Extended abstracts on human factors in computing systems (pp. 2425–2428). https://doi.org/10.1145/1979742.1979575.

Dickerson, D. (2019, October 8). How I overcame impostor syndrome after leaving academia. *Nature*. Retrieved August 2, 2021, from https://www.nature.com/articles/d41586-019-03036-y.

Digital Communities Wales. (n.d.a). *Case studies*. Retrieved February 22, 2022, from https://www.digitalcommunities.gov.wales/case-studies-2/.

Digital Communities Wales. (n.d.b). Technology helps create a happy, friendly environment at Ty Gwyn Care Home. Retrieved February 22, 2022, from https://www.digitalcommunities.gov.wales/case-studies/ty-gwyn/.

Digital Health Central. (2020, December 5). *Are digital tattoos the future of wearables?* Retrieved October 13, 2021, from https://digitalhealthcentral.com/2020/12/05/what-are-digital-tattoos/.

Dikken, J., van den Hoven, R. F. M., van Staalduinen, W. H., Hulsebosch-Janssen, L. M. T., & van Hoof, J. (2020). How older people experience the age-friendliness of their city: Development of the age-friendly cities and communities questionnaire. *International Journal of Environmental Research and Public Health, 17*(18), 6867. http://dx.doi.org/10.3390/ijerph17186867.

DiMaggio, P., & Hargittai, E. (2011). *From the 'digital divide' to 'digital inequality': Studying internet use as penetration increases* (Vol. 15, pp. 1–23). Center for Arts and Cultural Policy Studies.

DiMaggio, P., Hargittai, E., Celeste, C., & Schafer, S. (2004). *Digital inequality: From unequal access to differentiated use*. In K. Neckerman (Ed.), *Social inequality* (pp. 355–400). Russell Sage Foundation. Retrieved April 5, 2017, from https://www.russellsage.org/research/reports/dimaggio.

Dimock, M. (2019, January 17). *Defining generations: Where millennials end and generation Z begins*. Pew Research Center. Retrieved November 12, 2021, from https://www.pewresearch.org/fact-tank/2019/01/17/where-millennials-end-and-generation-z-begins/.

Dixon, L. J., Correa, T., Straubhaar, J., Covarrubias, L., Graber, D., Spence, J., & Rojas, V. (2014). Gendered space: The digital divide between male and female users in Internet Public Access Sites. *Journal of Computer-Mediated Communication, 19*(4), 991–1009. https://doi.org/10.1111/jcc4.12088.

Dobransky, K., & Hargittai, E. (2006). The disability divide in internet access and use. *Information, Communication & Society, 9*(3), 313–334. doi:10.1080/13691180600751298.

Dorney, J. (2015). *The Northern Ireland Conflict 1968–1998 – An overview*. Retrieved August 16, 2021, from https://www.theirishstory.com/2015/02/09/the-northern-ireland-conflict-1968-1998-an-overview/#.YRpHCohKiUk.

Drachen, A., Mirza-Babaei, P., & Nacke, L. (2018). *Games user research*. OUP.

Duggan, M. (2015, August). *Mobile messaging and social media – 2015*. Pew Research Center. Retrieved January 16, 2021, from https://www.pewresearch.org/wp-content/uploads/sites/9/2015/08/Social-Media-Update-2015-FINAL2.pdf.

Dykstra, P. A., & Hagestad, G. O. (2007). Childlessness and parenthood in two centuries: Different roads–different maps? *Journal of Family Issues, 28*(11), 1518–1532. https://doi.org/10.1177/0192513X07303881.

Earle, S., & Blackburn, M. (2021). Young adults with life-limiting or life-threatening conditions: Sexuality and relationships support. *BMJ Supportive & Palliative Care, 11*(2), 163–169. http://dx.doi.org/10.1136/bmjspcare-2019-002070.

Earle, S., Marston, H., Hadley, R., & Banks, D. (2020). The use of menstruation and fertility app trackers: A scoping review of the evidence. *BMJ Sexual & Reproductive Health*. http://dx.doi.org/10.1136/bmjsrh-2019-200488.

Ed Lounge Ltd. (2020). *What is digital poverty?* Retrieved August 31, 2020, from https://blog.edlounge.com/what-is-digital-poverty/.

Edwards, D. (2020, January 21). *Amazon now has 200,000 robots working in its warehouses*. Robotics & Automation. Retrieved January 5, 2022, from roboticsandautomation-news.com.

Edwards, J. D., Perkins, M., Ross, L. A., & Reynolds, S. L. (2009). Driving status and three-year mortality among community-dwelling older adults. *Journals of Gerontology: Series A, 64A*(2), 300–305. https://doi.org/10.1093/gerona/gln019.

Elder, G. H., Jr. (Ed.). (1985). Perspectives on the life course. In *Life course dynamics: Trajectories and transitions, 1968–1980* (chapter 1, pp. 23–49). Cornell University Press.

Elder, G. H., Johnson, M. K., & Crosnoe, R. (2003). The emergence and development of life course theory. In J. T. Mortimer & M. J. Shanahan (Eds), *Handbook of the life course. Handbooks of sociology and social research*. Springer. https://doi.org/10.1007/978-0-306-48247-2_1.

Ellis, D., & Tucker, I. (2020). *Emotion in the digital age: Technologies, data and psychosocial life*. Taylor & Francis Group.

Entertainment Software Association. (2004). *Essential facts about the computer and video game industry*. Retrieved January 5, 2022, from https://www.scribd.com/document/125494009/ESA-Essential-Facts-2004.

Entertainment Software Association. (2006). *Essential facts about the computer and video game industry*. Retrieved August 23, 2021, from https://library.princeton.edu/sites/default/files/2006.pdf.

Entertainment Software Association. (2007). *Essential facts about the computer and video game industry*. Retrieved August 23, 2021, from https://www.org.id.tue.nl/IFIP-TC14/documents/ESA-Essential-Facts-2007.pdf.

Entertainment Software Association. (2008). *Essential facts about the computer and video game industry*. Retrieved August 23, 2021, from https://www.yumpu.com/en/document/read/25040323/2008-essential-facts-about-the-computer-and-video-game-industry.

Entertainment Software Association. (2010). *Essential facts about the computer and video game industry*. Retrieved August 23, 2021, from https://www.org.id.tue.nl/IFIP-TC14/documents/ESA-Essential-Facts-2010.pdf.

Entertainment Software Association. (2011). *Essential facts about the computer and video game industry*. Retrieved August 23, 2021, from https://etcjournal.files.wordpress.com/2011/11/esa_ef_2011.pdf.

Entertainment Software Association. (2013). *Essential facts about the computer and video game industry*. Retrieved August 23, 2021, from https://issuu.com/exame/docs/esa____essential_facts_about_the_c.

Entertainment Software Association. (2014). *Essential facts about the computer and video game industry*. Retrieved August 23, 2021, from https://time.com/wp-content/uploads/2015/03/esa_ef_2014.pdf.

Entertainment Software Association. (2015). *Essential facts about the computer and video game industry*. Retrieved August 23, 2021, from https://templatearchive.com/esa-essential-facts/.

Entertainment Software Association. (2016). *Essential facts about the computer and video game industry*. Retrieved August 23, 2021, from https://cdn.arstechnica.net/wp-content/uploads/2017/04/esa_ef_2016.pdf.

Entertainment Software Association. (2018). *Essential facts about the computer and video game industry*. Retrieved August 23, 2021, from https://www.theesa.com/resource/2018-essential-facts-about-the-computer-and-video-game-industry/.

Entertainment Software Association. (2020). *Essential facts about the computer and video game industry*. Retrieved August 23, 2021, from https://www.theesa.com/wp-content/uploads/2021/03/Final-Edited-2020-ESA_Essential_facts.pdf.

European Commission. (2014). *Population ageing in Europe – Facts, implications and policies*. Retrieved August 23, 2021, from https://ec.europa.eu/research/social-sciences/pdf/policy_reviews/kina26426enc.pdf.

Fairlie, R. (2014). *Race and the digital divide*. Department of Economics, UCSC. Retrieved August 23, 2021, from https://escholarship.org/uc/item/48h8h99w.

Featherstone, M. (1999). Body modification: An introduction. *Body & Society, 5*(2–3), 1–13. https://doi.org/10.1177/1357034X99005002001.

Feit, D. (2012, September 5). How virtua fighter saved playstation's Bacon. *Wired*. Retrieved August 31, 2020, from https://www.wired.com/2012/09/how-virtua-fighter-saved-playstations-bacon/.

Fencott, C. (1999b). Towards a design methodology for virtual environments. In *Proceedings of the international workshop on user friendly design of virtual environments*, York.

Fencott, C. (2001a). Virtual storytelling as narrative potential: Towards an ecology of narrative. In O. Balet, G. Subsol, & P. Torguet (Eds), *Virtual storytelling using virtual reality technologies for storytelling*. Lecture Notes in Computer Science (Vol. 2197). Springer. https://doi.org/10.1007/3-540-45420-9_11.

Fencott, C. (2001b). Comparative content analysis of virtual environments using perceptual opportunities. In R. Earnshaw & J. Vince (Eds), *Digital content creation*. Springer. https://doi.org/10.1007/978-1-4471-0293-9_4.

Fencott, C., Clay, M., Lockyer, M., & Massey, P. (2012). *Game invaders: The theory and understanding of computer games*. Wiley-IEEE Computer Society.

Fernández-Ardèvol, M. (2019). One phone, two phones, four phones: Older women and mobile telephony in Lima, Peru. In C. W. Larsson & L. Stark (Eds), *Gendered power and mobile technology: Intersections in the global south* (pp. 93–107). Routledge. doi:10.4324/9781315175904-5.

Fernández-Ardèvol, M. (2020). Older people go mobile. In R. Ling, L. Fortunati, G. Goggin, S. S. Lim, & Y. Li (Eds), *The oxford handbook of mobile communication and society* (pp. 186–199). Oxford University Press. doi:10.1093/oxfordhb/9780190864385.013.13.

Fernández-Ardèvol, M., & Ivan, L. (2015). Why age is not that important? An ageing perspective on computer anxiety. In J. Zhou & G. Salvendy (Eds), *Human aspects of IT for the aged population. Design for aging*. Lecture Notes in Computer Science (Vol. 9193). Springer. https://doi.org/10.1007/978-3-319-20892-3_19.

Ferrant, G., Maria, L., & Nowacka, K. (2014). *Unpaid care work: The missing link in the analysis of gender gaps in labour outcomes*. OECD. Retrieved August 3, 2021, from https://www.oecd.org/dev/development-gender/Unpaid_care_work.pdf.

Ferrara, G., Kim, J., Lin, S., Hua, J., & Seto, E. (2019). A focused review of smartphone diet-tracking apps: Usability, functionality, coherence with behavior change theory, and comparative validity of nutrient intake and energy estimates. *JMIR mHealth and uHealth, 7*(5). https://doi.org/10.2196/mhealth.9232.

Ferretti, L., Wymant, C., Kendall, M., Zhao, L., Nurtay, A., Abeler-Dorner, L., Parker, M., Bonsall, D., & Fraser, C. (2020). Quantifying SARS-CoV-2 transmission suggests epidemic control with digital contact tracing. *Science, 368*(6491). doi:10.1126/science.abb6936.

Fisk, A., D., Rogers, W. A., Charness, N., Czaja, S. J., & Sharit, J. (2004). *Designing for older adults: Principles and creative human factors approaches*. CRC Press.

Fisk, M. (2015). Surveillance technologies in care homes: Seven principles for their use. *Working with Older People, 19*(2), 51–59. https://doi.org/10.1108/WWOP-11-2014-0037.

Fisk, M., & Flórez-Revuelta, F. (2016). The ethics of using cameras in care homes. *Nursing Times, 112*(10), 12–13.

Fisk, M., Livingstone, A., & Pit, S. W. (2020). Telehealth in the context of COVID-19: Changing perspectives in Australia, the United Kingdom, and the United States. *Journal of Medical Internet Research, 22*(6), e19264. doi:10.2196/19264.

Flynn, B. (2003). Geography of the digital hearth. *Information, Communication & Society, 6*(4), 551–576. doi:10.1080/1369118032000163259.

Flynn, D., Schaik, P., Blackman, T., Fencott, C., Hobbs, B., & Calderon, C. (2003). Developing a virtual reality-based methodology for people with dementia: A feasibility study. *Cyberpsychology & Behavior: The Impact of the Internet, Multimedia and Virtual Reality on Behavior and Society, 6*(6), 591–611.

Forbes, D., Pedlar, D., Adler, A. B., Bennett, C., Bryant, R., Busuttil, W., Cooper, J., Creamer, M. C., Fear, N. T., Greenberg, N., Heber, A., Hinton, M., Hopwood, M., Jetly, R., Lawrence-Wood, E., McFarlane, A., Metcalf, O., O'Donnell, M., Phelps, A., & Wessely, S. (2019). Treatment of military-related post-traumatic stress disorder: Challenges, innovations, and the way forward. *International Review of Psychiatry, 31*(1), 95–110. https://doi.org/10.1080/09540261.2019.1595545.

Fox, S. (2011, January 21). *Americans living with disability and their technology profile*. Pew Research Center, Internet, Science & Tech. Retrieved October 13, 2021, from https://www.pewresearch.org/internet/2011/01/21/americans-living-with-disability-and-their-technology-profile/.

Fox, S., & Duggan, M. (2012). *Mobile Health 2012*. Pew Internet. Retrieved November 21, 2019, from https://www.pewinternet.org/wp-content/uploads/sites/9/media/Files/Reports/2012/PIP_MobileHealth2012_FINAL.pdf.

Francis, J., Ball, C., Kadylak, T., & Cotten, S. R. (2019). Ageing in the digital age: Conceptualising technology adoption and digital inequalities. In B. Barbosa Neves & F. Vetere (Eds), *Ageing and digital technology – Designing and evaluating emerging technologies for older adults* (1st ed.). Springer Nature.

Frank, J. B. (2002). *The paradox of aging in place in assisted living*. Bergin & Garvey.

Freeman, S., Marston, H. R., Olynick, J., Musselwhite, C., Kulczycki, C., Genoe, R., & Xiong, B. (2020). Intergenerational effects on the impacts of technology use in later life: Insights from an international, multi-site study. *International Journal of Environmental Research and Public Health, 17*(16), 5711. http://dx.doi.org/10.3390/ijerph17165711.

Friemal, T. N. (2016). The digital divide has grown old: Determinants of a digital divide among seniors. *New Media & Society, 18*(2), 313–331. https://doi.org/10.1177/1461444814538648.

Fry, R. (2018). *Millennials approach Baby Boomers as America's largest generation in the electorate,* 4. Retrieved March 15, 2021, from http://www.pewresearch.org/fact-tank/2018/04/03/millennials-approach-baby-boomers-aslargest-generation-in-u-s-electorate/.

Fulmer, T., Patel, P., Levy, N., Mate, K., Berman, A., Peloton, L., Beard, J., Kalache, A. Auerbach, J. (2020). Moving toward a global age-friendly ecosystem. *Journal of the American Geriatrics Society, 68,* 1936–1940. Doi: 10.1111/jgs.16675. .

Gajadhar, B.J., de Kort, Y.A.W., IJsselsteijn, W.A., 2008. Shared fun is doubled fun: player enjoyment as a function of social setting. In P. Markopoulos, B. de Ruyter, W. IJsselsteijn, D. Rowland (Eds.), *Proceedings of the Second International Conference on Fun and Games,* Springer, New York pp. (106–117).

Gajadhar, B. J., Nap, H. H., De Kort, Y. A. W., & Ijsselsteijn, W. A. (2010). Out of sight, out of mind: Co-player effects on seniors' player experience. *fun and games '10: proceedings of the 3rd international conference on fun and games,* September (pp. 74–83). https://doi.org/10.1145/1823818.1823826.

Gallistl, V., Rohner, R., Seifert, A., & Wanka, A. (2020). Configuring the older non-user: Between research, policy and practice of digital exclusion. *Social Inclusion, 8,* 233–243. doi:10.17645/si.v8i2.2568.

Gannes, L. (2012, April 4). *Google unveils Project Glass: Wearable augmented-reality glasses.* AllThings. Retrieved October 27, 2020, from http://allthingsd.com/20120404/google-unveils-project-glass-wearable-augmented-reality-glasses/.

Garçon, L., Khasnabis, C., Walker, L., Nakatani, Y., Lapitan, J., Borg, J., Ross, A., & Velazquez Berumen, A. (2016). Medical and assistive health technology: Meeting the needs of aging populations. *The Gerontologist, 56*(Suppl. 2), S293–S302. https://doi.org/10.1093/geront/gnw005.

Gega, L., & Aboujaoude, E. (2021, September 14). How digital technology mediated the effects of the COVID-19 pandemic on mental health: The good, the bad, and the indifferent. *Frontiers in Digital Health.* https://doi.org/10.3389/fdgth.2021.733151.

Gelfand, A. (2019). How Wearable and Implantable Technology is Changing the Future of Health Care. *Hopkins Bloomberg Public Health,* 13th February 2019. Retrieved 13th October 2021 from https://magazine.jhsph.edu/2019/how-wearable-and-implantable-technology-changing-future-health-care.

Genoe, M. R., Kulczycki, C., Marston, H., Freeman, S., Musselwhite, C., & Rutherford, H. (2018). E-leisure and older adults: Findings from an international exploratory study. *Therapeutic Recreation Journal,* Vol. LII(1). doi.org/10.18666/TRJ-2018-V52-I1-8417.

Gerling, K., de Schutter, B., Brown, J. A., & Allaire, J. (2015). Ageing playfully: Advancing research on games for older adults beyond accessibility and health benefits. In A. L. Cox, P. Cairns, R. Bernhaupt, & L. Nacke (Eds), *Proceedings of the 2015 annual symposium on computer–human interaction in play* (pp. 817–820). Association for Computing Machinery. doi:10.1145/2793107.2810262.

Gerling, K., Schild, J., and Masuch, M. (2010). Exergame design for elderly users: the case study of SilverBalance. *In 7th International Conference on Advances in Computer Entertainment Technology*, ACE 2010, 17–19 November 2010, Taipei, Taiwan. http://dx.doi.org/10.1145/1971630.1971650.

Gibson, G., Dickinson, C., Brittain, K., & Robinson, L. (2019). Personalisation, customisation and bricolage: How people with dementia and their families make assistive technology work for them. *Ageing and Society*, *39*(11), 2502–2519.

Gibson, G., Newton, L., Pritchard, G., Finch, T., Brittain, K., & Robinson, L. (2016). The provision of assistive technology products and services for people with dementia in the United Kingdom. *Dementia*, *15*(4), 681–701.

Gilbert, C. (2022). *Smarter homes for independent living: Putting people in control of their lives.* Policy Connect.

Gilleard, C., Jones, I., & Higgs, P. (2015). Connectivity in later life: The declining age divide in mobile cell phone ownership. *Sociological Research Online*, *20*, 3. doi:10.5153/sro.3552.

Gillett, J. E., & Crisp, D. A. (2017). Examining coping style and the relationship between stress and subjective well-being in Australia's 'sandwich generation'. *Australasian Journal on Ageing*, *36*(3), 222–227. https://doi.org/10.1111/ajag.12439.

Gish, J., Vrkljan, B., Grenier, A., & Van Miltenburg, B. (2017). Driving with advanced vehicle technology: A qualitative investigation of older drivers' perceptions and motivations for use. *Accident Analysis and Prevention*, *106*, 498–504. https://doi.org/10.1016/j.aap.2016.06.027.

Goedhart, N. S., Broerse, J. E., Kattouw, R., & Dedding, C. (2019). 'Just having a computer doesn't make sense': The digital divide from the perspective of mothers with a low socio-economic position. *New Media & Society*, *21*(11–12), 2347–2365. https://doi.org/10.1177/1461444819846059.

Golant, S. M. (2015). *Aging in the right place.* Health Professions Press.

Graafmans, J. A. M., Taipale, V., & Charness, N. (1998). *Gerontechnology. A sustainable investment in the future.* IOS Press.

Graafmans, J. A., Fozard, J. L., Rietsema, J., van Berlo, G., & Bouma, H. (1996). *Gerontechnology: Matching the technological environment to the needs and capacities of the elderly.* Eindhoven University of Technology.

Graff, G. M. (2019, September 10). On 9/11, Luck meant everything. *The Atlantic.* Retrieved August 14, 2021, from https://www.theatlantic.com/ideas/archive/2019/09/september-11-blind-luck-decided-who-lived-or-died/597688/.

Graner Ray, S. (2004). *Gender inclusive game design: Expanding the market.* Cengage Learning.

Green, C. S., & Bavelier, D. (2003). Action video game modifies visual selective attention. *Nature*, *29*, 534–537. doi:10.1038/nature01647.

Green, C. S., Li, R., & Bavelier, D. (2010). Perceptual learning during action video game playing. *Topics in Cognitive Science*, *2*(2), 202–216. doi:10.1111/j.1756-8765.2009.01054.x.

Green, J. (2020, October 16). Singletons' lockdown nightmare: Millions face heartbreak during weeks of Tiers 2 and 3 restrictions … so CAN you still see your partner and where can you on dates? *The Daily Mail.* Retrieved November 1, 2020, from https://www.dailymail.co.uk/femail/article-8846927/FEMAIL-answers-questions-looking-love-Tier-2-lockdown.html.

Green, L. (2017). *Understanding the life course: Sociological and psychological perspectives* (2nd ed.). Polity Press.

Green, L., Morgan, L., Azam, S., Evan, L., Parry-Williams, L., Petchey, L., & Bellis, M. A. (2020). A health impact assessment of the 'Staying at Home and Social Distancing

Policy' in Wales in response to the COVID-19 pandemic. *Public Health Wales.* Retrieved October 8, 2020, from https://phw.nhs.wales/news/staying-at-home-policy-has-reduced-spread-of-coronavirus-but-has-also-had-other-positive-and-negative-impacts-on-the-well-being-of-welsh-society/a-health-impact-assessment-of-the-staying-at-home-and-social-distancing-policy-in-wales-in-response-to-th/.

Greene, B. (2011, April 3). 38 Years ago he made the first cell phone call. *CNN.* Retrieved September 28, 2021, from http://edition.cnn.com/2011/OPINION/04/01/greene. first.cellphone.call/index.html.

Greenhalgh, T., Rosen, R., Shaw, S. E., Byng, R., Faulkner, S., Finlay, T., Grundy, E., Husain, L., Hughes, G., Leone, C., Moore, L., Papoutsi, C., Pope, C., Rybczynska-Bunt, S., Rushforth, A., Wherton, J., Wieringa, S., & Wood, G. W. (2021). Planning and evaluating remote consultation services: A new conceptual framework incorporating complexity and practical ethics. *Frontiers in Digital Health, 13*(3), 726095. doi:10.3389/fdgth.2021.726095.

Griffith, E., Colon, A., & Moscaritolo, A. (2021, April 26). The best smart home devices for 2021. *PC Magazine.* Retrieved April 30, 2021, from https://uk.pcmag.com/ smart-home/85/the-best-smart-home-devices-for-2020.

Gschwind, Y. J., Eichberg, S., Marston, H. R., de Rosario, H., Aal, K., Ejupi, A., de Rosario, H., Kroll, M., Drobics, M., Annegarn, J., Wieching, R., Lord, S. R., Aal, K., & Delbaere, K. (2014). ICT-based system to predict and prevent falls (iStopp-Falls): Study protocol for an international multicenter randomized controlled trial. *BMC Geriatrics.* doi:10.1186/1471-2318-14-91.

Gschwind, Y., Eichberg, S., Ejupi, A., de Rosario, H., Kroll, M., Marston H., Drobics, M., Annegarn, J., Wieching, R., Lord, S. R., Aal, K., Vaziri, D., Woodbury, A., Fink, D., & Delbaere, K. (2015). ICT-based system to predict and prevent falls (iStoppFalls): Results from an international multicenter randomized controlled trial. *European Review of Aging and Physical Activity (EURAPA), 12*(10). doi:10.1186/ s11556-015-0155-6.

Gulf News. UAE. (2017, September 16). New Dubai traffic signs use emojis. *Gulf News.* Retrieved October 19, 2021, from https://gulfnews.com/uae/transport/new-dubai-traffic-signs-use-emojis-1.2090806.

Hadley, R. (2020b, September 22). *Written evidence (LBC0114).* COVID-19 Committee. Retrieved March 3, 2021, from https://committees.parliament.uk/committee/460/ covid19-committee/publications/written-evidence/?page=8.

Hadley, R. A. (2018a). The lived experience of older involuntary childless men. *The Annual Journal of the British Sociological Association Study Group on Auto/Biography,* 93–108.

Hadley, R. A. (2018b). Ageing without children, gender and social justice. In S. Westwood (Ed.), *Ageing, diversity and equality: Social justice perspectives* (pp. 66–81). Routledge.

Hadley, R. A. (2019). Deconstructing dad. In J. Barry, R. Kingerlee, M. Seager, & L. Sullivan (Eds), *The Palgrave handbook of male psychology and mental health* (pp. 47–66). Palgrave Macmillan.

Hadley, R. A. (2020a). Men and me(n). *Methodological Innovations, 13*(2). https://doi. org/10.1177/2059799120918336.

Hadley, R. A. (2021). *How is a man supposed to be a man? Male childlessness – A life course disrupted.* Berghahn.

Hall, A. K., Chavarria, E., Maneeratana, V., Chaney, B. H., & Bernhardt, J. M. (2012). Health benefits of digital videogames for older adults: A systematic review of the literature. *Games for Health Journal, 1,* 402–410. doi:10.1089/g4h.2012.0046.

Hargittai, E., & Dobransky, K. (2017). Old dogs, new clicks: Digital inequality in skills and uses among older adults. *Canadian Journal of Communication, 42*(2). https://doi. org/10.22230/cjc.2017v42n2a3176.

Hargittai, E., Redmiles, E., Vitak, J., & Zimmer, M. (2020). Americans' willingness to adopt a COVID-19 tracking app: The role of app distributor. *First Monday*, *25*, 11.

Harrington, C. N., Wilcox, L., Connelly, K., Rogers, W., & Sanford, J. (2018). Designing health and fitness apps with older adults: Examining the value of experience-based co-design. *Proceedings of the 12th EAI international conference on pervasive computing technologies for healthcare*.

Harrington, T. L., & Harrington, M. K. (2000). *Gerontechnology why and how*. Shaker Verlag GmbH.

Haskins, B. L., Lesperance, D., Gibbons, P., & Boudreaux, E. D. (2017). A systematic review of smartphone applications for smoking cessation. *Translational Behavioral Medicine*, *7*(2), 292–299. https://doi.org/10.1007/s13142-017-0492-2.

Hawkins, M. (2005, May 6). Go to synesthesia … Jake Kazdal's journey through the heart of REZ. *Game Developer*. Retrieved December 13, 2021, from https://www.gamedeveloper.com/design/go-to-synesthesia-jake-kazdal-s-journey-through-the-heart-of-i-rez-i-.

Haworth, R. (2020, October 28). For the millions in digital poverty, local lockdowns mean utter isolation. *City A.M.* Retrieved February 19, 2021, from https://www.cityam.com/for-the-millions-in-digital-poverty-local-lockdowns-mean-utter-isolation/.

Health and Wellbeing SRA. (2017–2019). *'Talking about … Sex and relationships: Young people speak out' project webpage*. Retrieved August 31, 2020, from https://health-wellbeing.open.ac.uk/related-projects/talking-about-sex-and-relationships-young-people-speak-out/.

Health and Wellbeing SRA. (2020b). *'COVID-19: Vulnerable young people living with life-limiting/life-threatening conditions and their families' project webpage*. Retrieved June 15, 2022,, from https://healthwellbeing.kmi.open.ac.uk/covid-19/vulnerable-young-people-living-with-life-limiting-life-threatening-conditions-and-their-families/.

HEFCE. (2016). Landscape Review of Interdisciplinary Research in the UK. Report to HEFCE and RCUK by Technopolis and the Science Policy Research Unit (SPRU). University of Sussex. Retrieved May 17, 2021, from https://webarchive.national-archives.gov.uk/20170712122426/http://www.hefce.ac.uk/pubs/rereports/year/2016/interdis/.

Helsper, E. J. (2010). Gendered Internet use across generations and life stages. *Communication Research*, *37*, 352–374. https://doi.org/10.1177/0093650209356439.

Helsper, E. J. (2021). *The digital disconnect* (1st ed.). SAGE Publications Ltd.

Helsper, E. J., & van Deursen. A. J. A. M. (2017). Do the rich get digitally richer? Quantity and quality of support for digital engagement. *Information, Communication & Society*, *20*(5), 700–714. doi:10.1080/1369118X.2016.1203454.

Henwood, F., & Marent, B. (2019). Understanding digital health: Productive tensions at the intersection of sociology of health and science and technology studies. *Sociology of Health and Illness*, *41*, 1–15. doi:10.1111/1467-9566.12898.

Herman, L. (2001). *Phoenix: The fall and rise of videogames*. Rolenta Press.

Herz, J. C., & Macedonia, M. R. (2002, April). Computer games and the military: Two views. *Defense Horizons*. Retrieved February 23, 2020, from https://www.files.ethz.ch/isn/135079/DH11.pdf.

Heutinck, L., Jansen, M., van den Elzen, Y., van der Pijl, D., & de Groot, I. J. M. (2018). Virtual reality computer gaming with dynamic arm support in boys with Duchenne muscular dystrophy. *Journal of Neuromuscular Diseases*, *5*(3), 359–372. doi:10.3233/JND-180307.

Hilbert, M. (2011a). The end justifies the definition: The manifold outlooks on the digital divide and their practical usefulness for policy-making. *Telecommunications Policy*, *35*(8), 715–736. https://doi.org/10.1016/j.telpol.2011.06.012.

Hilbert, M. (2011b). Digital gender divide or technologically empowered women in developing countries? A typical case of lies, damned lies, and statistics. *Women's Studies International Forum*, *34*(6), 479–489. doi:10.1016/j.wsif.2011.07.001.

History of Information.com. (n.d.). Retrieved January 18, 2022, from https://www.history-ofinformation.com/detail.php?entryid=607.

Hive. (n.d.). Make your home a smarter place, product range. Retrieved June 15, 2021, from https://www.hivehome.com/?cid=ppc.cid_tool=goo.cid_ctype=bran.cid_cname= UK_Brand_Hive_Pure%20Brand_Exact&gclid=Cj0KCQjw1a6EBhC0ARIs AOiTkrFfwPngOa2JOs72R4WaSaiiiL91499M-J6fUHVPPhZIGHtIBQm1G9 waAmndEALw_wcB&gclsrc=aw.ds.

Holt, N., Neumann, J., McNeil, J., & Cheng, A. (2020). Implications of COVID-19 for an ageing population. *Medical Journal of Australia, 213*, 342–344.

House of Lords. (2021, April 21). Beyond digital: Planning for a hybrid world. *1st Report o Session 2019–21.* HL Paper 263. Retrieved February 28, 2022, from https:// publications.parliament.uk/pa/ld5801/ldselect/ldcvd19/263/263.pdf.

Howe, N., & Strauss, W. (2000). *Millennials rising: The next great generation.* Vintage Original.

Hung, L., Liu, C., Woldum, E., Au-Yeung, A., Berndt, A., Wallsworth, Horne, N., Gregorio, M., Mann, J., & Chaudhury, H. (2019). The benefits of and barriers to using a social robot PARO in care settings: A scoping review. *BMC Geriatrics, 19*, 232. https://doi.org/10.1186/s12877-019-1244-6.

Ijsselsteijn, W., Nap, H. H. De Kort, Y., & Poels, K. (2007). Digital game design for elderly users. In *Proceedings of the 2007 conference on future play, future play'07* (pp. 17–22). https://doi.org/10.1145/1328202.1328206.

International Society for Gerontechnology (ISG). (2016). *Articles of Association, English.* Retrieved July 31, 2021, from https://www.gerontechnology.org/reports /Articles%20of%20Association%20ISG%20(ENGLISH).pdf.

International Society of Gerontechnology. (n.d.). *Past conferences.* Retrieved November 12, 2021, from https://www.gerontechnology.org/pastconference.html.

Interreg Europe. (2021). *Active and healthy ageing.* Retrieved January 15, 2022, from https://www.interregeurope.eu/policylearning/news/11071/active-and-healthy-ageing/?id=4203#:~~:text=The%20promotion%20of%20healthy%20ageing, society'%20(European%20Commission).

Isler, Y. Olcuoglu, L. T., & Yeniad, M. (2018). Data security and privacy issues of implantable medical devices. *International Journal of Natural and Engineering Sciences, 3*(3), 12–22.

Ismail, A. W., & Sunar, M. S. (2009). Collaborative augmented reality: Multi-user interaction in urban simulation. In H. Badioze Zaman, P. Robinson, M. Petrou, P. Olivier, H. Schröder, & T. K. Shih (Eds), *Visual informatics: Bridging research and practice.* IVIC 2009. Lecture Notes in Computer Science, *5857*. Springer. https://doi. org/10.1007/978-3-642-05036-7_36.

Jackson, P. (2021, August 3). September 11 attacks: What happened that day and after. *BBC News.* Retrieved August 14, 2021, https://www.bbc.co.uk/news/world-us-canada-57698668.

Johnson, T. (2015, March 18). Desert storm: The first war televised live around the world (and around the clock). *Atlanta Magazines.* Retrieved August 14, 2021, from https:// www.atlantamagazine.com/90s/desert-storm-the-first-war-televised-live-around-the-world-and-around-the-clock/.

Jonaitis, A. (1988). *From the Land of the Totem Poles: The Northwest Coast Indian Art Collection at the American Museum of Natural History.* Renaissance Books.

Jones, C., Smith-MacDonald, L., Miguel-Cruz, A., Pike, A., van Gelderen, M., Lentz, L., Shiu, M.Y., Tang, E., Sawalha, J., Greenshaw, A., Rhind, S. G., Fang, X., Norbash, A., Jetly, R., Vermetten, E., & Brémault-Phillips, S. (2020). Virtual reality-based treatment for military members and veterans with combat-related posttraumatic stress disorder: Protocol for a multimodular motion-assisted memory desensitization and reconsolidation randomized controlled trial. *JMIR Research Protocols*, *9*(10). doi:10.2196/20620.

Jones, E., & Fear, N. T. (2011). Alcohol use and misuse within the military: A review. *International Review of Psychiatry*, *23*(2), 166–172. https://doi.org/10.3109/095402 61.2010.550868.

Juul, J. (2010). *A casual revolution*. MIT Press.

Kafai, Y. B., Heeter, C., Denner, J., & Sun, J. Y. (2008). *Beyond Barbie and Mortal Kombat: New perspectives on gender and gaming*. MIT Press.

Katz, S., & Marshall, B. L. (2018). Tracked and fit: FitBits, brain games, and the quantified aging body. *Journal of Aging Studies*, *45*, 63–68. https://doi.org/10.1016/j.jaging.2018.01.009.

Katz, S., Ford, A. B., Moskowitz, R. W., Jackson, B. A., & Jaffe, M. W. (1963). Studies of illness in the aged: The index of ADL: A standardized measure of biological and psychosocial function. *JAMA*, *185*(12), 914–919.

Keeling, S. (1999). Ageing in (a New Zealand) place: Ethnography, policy and practice. *Social Policy Journal of New Zealand*, *13*, 95–114.

Kendig, H., Browning, C., Pedlow, R., Wells, Y., & Thomas, S. (2010). Health, social and lifestyle factors in entry to residential aged care: An Australian longitudinal analysis. *Age Ageing*, *39*(3), 342–349. doi:10.1093/ageing/afq016.

Kendig, H., Dykstra, P. A., van Gaalen, R. I., & Melkas, T. (2007). Health of aging parents and childless individuals. *Journal of Family Issues*, *28*(11), 1457–1486. https://doi.org/10.1177/0192513X07303896.

Kent, S. L. (2000). *The first quarter: A 25-year history of video games*. BWD Press.

Kiernan, M. D., Osbourne, A., McGill, G., Greaves, J. P., Wilson, G., & Hill, M. (2018). Are veterans different? Understanding veterans' help-seeking behaviour for alcohol problems. *Health & Social Care in the Community*. doi:10.1111/hsc.12585.

Kim, Y. S. (2008). Reviewing and critiquing computer learning and usage among older adults. *Educational Gerontology*, *34*, 709–735. https://doi.org/10.1080/03601270802000576.

King's College London. (2020, March 12). *Veterans' mental health conference 2020: Bridging the gap*. Retrieved January 4, 2022, from https://www.kcl.ac.uk/news/veterans-mental-health-conference-2020-bridging-the-gap.

Klebnikov, S. (2022, January 5). Stocks plunch after fed minutes show central bank could remove more stimulus. *Forbes*. Retrieved January 6, 2022, from https://www.forbes.com/sites/sergeiklebnikov/2022/01/05/stocks-plunge-after-fed-minutes-show-central-bank-could-remove-more-stimulus/?sh=55ce22f44448.

Knowledge Exchange Seminar Series (KESS). (2012–2018). *Northern Ireland Assembly*. Retrieved February 28, 2022, from https://kess.org.uk/.

Kowert, R., & Quandt, T. (2020). *The video game debate 2: Revisiting the physical, social, and psychological effects of video games*. Routledge.

Krauss Whitbourne, S., & Willis, S. L. (2006). *The Baby Boomers grow up: Contemporary perspectives on midlife* (1st ed.). Routledge.

Lagacé, M., Charmarkeh, H., Laplante, J., & Tanguay, A. (2015). How ageism contributes to the second level digital divide: The case of Canadian seniors. *Journal of Technologies and Human Usability*, *11*, 1–13. doi:10.18848/2381-9227/CGP/v11i04/56439.

Lallanilla, M. (2013, November 1). 'Biohacker' Implants Chip in Arm. *NBC News*. Retrieved January 15, 2022, from https://www.nbcnews.com/id/wbna53438000.

Lane, G. W., Noronha, D., Rivera, A., Craig, K., Yee, C., Mills, B., & Villanueva, E. (2016). Effectiveness of a social robot, "Paro," in a VA long-term care setting. *Psychological Services*, *13*, 292–299.

Laranjo, L., Ding, D., Heleno, B., Kocaballi, B., Quiroz, J. C., Huong Ly, T., Chahwan, B., Neves, A. L., Gabarron, E., Dao, K. P., Rodrigues, D., Neves, G. C., Antunes, M. L., Coiera, E., & Bates, D.W. (2021). Do smartphone applications and activity trackers increase physical activity in adults? Systematic review, meta-analysis and meta regression. *British Journal of Sports Medicine, 55*, 422–432.

Lavallière, M., D'Ambrosio, L., Gennis, A., Burstein, A., Godfrey, K. M., Waerstad, H., Puleo, R. M., Lauenroth, A., & Coughlin, J. F. (2017). Walking a mile in another's shoes: The impact of wearing an Age Suit. *Gerontology & Geriatrics Education, 38*(2), 171–187. https://doi.org/10.1080/02701960.2015.1079706.

Laws, G. (1993). The land of old age: Society's changing attitudes toward urban built environments for elderly people. *Annals of the Association of American Geographers, 83*, 672–693. https://www.jstor.org/stable/2563599.

Learner, S. (2018). Nearly a third of care home staff want CCTV cameras in care homes. *Care Home*, July 12, 2019. Retrieved January 30, 2022, from https://www.carehome.co.uk/news/article.cfm/id/1612213/nearly-third-care-home-staff-cctv-cameras.

Leask, C. F., Sandlund, M., Skelton, D. A., & Chastin, S. F. M. (2017). Co-creating a tailored public health intervention to reduce older adults' sedentary behaviour. *Health Education Journal, 76*(5), 595–608. https://doi.org/10.1177/0017896917707785.

Leszczynski, Chaieb, L., Reber, T. P., Derner, M., Axmacher, N., & Fell, J. (2017). Mind wandering simultaneously prolongs reactions and promotes creative incubation. *Scientific Reports, 7*(1), 10197–10197. https://doi.org/10.1038/s41598-017-10616-3.

Levy, S. (n.d.). Graphical user interfaces. *Britannica*. Retrieved January 15, 2022, from https://www.britannica.com/technology/graphical-user-interface.

Lewis-Evans, B. (2018). A short guide to user testing for simulation sickness in Virtual Reality. Chapter 30. In A. Drachen, P. Mirza-Babaei, & L. Nacke (Eds), *Games user research*. OUP.

Liechty, T., Genoe, M. R., & Marston, H. R. (2017). Physically active leisure and the transition to retirement: The value of context. *Annals of Leisure Research, 20*(1), 23–38. doi:10.1080/11745398.2016.1187570.

Lissitsa, S., Zychlinski, E., & Kagan, M. (2022). The Silent Generation vs Baby Boomers: Socio-demographic and psychological predictors of the "gray" digital inequalities. *Computers in Human Behavior, 128*, 107098. https://doi.org/10.1016/j.chb.2021.107098.

Lloyds Bank. (2018). *UK Consumer Digital Index 2018*. Retrieved May 15, 2020, from https://www.lloydsbank.com/assets/media/pdfs/banking_with_us/whats-happening/LB-Consumer-Digital-Index-2018-Report.pdf.

Lloyds Bank. (2021, May). *Lloyds Consumer Digital Index*. Retrieved August 26, 2021, from 21 0513-lloyds-consumer-digital-index-2021-report.pdf.

Loftin, R. B., & Kenney, P. (1995). Training the Hubble space telescope flight team. *IEEE Computer Graphics and Applications, 15*(5), 31–37. doi:10.1109/38.403825.

Loos, E. (2012). Senior citizens: Digital immigrants in their own country? *Observatorio, 6*.

Loos, E., Haddon, L., & Mante-Meijer, E. (Eds). (2012). *Generational use of new media*. Ashgate.

Marston, H. R. (2010). *Wii like to play too: Computer gaming habits of older adults*. PhD thesis, Teesside University, North Yorkshire.

Marston, H. R. (2012). Older adults as 21st century game designers (pp. 90–102). *Whitsun: The Computer Games Journal*. https://doi.org/10.1007/BF03392330.

Marston, H. R. (2013a). Design recommendations for digital game design within an aging society. *Educational Gerontology, 39*(2), 103–118. doi:10.1080/03601277.2012.689936.

Marston, H. R. (2013b). Digital gaming perspectives of older adults: Content vs. interaction. *Educational Gerontology, 39*(3), 194–208. https://doi.org/10.1080/03601277.2012.700817.

Marston, H. R. (2019). Millennials and ICT—Findings from the Technology 4 Young Adults (T4YA) project: An exploratory study. *Societies, 9*(4), 80. https://doi.org/10.3390/soc9040080.

Marston, H. R., & Azadvar, A. (2020). Defeating the boss level … Exploring inter-and-multigenerational gaming experiences. *Computer Games Journal, 9*(4). https://doi.org/10.1007/s40869-020-00098-1.

Marston, H. R., & del Carmen Miranda Duro, M. (2020). Revisiting the twentieth century through the lens of Generation X and digital games: A scoping review. *Computer Games Journal.* https://doi.org/10.1007/s40869-020-00099-0.

Marston, H. R., & Hall, A. K. (2016). Gamification: Applications for health promotion and health information technology engagement. In D. Novák, B. Tulu, & H. Brendryen. (Eds), *Handbook of research on holistic perspectives in gamification for clinical practice* (pp. 78–104). IGI Global. http://doi:10.4018/978-1-4666-9522-1.ch005.

Marston, H. R., & Kowert, R. (2020). What role can videogames play in the COVID-19 pandemic? [version 1; peer review: 2 approved]. *Emerald Open Research, 2,* 34 https://doi.org/10.35241/emeraldopenres.13727.1.

Marston, H. R., & Morgan, D. J. (2020a). Technology & social media during COVID-19 pandemic. Special Issue: COVID-19 & Geriatric Mental Health Worldwide. *IPA Bulletin, 3*(2). Retrieved September 2, 2020, from https://www.ipa-online.org/publications/ipa-bulletin/featured-articles/covid-19-bulletin-articles/technology-social-media-during-covid19.

Marston, H. R., & Morgan, D. J. (2020b, November 2). Lockdown 2.0: Gunpowder plot, digital christmas, sex and relationships. *Ageing Issues Blog.* Retrieved August 24, 2021, from https://ageingissues.wordpress.com/2020/11/02/lockdown-2-0-gunpowder-plot-digital-christmas-sex-and-relationships/.

Marston, H. R., & Samuels, J. (2019). A review of age friendly virtual assistive technologies and their effect on daily living for carers and dependent adults. Special Issue "Creating Age-friendly Communities: Housing and Technology" *Healthcare, 7*(1). doi:10.3390/healthcare7010049.

Marston, H. R., & Smith, S. T. (2012). Interactive videogame technologies to support independence in the elderly: A narrative review. *Games for Health Journal, 1*(2), 139–152. doi:10.1089/g4h.2011.0008.

Marston, H. R., & van Hoof, J. (2019). "Who doesn't think about technology when designing urban environments for older people?" A case study approach to a proposed extension of the WHO'S age-friendly cities model. *International Journal Environmental Research Public Health, 16*(19), 3525. doi:10.3390/ijerph16193525.

Marston, H. R., Freeman, S., Bishop, A. K., & Beech, C. L. (2016). Utilization of digital games for older adults aged 85+ years: A scoping review. *Games for Health Journal, 5*(3), 157–174. doi:10.1089/g4h.2015.0087.

Marston, H. R., Freeman, S., Genoe, R., Kulcyzki, C., & Musselwhite, C. (2018). *The cohesiveness of technology in later life: Findings from the Technology in Later Life (TILL) Project Knowledge Exchange Seminar Series 2017–2018.*

Marston, H., & Graner-Ray, S. (2016). Older women on the game: Understanding digital game perspectives from an ageing cohort. In E. Domínguez-Rué & L. Nierling (Eds), *Ageing and technology* (pp. 67–92). Transcript Verlag. https://doi.org/10.14361/9783839429570-004.

Marston, H. R., Genoe, R., Freeman, S., Kulczycki, C., & Musselwhite, C. (2019). Older adults perceptions of ICT: Main findings from the Technology in Later Life (TILL) an initial study. *Healthcare, 7*(3). doi:10.3390/healthcare7030086.

Marston, H. R., Greenlay, S., & van Hoof, J. (2013). Understanding the Nintendo Wii console in long-term care facilities. *Technology & Disability, 25*(2), 77–85. doi:10.3233/TAD-130369.

Marston, H. R., Hadley, R., Banks, D., & Duro Miranda, M. D. C. (2019). Mobile self-monitoring ECG devices to diagnose arrhythmia that coincide with palpitations: A scoping review. *Healthcare, 7*(3), 96. doi:10.3390/healthcare7030096.

Marston, H. R., Hadley, R., Pike, G., & Hesketh, I. (2020). Games for health & mHealth apps for police & blue light personnel: A research review. *The Police Journal, 94*(3). https://doi.org/10.1177/0032258X20937327.

Marston, H. R., Ivan, L., Fernández-Ardèvol, M., Rosales Climent, A., Gómez-León, M., Blanche, D., Earle, s., Ko, P.-C., Colas, S., Bilir, B., Çalikoglu, H. O., Arslan, H.,

Kriebernegg, U., Großschädl, F., Reer, F., Quandt, T., Buttigieg, S. C., Silva, P. A., Gallistl, V., & Rohner, R. (2020). COVID-19: Technology, social connections, loneliness & leisure activities: An international study protocol. *Frontiers in Sociology.* https://doi.org/10.3389/fsoc.2020.574811.

Marston, H. R., Kroll, M., Fink, D., & de Rosario, H., Gschwind, Y. J. (2016). Technology use, adoption and behaviour in older adults: results from the iStoppFalls Project. *Educational Gerontology.* doi: 1080/03601277.2015.1125178.

Marston, H. R., Kroll, M., Fink, D., & Eichberg S. (2014). *Digital game aesthetics of the iStoppFalls Exergame.* In B. Schouten, S. Fedtke, M. Schijven, M. Vosmeer, & A. Gekker (Eds), *Games for health 2014.* Springer Vieweg. https://doi.org/10.1007/978-3-658-07141-7_12.

Marston, H. R., Kroll, M., Fink, D., & Gschwind, Y. J. (2016). Flow experience of older adults using the iStoppFalls Exergame. *Games and Culture, 11*(1–2), 201–222. https://doi.org/10.1177/1555412015605219.

Marston, H. R., Morgan, D. J., Wilson-Menzfeld, G., Gates, J. R., & Turner, R. (2021, July 6). Written Evidence [PTC0018]. The long-term impact of the pandemic on towns and cities. UK Parliament. Retrieved July 14, 2021, from https://committees.parliament.uk/writtenevidence/37464/pdf/.

Marston, H. R., Musselwhite, C., & Hadley, R. A. (2020). COVID-19 vs Social Isolation: The impact technology can have on communities, social connections and citizens. British Society of Gerontology. *Ageing Issues.* Retrieved March 3, 2021, from https://ageingissues.wordpress.com/2020/03/18/covid-19-vs-social-isolation-the-impact-technology-can-have-on-communities-social-connections-and-citizens/?fbclid=IwAR1sUsffKNd_G5u6d_oc0Z56u4Es7HyoCJYKr0qSnqFxX68pD3PY5Ja-SI7g.

Marston, H. R., Niles-Yokum, K., & Silva, P. A. (2021). A commentary on Blue Zones®: A critical review of age-friendly environments in the 21st century and beyond. *International Journal of Environmental Research & Public Health, 18*, 837. https://doi.org/10.3390/ijerph18020837.

Marston, H. R., Niles-Yokum, K., Earle, S., Gomez, B., & Lee, D. M. (2020). OK Cupid, stop bumbling around and match me tinder: Using dating apps across the life course. *Gerontology and Geriatric Medicine.* https://doi.org/10.1177/2333721420947498.

Marston, H. R., Shore, L., & White, P. J. (2020). How does a (Smart) age-friendly ecosystem look in a post-pandemic society? *International Journal of Environmental Research & Public Health, 17*(21), 8276. http://dx.doi.org/10.3390/ijerph17218276.

Marston, H. R., Wilson, G., Morgan, D. J., & Gates, J. (2020, December 4). *Research evidence – LOL0017 – Living online: The long-term impact on wellbeing.* Covid 19 Committee. Retrieved January 15, 2022, from https://committees.parliament.uk/writtenevidence/18490/pdf/.

Marston, H. R., Woodbury, A., Gschwind, Y. J., Kroll, M., Fink, D., Eichberg, S., Kreiner, K., Ejupi, A., Annegarn, J., de Rosario, H., Wienholtz, A., Wieching, R., & Delbaere, K. (2015). The design of a purpose-built exergame for fall prediction and prevention for older people. *European Review of Aging and Physical Activity, 12*, 13. https://doi.org/10.1186/s11556-015-0157-4.

Martin, K., & Shilton, K. (2016). Putting mobile application privacy in context: An empirical study of user privacy expectations for mobile devices. *The Information Society, 32*(3), 200–216. doi:10.1080/01972243.2016.1153012.

McCosker, H., Barnard, A., & Gerber, R. (2001). Undertaking Sensitive Research: Issues and Strategies for meeting the safety needs of all participants [41 paragraphs]. *Forum Qualitative Sozialforschung/Forum: Qualitative Social Research, 2*(1), Article 22. http://nbn-resolving.de/urn:nbn:de:0114-fqs0101220.

McGill, G., Wilson, G., Caddick, N., Forster, N., & Kiernan, M. D. (2020). Rehabilitation and transition in military veterans after limb-loss. *Disability and Rehabilitation.* doi:10.1080/09638288.2020.1734875.

McGlynn, S. A., Kemple, S., Mitzner, T. L., King, C.-H. A., & Rogers, W. A. (2017). Understanding the potential of PARO for healthy older adults. *International Journal of Human–Computer Studies, 100*, 33–47. https://doi.org/10.1016/j.ijhcs. 2016.12.004.

McLaughlin, A., Gandy, M., Allaire, J., & Whitlock, L. (2012). Putting Fun into Video Games for Older Adults. *Ergonomics in Design, 20*(2), 13–22. https://doi.org/10.1177/1064804611435654.

McMillan, B. (2016, April 18). Think like an impostor, and you'll go far in academia. *Times Higher Education*. Retrieved August 3, 2021, from https://www.timeshighereducation.com/blog/think-impostor-and-youll-go-far-academia.

McNeill, A., & Coventry, L. (2015). An appraisal-based approach to the stigma of walker-use. In J. Zhou & G. Salvendy (Eds), *Human aspects of IT for the aged population. Design for aging.* Lecture Notes in Computer Science (Vol. 9193). Springer. https://doi.org/10.1007/978-3-319-20892-3_25.

McVeigh, K. (2015, March 3). Grimethorpe, the mining village that hit rock bottom – Then bounced back. *The Guardian*. Retrieved September 28, 2021, from https://www.theguardian.com/politics/2015/mar/03/grimethorpe-hit-rock-bottom-then-bounced-back.

Means, R. (2007). Safe as houses? Ageing in place and vulnerable older people in the UK. *Social Policy and Administration, 41*, 65–85.

Men's Sheds Association. (n.d.a). Retrieved August 27, 2021, from https://menssheds.org.uk/.

Men's Sheds Association. (n.d.b). *What is a men's shed?* Retrieved August 27, 2021, from https://menssheds.org.uk/about/what-is-a-mens-shed/.

Men's Sheds Association (n.d.c). *Men's sheds FAQ.* Retrieved August 27, 2021, from https://menssheds.org.uk/about/what-is-a-mens-shed/mens-sheds-faq/.

Mencap NI. (n.d.). Retrieved December 29, 2021, from https://northernireland.mencap.org.uk/.

Mental Health Foundation. (2021). *Pandemic one year on: Landmark mental health study reveals mixed picture.* Mental Health Foundation. Retrieved July 31, 2021, from https://www.mentalhealth.org.uk/news/pandemic-one-year-landmark-mental-health-study-reveals-mixed-picture.

Merkel, S., & Kucharski, A. (2019). Participatory design in gerontechnology: A systematic literature review. *The Gerontologist, 59*(1), e16–e25. https://doi.org/10.1093/geront/gny034.

Michailidis, L., Balaguer-Ballester, E., & He, X. (2018). Flow and immersion in video games: The aftermath of a conceptual challenge. *Frontiers in Psychology.* https://doi.org/10.3389/fpsyg.2018.01682.

Mielke, J. (2006, July 26). Tetsuya Mizuguchi Reexaming *REZ* and Space Channel 5. Retrieved December 13, 2021, from https://web.archive.org/web/20120711001554/http://www.1up.com/features/northern-lights-retroactive-rez-space.

Military Wikia. (n.d.). *Catterick Garrison.* Retrieved October 21, 2021, from https://military.wikia.org/wiki/Catterick_Garrison.

Miller, J., & Glassmer, B. (2011). *The "inside" and the "outside": Finding realities in interviews.* In D. Silverman (Ed.) *Qualitative research: Issues of theory, method and practice* (chapter 8, 3rd ed.). SAGE.

Miller, K. J., Adair, B. S., Pearce, A. J., Said, C. M., Ozanne, E., & Morris, M. M. (2014). Effectiveness and feasibility of virtual reality and gaming system use at home by older adults for enabling physical activity to improve health related domains: A systematic review. *Age Ageing, 43*, 188–195. doi:10.1093/ageing/aft194.

Ministry of Defence. (2014, May 12). *Mental health awareness app for veterans.* Retrieved January 4, 2022, https://www.gov.uk/government/news/mental-health-awareness-app-for-veterans.

Ministry of Defence. (2017). *Defence people mental health and wellbeing strategy 2017–2022*. Retrieved October 11, 2021, from https://assets.publishing.service.gov.uk/government/uploads/system/uploads/attachment_data/file/689978/20170713-MHW_Strategy_SCREEN.pdf.

Ministry of Defence. (2020a). *UK armed forces mental health: Annual summary & trends over time, 2007/08–2019/20*. Retrieved October 11, 2021, from https://assets.publishing.service.gov.uk/government/uploads/system/uploads/attachment_data/file/892426/20200618_Annual_Report_19-20_O.pdf.

Ministry of Defence. (2020b, April 27). *New mental fitness tool launched to help military enhance mental wellbeing*. Retrieved January 4, 2022, from https://www.gov.uk/government/news/new-mental-fitness-tool-launched-to-help-military-enhance-mental-wellbeing.

Mitzner, T. L., Sanford, J. A., & Rogers, W. A. (2018). Closing the capacity-ability gap: Using technology to support aging with disability. *Innovation in Aging, 2*, 1–8. https://doi.org/10.1093/geroni/igy008.

Molina, K. I., Ricci, N. A., de Moraes, S. A., & Rodrigues Perracini, M. (2014). Virtual reality using games for improving physical functioning in older adults: A systematic review. *Journal of NeuroEngineering and Rehabilitation, 11*, 156. https://doi.org/10.1186/1743-0003-11-156.

Mollenkopf, H. (2004). Aging and technology – Social science approaches. In D. Burdick & S. Kwon (Eds), *Gerotechnology: Research and practice in technology and aging* (pp. 54–67). Springer Publishing.

Moore, P., & Conn, C. P. (1985). *Disquised – A true story*. World Books.

Moreau, E. (2020, September 24). What does it mean to go viral online? *Lifewire*. Retrieved January 6, 2022, from https://www.lifewire.com/what-does-it-mean-to-go-viral-3486225.

Morgan, D. J. (2021, November 10). Design for age – Doing co-design better. *Podcast*. Retrieved December 13, 2021, from https://soundcloud.com/user-54146754/design-for-age-doing-co-design-better?si=b6e40be1a440461bac92ce09a2b5bd61.

Morgan, D. J., Marston, H. R., & Hadley, R. (2020, September 18). *Written evidence [LBCO135] – Life beyond COVID*. COVID-19 Committee, UK Government. Retrieved January 10, 2022, from https://committees.parliament.uk/writtenevidence/10153/pdf/.

Morgan, T. (2019, October 1). Virtual reality PTSD treatment has 'big impact' for veterans. *BBC Wales News*. Retrieved January 15, 2022, https://www.bbc.co.uk/news/uk-wales-49880915#:~:text=Virtual%20reality%20could%20be%20used,the%20type%20of%20trauma%20experienced.

Morris, S., Sherwood, S., & Morris, J. (1996). A dynamic model for explaining changes in use of IADL/ADL care in the community. *Journal of Health and Social Behavior, 37*(1), 91–103. https://doi.org/10.2307/2137233.

Moscaritolo, A. (2020). *Peloton Bike+. PC Magazine*. Retrieved May 3, 2021, from https://uk.pcmag.com/health-fitness/129876/peloton-bike.

Muriel, D., & Crawford, G. (2018). *Video games as culture*. Routledge.

Murphy, M. (2019, October 29). From dial-up to 5G: A complete guide to logging onto the internet. *Quartz*. Retrieved August 14, 2021, from https://qz.com/1705375/a-complete-guide-to-the-evolution-of-the-internet/.

Murray, A., & Musselwhite, C. (2019). Older peoples' experiences of informal support after giving up driving. *Research in Transportation Business & Management, 30*. https://doi.org/10.1016/j.rtbm.2019.100367.

Murray, J. (2020a, March 25). Care workers move into Sheffield dementia home to shield residents. *The Guardian*. Retrieved August 10, 2021, from https://www.theguardian.com/world/2020/mar/25/care-workers-move-into-sheffield-dementia-home-to-shield-residents.

Murray, J. (2020b, April 28) 'We did what we set our to achieve': The staff who moved into care homes. *The Guardian.* Retrieved August 10, 2021, from https://www.theguardian. com/society/2020/apr/28/we-did-what-we-set-out-to-achieve-the-staff-who-moved-into-care-homes.

Murray, J. H. (2017). *Hamlet on the Holodeck: The future of narrative in cyberspace.* MIT Press.

Nacke, L. E., & Lindley, C. A. (2008a). Flow and immersion in first-person shooters: Measuring the player's. *Future Play '08: Proceedings of the 2008 conference on future play: Research, play* (pp. 81–88). https://doi.org/10.1145/1496984.1496998.

Nacke, L. E., & Lindley, C. A. (2010). *Affective ludology, flow and immersion in a first-person shooter: Measurement of player experience.* Retrieved June 15, 2021, from https:// arxiv.org/abs/1004.0248.

Nacke, L., & Lindley, C. (2008b). Boredom, immersion, flow – A pilot study investigating player experience. Presented at the IADIS international conference gaming 2008: Design for engaging experience and social interaction, IADIS Press.

Nafus, D. (2016). *Quantified: Biosensing technologies in everyday life.* The MIT Press.

Nap, H. H., de Kort, Y. A. W., & Ijsselsteijn, W. A. (2009a). Senior gamers: Preferences, motivations and needs. *Gerontechnology,* 8(4), 247–262. https://doi.org/10.4017/ gt.2009.08.04.003.00.

Nap, H. H., Ijsselsteijn, W. A. W., & de Kort, Y. A. W. (2009b). Age differences in associations with digital gaming. In *Breaking new ground: Innovation in games, play, practice and theory. Proceedings of DiGRA 2009.* http://www.digra.org/dl/db/09287.31341. pdf.

National Geographic. (n.d.). *Y2K bug. Resource library, encyclopaedic entry.* Retrieved August 14, 2021, from https://www.nationalgeographic.org/encyclopedia/Y2K-bug/.

NCIA. (n.d.). Not-For-Profit-Framework (NFPF). Retrieved 21st June 2022 from https:// www.ncia.nato.int/business/do-business-with-us/notforprofit-framework-nfpf.html.

Neves, B. B., & Franz, R. L., Munteanu, C., & Baecker, R. (2018). Adoption and feasibility of a communication app to enhance social connectedness amongst frail institutionalized oldest old: An embedded case study. *Information, Communication & Society,* 21, 1681–1699.

Neves, B. B., Amaro, F., & Fonseca, J. R. (2013). Coming of (Old) age in the digital age: ICT usage and non-usage among older adults. *Sociological Research Online, 18,* 1–14.

Newbury-Birch, D., & Allan, K. (Eds). (2019). *Co-creating and co-producing research evidence: A guide for practitioners and academics in health, social care and education settings* (1st ed.). Routledge.

Newman, J. (2012). *Videogames* (2nd ed.). Routledge.

Newton, L., Dickinson, C., Gibson, G., Brittain, K., & Robinson, L. (2016). Exploring the views of GP's, people with dementia and their carers on assistive technology: A qualitative study. *BMJ Open, 6,* e011132. http://dx.doi.org/10.1136/bmjopen-2016-011132.

Nguyen, M. H., Gruber, J., Fuchs, J., Marler, W., Hunsaker, A., & Hargittai, E. (2020). Changes in digital communication during the COVID-19 global pandemic: Implications for digital inequality and future research. *Social Media + Society.* https://doi.org/10.1177/2056305120948255.

NHS. (n.d.a). *Contraceptive implant.* Retrieved October 13, 2021, from https://www.nhs.uk/ conditions/contraception/contraceptive-implant/.

NHS. (n.d.b). Intrauterine device (IUD). Retrieved October 13, 2021, from https://www. nhs.uk/conditions/contraception/iud-coil/.

NI Direct Government Services. (n.d.). *Coronavirus (COVID-19): StopCOVID NI proximity app.* Retrieved May 4, 2021, from https://www.nidirect.gov.uk/articl es/coronavirus-covid-19-stopcovid-ni-proximity-app.

Nielsen. (2014). *Millennials-breaking the myths*. Nielsen Company.

Noelker, L. S., Browdie, R., & Katz, S. (2014). A new paradigm for chronic illness and long-term care. *The Gerontologist, 54*(1), 13–20. https://doi.org/10.1093/geront/gnt086.

Norman, D. A. (2005). *Emotional design: Why we love (or hate) everyday things*. Basic Books.

Norman, D. A. (2007). *The design of future things*. Basic Books.

Norman, J. (1991, January 17). *Peter Arnett at CNN Broadcasts the First Live Television Coverage of War*. Retrieved August 14, 2021, from https://historyofinformation.com/detail.php?entryid=4627.

Northern Ireland Assembly. (2013, November 21). Research and information service research paper. Written by Dr Raymond Russell. Retrieved April 5, 2022, from http://www.niassembly.gov.uk/globalassets/documents/raise/publications/2013/general/13813.pdf.

Nuwer, R. (2014, April 8). Andy Warhol probably never said his celebrated "fifteen minutes of fame" line. *Smithsonian*. Retrieved January 6, 2022, from https://www.smithsonianmag.com/smart-news/andy-warhol-probably-never-said-his-celebrated-fame-line-180950456/.

Nygård, L. (2008). The meaning of everyday technology as experienced by people with dementia who live alone. *Dementia, 7*, 481–502.

Nygård, L., & Starkhammar, S. (2007). The use of everyday technology by people with dementia living alone: Mapping out the difficulties. *Aging & Mental Health, 11*(2), 144–155. doi:10.1080/13607860600844168.

Ofcom. (2018). *Adults' media use and attitudes report*. Ofcom. Retrieved May 4, 2020, from https://www.ofcom.org.uk/__data/assets/pdf_file/0011/113222/Adults-Media-Use-and-Attitudes-Report-2018.pdf.

Ofcom. (2020–2021, April 28). *Adults' media use and attitudes report*. Retrieved May 4, 2021, from https://www.ofcom.org.uk/__data/assets/pdf_file/0025/217834/adults-media-use-and-attitudes-report-2020-21.pdf.

Office for National Statistics. (2020a, August 17). *Living longer: Implications of childlessness among tomorrow's older population*. Retrieved August 24, 2021, from https://www.ons.gov.uk/releases/livinglongerimplicationsofchildlessnessamongtomorrowsolderpopulation.

Office for National Statistics. (2020b, June 29). *Household projections for England: Detailed data for modelling and analysis*. Retrieved August 24, 2021, from https://www.ons.gov.uk/peoplepopulationandcommunity/populationandmigration/populationprojections/datasets/householdprojectionsforenglanddetaileddataformodellingandanalysis.

Office for National Statistics. (2018). Internet users, UK: 2018. Retrieved August 31, 2021, from https://www.ons.gov.uk/businessindustryandtrade/itandinternetindustry/bulletins/internetusers/2018.

Office for National Statistics. (2019a, May 24). *Internet users, UK: 2019*. Retrieved August 29, 2021, from https://www.ons.gov.uk/businessindustryandtrade/itandinternetindustry/bulletins/internetusers/2019.

Office for National Statistics. (2019b). *Exploring the UK's digital divide*. Retrieved February 14, 2021, from https://www.ons.gov.uk/peoplepopulationandcommunity/householdcharacteristics/homeinternetandsocialmediausage/articles/exploringtheuksdigitaldivide/2019-03-04.

Office for National Statistics. (2020c, August 7). Internet access – Households and individuals, Great Britain: 2020. Retrieved May 4, 2021, from https://www.ons.gov.uk/peoplepopulationandcommunity/householdcharacteristics/homeinternetandsocialmediausage/bulletins/internetaccesshouseholdsandindividuals/2020.

Office for Veterans' Affairs. (2020). *Veterans factsheet 2020*. Retrieved October 11, 2021, from https://assets.publishing.service.gov.uk/government/uploads/system/uploads/

attachment_data/file/874821/6.6409_CO_Armed-Forces_Veterans-Factsheet_v9_ web.pdf.

Okada, A., & Sheehy, K. (2020, December 11). Factors and recommendations to support students' enjoyment of online learning with fun: A mixed method study during COVID-19. *Frontiers in Education.* https://doi.org/10.3389/feduc.2020.584351.

Olanrewaju, O. A., Faieza, A. A., & Syakirah, K. (2013). Current trend of robotics application in medical. *IOP Conference Series: Materials Science and Engineering, 46,* 012041.

Oliveira, J. S., Sherrington, C., Zheng, E. R. Y., Franco, M. R., & Tiedemann, A. (2020). Effect of interventions using physical activity trackers on physical activity in people aged 60 years and over: A systematic review and meta-analysis. *British Journal of Sports Medicine, 54,* 1188–1194.

Olmstead, K., & Atkinson, M. (2015, October). *Apps permissions in the Google Play Store.* Pew Research Center. Retrieved January 4, 2021, from http://www.pewinternet. org/2015/11/10/apps-permissions-in-the-google-play-store/.

Olsen, J. E., Thach And, L., & Nowak, L. (2007). Wine for my generation: Exploring how US wine consumers are socialized to wine. *Journal of Wine Research, 18*(1), 1–18.

Orpwood, R., Chadd, J., Howcroft, D., Sixsmith, A., Torrington, J., Gibson, G., & Chalfont G. (2010). Designing technology to improve quality of life for people with dementia; User led approaches. *Universal Access in the Information Society, 9*(3), 249–259.

Oswald, F., Jopp, D., Rott, C., & Wahl, H. (2010). Is aging in place a resource for or risk to life satisfaction? *The Gerontologist, 51,* 238–250. doi:10.1093/geront/gnq096.

Oxford Reference. (n.d.). *Graphical user interface.* Retrieved February 18, 2022, from https://www.oxfordreference.com/view/10.1093/oi/authority.20110803095904199.

Paczynski A., Diment L., Hobbs D., & Reynolds K. (2017) Using technology to increase activity, creativity and engagement for older adults through visual art. In H. Marston, S. Freeman, & C. Musselwhite (Eds), *Mobile e-Health. Human–Computer Interaction Series.* Springer. https://doi.org/10.1007/978-3-319-60672-9_5.

PAHO. *Age-friendly cities and communities.* Retrieved November 12, 2021, from https://www3.paho.org/hq/index.php?option=com_content&view=article&id= 13765:age-friendly-cities&Itemid=42450&lang=en.

Pancani, L., Marinucci, M., Aureli, N., & Riva, P. (2021). Forced social isolation and mental health: A study on 1,006 Italians under COVID-19 lockdown. *Frontiers in Psychology, 12,* 1540.

Panda, D., Narayanaswamy, M. B., Krishnamurthy, S., Stefani, S., Sengupta, S., & Papakonstantinou, Y. (2020, December 8). Create, train, and deploy machine learning models in Amazon Redshift using SQL with Amazon Redshift ML. *AWS Big Data Blog.* Retrieved January 5, 2022, from Create, train, and deploy machine learning models in Amazon Redshift using SQL with Amazon Redshift ML | AWS Big Data Blog.

Pandya, A., & Lodha, P. (2021, July). Social connectedness, excessive screen time during COVID-19 and mental health: A review of current evidence. *Frontiers in Human Dynamics, 22.* https://doi.org/10.3389/fhumd.2021.684137.

Pantri. (n.d.). Retrieved June 15, 2021, from https://pantri.net/.

Paradiso, J. A., & Landay, J. A. (2009, July–September 14–15). Guest editors' introduction: Cross-reality environments. *IEEE Pervasive Computing, 8*(3). doi:10.1109/ MPRV.2009.47.

Peace, S., Werner-Wahl, H., Oswald, F., & Mollenkoph, H. (2007). Environment and ageing. In J. Bond, S. Peace, F. Dittmarr-Kohli, & G. Westerhof (Eds), *Ageing in society: European perspectives on gerontology* (pp. 209–234). Sage Publications.

Pearce, C. (2008). The truth about Baby Boomer Gamers: A study of over-forty computer game players. *Games and Culture, 3*(2), 142–174. https://doi.org/10.1177/ 1555412008314132.

Peine, A., Marshall, B. L., Martin, W., & Neven, L. (2021). *Socio-gerontechnology – Interdisciplinary critical studies of ageing and technology*. Routledge. https://doi. org/10.4324/9780429278266.

Pennington, N. (2021). Communication outside of the home through social media during COVID-19. *Computers in Human Behavior Reports, 4,* 100118. https://doi. org/10.1016/j.chbr.2021.100118.

Penninx, B. W., & Comijs, H. C. (2012). Depression and other common mental health disorders in old age. In A. B. Newman & J. A. Cauley (Eds), *The epidemiology of aging.* Springer. https://doi.org/https://doi.org/10.1007/978-94-007-5061-6.

Petersen, S., Houston, S., Qin, H., Tague, C., & Studley, J. (2017). The utilization of robotic pets in dementia care. *Journal of Alzheimer's disease: JAD, 55*(2), 569–574. https:// doi.org/10.3233/JAD-160703.

Philips, J., Walford, N., Hockey, A., & Sparks, L. (2021). Older people, town centres and the revival of the 'High Street'. *Planning Theory & Practice, 22*(1), 11–26. doi:10.1080/14649357.2021.1875030.

Philips. (n.d.). *Philips Hue.* Retrieved June 15, 2021, from https://www.philips-hue.com/en-gb?&origin=p62607951824&pcrid=314095778836%7cmckv%7csp62607951824_dc%7cplid%7c%7cslid%7c%7cpgrid%7c27017771688%7cptaid%7ckwd-54872 621899%7cproduct%7c%7c&gclid=Cj0KCQjw1a6EBhC0ARIsAOiTkrGuuSt zd26Ri4EYDddX942bH1wDd5VPbffjzsTF6_Faug3-CWhB2d4aAlY9EALw_ wcB&gclsrc=aw.ds.

Phillipson, C., & Baars, J. (2007). Social theory and social ageing. In J. Bond, S. Peace, F. Dittmarr-Kohli, & G. Westerhof (Eds), *Ageing in society: European perspectives on gerontology* (pp. 68–84). Sage Publications.

Phinney, L. M. (2009, March 27). What I wish I'd known about tenure. *Inside Higher Education.* Retrieved August 3, 2021, from https://www.insidehighered.com/ advice/2009/03/27/what-i-wish-id-known-about-tenure.

Pieper, R., Vaarama, M., & Fozard, J. L. (2002). *Gerontechnology: Technology and aging – Starting into the third millennium.* Shaker Verlag GmbH.

Pigliautile, M., Tiberio, L., Mecocci, P., & Federici, S. (2012). The geriatrician. In S. Federici & M. J. Scherer (Eds), *The assistive technology assessment handbook* (pp. 269–299). CRC Press.

Pirkl, J. J. (1994). *Transgenerational design: Products for an aging population.* Van Nostrand Reinhold.

Pittam, D. (2019, March 6). Miners' strike: The decades-old feud that still divides communities. *BBC News.* Retrieved August 30, 2020, from https://www.bbc.co.uk/news/ uk-england-nottinghamshire-47401859.

Pitts, V. (2003). *In the flesh – The cultural politics of body modification.* Palgrave Macmillan.

Plater, R. (2022, March 7). Dr. Alexa? Teladoc teams up with Amazon for Telehealth Services. *Healthline.* Retrieved March 14, from https://www.healthline.com/health-news/dr-alexa-teladoc-teams-up-with-amazon-for-virtual-healthcare-services.

Policy Connect. (2021, September 9). *Public call for evidence: How can smart home technologies enhance independent living?* Retrieved March 3, 2022, from https://www. policyconnect.org.uk/news/public-call-evidence-how-can-smart-home-technologies-enhance-independent-living.

Polikoff, M., Saavedra, A. R., & Korn, S. (2020). Not all kids have computers – And they're being left behind with schools closed by the coronavirus. *The Conversation,* May 8. Retrieved January 4, 2021, from https://theconversation. com/not-all-kids-have-computers-and-theyre-being-left-behind-with-schools-closed-by-the-coronavirus-137359.

Power, V., O'Sullivan, L., de Eyto, A., Schülein, S., Nikamp, C., Bauer, C., Mueller, J., & Ortiz, J. (2016). Exploring user requirements for a lower body soft exoskeleton to assist mobility. In *Proceedings of the 9th ACM international conference on*

PErvasive technologies related to assistive environments (PETRA '16). Association for Computing Machinery, New York, NY, Article 69 (pp. 1–6). https://doi. org/10.1145/2910674.2935827.

Pratty, F. (2021, June 2). The Big Idea: Injectable, health-monitoring implants. *Sifted*. Retrieved October 13, 2021, from https://sifted.eu/articles/dsruptive-injectable-implants/.

Prensky, M. (2001a). True Believers: Digital Game-Based Learning the Military. In *Digital Game-Based Learning* (Ch. 10). McGraw-Hill. Retrieved 15th June 2022 from https://marcprensky.com/writing/Prensky%20-%20Digital%20Game-Based%20 Learning-Ch10-Military.pdf. .

Prensky, M. (2001b). Digital natives, digital immigrants. *Horizon*, *9*, 1–6.

Prescott, J., & Bogg, J. (2013). *Gender divide and the computer game industry*. IGI Global.

Price, B. A., Stuart, A., Calikli, G., Mccormick, C., Mehta, V., Hutton, L., Bandara, A. K., Levine, M., & Nuseibeh, B. (2017). Logging you, Logging me: A replicable study of privacy and sharing behaviour in groups of visual lifeloggers. *Proceedings of the ACM on interactive mobile wearable and ubiquitous technologies*, *1*(2), Article no. 22. doi:10.1145/3090087.

Principe, L. M. (2021, December 27). Robert Boyle. *Encyclopaedia Britannica*. https://www. britannica.com/biography/Robert-Boyle.

Prunk, J. (2001). *Path to Slovene State. Public relations and media office, government of the Republic of Slovenia*. Retrieved August 14, 2021, from http://www.slovenija2001. gov.si/10years/path/.

Pu, L., Moyle, W., & Jones, C. (2020). How people with dementia perceive a therapeutic robot called PARO in relation to their pain and mood: A qualitative study. *Journal of Clinical Nursing*, *29*(3–4), 437–446. doi:10.1111/jocn.15104.

Public Health England. (2019). *An evidence summary of health inequalities in older populations in coastal and rural areas. Executive summary and main messages*. Retrieved August 11, 2021, from https://assets.publishing.service.gov.uk/government/uploads/ system/uploads/attachment_data/file/824717/Health_Inequalities_in_Ageing_in_ Rural_and_Coastal_Areas-Messages_and_summary.pdf.

Public Health England. (2021, July 16). *Admission and care of residents in a care home during COVID-19*. UK Government, Department of Health and Social Care. Retrieved August 10, 2021, from https://www.gov.uk/government/publications/coronavirus-covid-19-admission-and-care-of-people-in-care-homes/coronavirus-covid-19-admission-and-care-of-people-in-care-homes.

Public Health Wales. (2021a, August 6). Guidance to prevent COVID-19 and manage cases, incidents & outbreaks in care homes, supported living and supported accommodation settings in Wales. *Interim Revision to Reflect Changes to Alert Level Zero*. Retrieved August 10, 2021, from https://phw.nhs.wales/topics/latest-information-on-novel-coronavirus-covid-19/information-for-health-and-social-care/gui-001-covid-19-in-residential-care-settings/.

Public Health Wales. (2021b, June 23). *Action care – Visitors to care homes*. Retrieved August 10, 2021, from https://gov.wales/sites/default/files/publications/2021-06/ action-card-visitors-to-care-homes.pdf.

Push Doctor. (n.d.b). *Service update see a GP online, 7 days a week*. Retrieved March 14, 2022, from https://www.pushdoctor.co.uk/service-update.

Push Doctor. (n.d.a). *How it works*. Retrieved March 14, 2022, from https://www.pushdoctor.co.uk/how-it-works.

Push Doctor. (n.d.c). *Simple one-off cost*. Retrieved March 14, 2022, from https://www. pushdoctor.co.uk/pricing.

Rafalow, M. H. (2018). Disciplining play: Digital youth culture as capital at school. *American Journal of Sociology*, *123*, 1416–1452. doi:10.1086/695766.

Rawassizadeh, R., Price, B. A., & Petre, M. (2014). Wearables: Has the age of smart-watches finally arrived? *Communications of the ACM*, *58*(1), 45–47. https://doi.org/10.1145/2629633.

Redmiles, E. M. (2020). Behind the red lights: Methods for investigating the digital security and privacy experiences of sex workers, chapter 5. In E. Hargittai (Ed.), *Research exposed: How empirical social science gets done in the digital age*. Columbia University Press.

REZ – The Game. (n.d.). *REZ English website*. Retrieved December 13, 2021, from https://web.archive.org/web/20191030190746/http://rez.sega.jp/e/game/index.html.

Richardson, M., Zorn, T. E., & Weaver, C. K. (2011). Older people and new communication technologies. Narratives from the literature. In C. T. Salmon (Ed.), *Communication yearbook* (Vol. 35, pp. 121–154). Taylor and Francis.

Riley, M. W., Foner, A., & Riley, J. W. (1999). The aging and society paradigm. In V. L. Bengston & K. W. Schaie (Eds), *Handbook of theories of aging* (pp. 327–343). Springer.

Rogers, W. A., Meyer, B., Walker, N., & Fisk, A. D. (1998). Functional limitations to daily living tasks in the aged: A focus group analysis. *Human Factors*, *40*(1), 111–125.

Rolland, J. P., Biocca, F., Hamza-Lup, F., Ha, Y., & Martins, R. (2005). Development of head-mounted projection displays for distributed, collaborative, augmented reality applications. *Presence: Teleoperators and Virtual Environments*, *14*(5), 528–549. https://doi.org/10.1162/105474605774918741.

Romeo, A., Edney, S., Plotnikoff, R., Curtis, R., Ryan, J., Sanders, I., Crozier, A., & Maher, C. (2019). Can smartphone apps increase physical activity? Systematic review and meta-analysis. *Journal of Medical Internet Research*, *21*(3), e12053. doi:10.2196/12053.

Rosales, A., & Fernández-Ardèvol, M. (2016a). Beyond WhatsApp: Older people and smartphones. *Romanian Journal of Communication and Public Relations*, *18*, 27–47. doi:10.21018/rjcpr.2016.1.200.

Rosales, A., & Fernández-Ardèvol, M. (2016b). Smartphones, apps and older people's interests: From a generational perspective. In *Proceedings of the 18th international conference on human–computer interaction with mobile devices and services*, Florence (pp. 491–503). doi:10.1145/2935334.2935363.

Rosenberg, L., & Nygård, L. (2012). Persons with dementia become users of assistive technology: A study of the process. *Dementia*, *11*(2), 135–154. doi:10.1177/1471301211421257.

Roulstone, A. (2016). *Disability and technology. An interdisciplinary and international approach*. Palgrave Macmillan.

Rowe, J. W., & Kahn, R. L. (2015). Successful aging 2.0: Conceptual expansions for the 21st century. *Journals of Gerontology Series B: Psychological Sciences and Social Sciences*, *70*(4), 593–596. https://doi.org/10.1093/geronb/gbv025.

Rowles, G. D., & Bernard, M. (2013). *Environmental gerontology: Making meaningful places in old age* (p. 320). Springer Publishing Company.

Rubinstein, R. L. (1989). The home environments of older people: A description of the psychosocial processes linking person to place. *Journal of Gerontology*, *44*(2), 45–53. doi:10.1093/geronj/44.2.S45.

Ryff, C. D. (2014). Psychological well-being revisited: Advances in the science and practice of Eudaimonia. *Psychotherapy and Psychosomatics*, *83*(1), 10–28. https://doi.org/10.1159/000353263.

Salminen, M., Hamari, J., & Ravaja, N. (2021). Empathizing with the end user: Effect of empathy and emotional intelligence on ideation. *Creativity Research Journal*, *33*(2), 191–201. https://doi.org/10.1080/10400419.2020.1864164.

Sanders, C. R. (2010). Customizing the body: The art and culture of tattooing. *Contemporary Sociology*, *19*(3), 445. https://doi.org/10.2307/2072496.

Saraiva, M., & Ayanoğlu, H. (2019). Emotions and emotions in design. In H. Ayanoğlu & E. Duarte (Eds), *Emotional design in human–robot interaction*. Human–Computer Interaction Series. Springer. https://doi.org/10.1007/978-3-319-96722-6_4.

Scambler, G., & Scambler, A. (1997). Afterword: Rethinking prostitution. In G. Scambler & A. Scambler (Eds), *Rethinking prostitution: Purchasing sex in the 1990s*. Routledge.

Scharf, T., Walsh, K., & O'Shea, E. (2016). Ageing in rural places. In M. Shucksmith & D. L. Brown (Eds), *Routledge international handbook of rural studies* (pp. 50–61). Routledge.

Schlomann, A., Seifert, A., Zank, S., Woopen, C., & Rietz, C. (2020). Use of information and communication technology (ICT) devices among the oldest-old: Loneliness, anomie, and autonomy. *Innovation in Aging*, *4*(2). https://doi.org/10.1093/geroni/igz050.

Schradie, J. (2011). The digital production gap: The digital divide and Web 2.0 collide. *Poetics*, *39*(2), 145–168. doi:10.1016/j.poetic.2011.02.003.

Schulzke, M. (2013). Rethinking military gaming: America's army and its critics. *Games and Culture*, *8*(2), 59–76. https://doi.org/10.1177/1555412013478686.

Science Service. (2018, July 12). *The future of wearables is implanted*. 2018. Retrieved October 13, 2021, from https://www.dr-hempel-network.com/digital-health-technolgy/implantable-wearables-in-healthcare/.

Scottish Government. (2012). A National Telehealth and Telecare Delivery Plan for Scotland to 2015. The Scottish Government, Edinburgh. Retrieved 15th June from https://www.gov.scot/binaries/content/documents/govscot/publications/advice-and-guidance/2012/12/national-telehealth-telecare-delivery-plan-scotland-2016-driving-improvement-integration-innovation/documents/00411586-pdf/00411586-pdf/govscot%3Adocument/00411586.pdf.

Scottish Government. (2021). Protect Scotland App user statistics: FOI release. Published 8th March 2021. Retrieved 15th June from https://www.gov.scot/publications/foi-202100149430/.

Scottish Government. (2020, May 15). *National clinical and practice guidance for adult care homes in Scotland during the COVID-19 pandemic*. Retrieved August 10, 2021, from https://www.gov.scot/binaries/content/documents/govscot/publications/advice-and-guidance/2020/03/coronavirus-covid-19-clinical-and-practice-guidance-for-adult-care-homes/documents/clinical-guidance-for-nursing-home-and-residential-care-residents/clinical-guidance-for-nursing-home-and-residential-care-residents/govscot%3Adocument/National%2BClinical%2BGuidance%2Bfor%2BCare%2BHomes%2BCOVID-19%2BPandemic-%2BMASTER%2BCOPY%2B-%2BFINAL%2B-%2B15%2BMay%2B2020.pdf.

Segen, J. C. (1992). *Dictionary of modern medicine*. CRC Press.

Seifert, A., & Schlomann, A. (2021). The use of virtual and augmented reality by older adults: Potentials and challenges. *Frontiers in Virtual Reality*, *2*, 639718. https://doi.org/10.3389/frvir.2021.639718.

Shah, S. G. S., Nogueras, D., Woerden, H., & van Kiparoglou, V. (2019). Effectiveness of digital technology interventions to reduce loneliness in adults: A protocol for a systematic review and meta-analysis. *BMJ Open*, *9*, e032455. doi:10.1136/bmjopen-2019-032455.

Shamim, U., Spinelli, G., Woodcock, A., & Nair, A. (2019). Enabling by voice: Voice enabled environmental control (EC) devices using interactive smart agents (ISA). *IEEE 23rd international symposium on consumer technologies (ISCT)*, Ancona (pp. 68–73). doi:10.1109/ISCE.2019.8901028.

Sharp, K., & Earle, S. (2003). Cyberpunters and cyberwhores: Prostitution on the internet. In Y. Jewkes (Ed.), *Dot.cons: Crime, deviance and identity on the internet* (pp. 36–52). Willan.

Shaw, A. (2014). *Gaming at the edge: Sexuality and gender at the margins of gamer culture.* University of Minnesota Press.

Sheerman, L., Marston, H. R., Musselwhite, C., & Morgan, D. (2020). COVID-19 and the secret virtual assistants: The social weapons for a state of emergency (version 1; peer review: 2 approved, 1 no approved). *Emerald Open Research, 2*, 19. https://doi.org/10.35241/emeraldopenres.13571.1.

Sheffield City Council. (2009–2018). Sources for the study of the miners' strike 1984–85. *Sheffield Libraries Archives and Information 2009–2018 (version 1.7)*. Retrieved August 30, 2020, from https://www.sheffield.gov.uk/content/dam/sheffield/docs/libraries-and-archives/archives-and-local-studies/research/Miners%27%20Strike%20Study%20Guide%20v1-7.pdf.

Shiels, M. (2003, April 21). A chat with the man behind mobiles. *BBC News*. Retrieved September 28, 2021, from http://news.bbc.co.uk/1/hi/uk/2963619.stm.

Shin, D.-H., & Park, Y. J. (2017). Understanding the internet of things ecosystem: Multi-level analysis of users, society, and ecology. *Digital Policy, Regulation and Governance, 19*, 77–100.

Shore, L. (2019). *Development of a design tool to optimise acceptance of exoskeletons by older adults.* University of Limerick.

Shore, L., De Eyto, A., & O'Sullivan, L. (2018b). Investigating perceptions related to technology acceptance & stigma of wearable robotic assistive devices by older adults – Preliminary findings. *Design research society conference 2018*, Limerick.

Shore, L., de Eyto, A., O'Sullivan, L. (2020, September 29). Technology acceptance and perceptions of robotic assistive devices by older adults – Implications for exoskeleton design. *Disability Rehabilitation: Assistive Technology* (pp. 1–9). doi:10.1080/17483107.2020.1817988.

Shore, L., Kiernan, L., DeEyto, A., Nic, A., Bhaird, D., White, P., Fahey, T., & Moane, S. (2018). Older adult insights for age friendly environments, products and service Systems. *Design and Technology Education: An International Journal, 23*(2), 40–58. Retrieved October 10, 2020, from https://ojs.lboro.ac.uk/DATE/article/view/2327.

Shore, L., Power, V., Hartigan, B., Schülein, S., Graf, E., de Eyto, A., O'Sullivan, L. (2019). Exoscore: A Design Tool to Evaluate Factors Associated with Technology Acceptance of Soft Lower Limb Exosuits by Older Adults. *Human Factors*. doi:10.1177/0018720819868122.

Shu, S., & Woo, B. K. (2021). Use of technology and social media in dementia care: Current and future directions. *World Journal of Psychiatry, 11*(4), 109–123. https://doi.org/10.5498/wjp.v11.i4.109.

Silva, P. A., Holden, K., & Jordan, P. (2015). Towards a list of heuristics to evaluate smartphone apps targeted at older adults: A study with apps that aim at promoting health and well-being. *Proceedings of Hawaii International Conference on System Sciences, 48*, 3237–3246.

Simons, D. J., Boot, W. R., Charness, N., Gathercole, S. E., Chabris, C. F., Hambrick, D. Z., & Stine-Morrow, E. A. L. (2016). Do "brain-training" programs work? *Psychological Science in the Public Interest, 17*(3), 103–186. https://doi.org/10.1177/1529100616661983.

Singh, N. A., Stavrinos, T. M., Scarbek, Y., Galambos, G., Liber, C., & Fiatarone Singh, M. A. (2005). A randomized controlled trial of high versus low intensity weight training versus general practitioner care for clinical depression in older adults. *The Journals of Gerontology Series A: Biological Sciences and Medical Sciences, 60*(6), 768–776. https://doi.org/10.1093/gerona/60.6.768.

Sixsmith, A. (1990). The meaning and experience of home in later life. In B. Bytheway & J. Johnson (Eds), *Welfare and the ageing experience*. Avebury.

Sixsmith, A. (2006). New technologies to support independent living and quality of life for people with dementia. *Alzheimer's Care Quarterly, 7*(3), 194–202.

Sixsmith, A., & Gutman, G. (2013). *Technologies for active ageing.* Springer. https://doi. org/10.1007/978-1-4419-8348-0. ISBN: 978-1-4419-8347-3.

Sixsmith, A., & Sixsmith, J. (1991). Transitions in home experience in later life. *Journal of Architectural and Planning Research, 8,* 181–191.

Sixsmith, A., & Sixsmith, J. (2008). Ageing in place in the United Kingdom. *Ageing International, 32,* 219–235. https://doi.org/10.1007/s12126-008-9019-y.

Sixsmith, R., Orpwood, R., & Torrington, J. (2007). Quality of life technologies for people with dementia. *Topics in Geriatric Rehabilitation, 23*(1), 85–93.

Smarr, C.-A., Mitzner, T. L., Beer, J. M., Prakash, A., Chen, T. L., Kemp, C. C., & Rogers, W. A. (2014). Domestic robots for older adults: Attitudes, preferences, and potential *International Journal of Social Robotics, 6*(2), 229–247. https://doi.org/10.1007/s12369-013-0220-0.

Smarter. (n.d.). Retrieved June 15, 2021, from https://smarter.am.

Smith, A. (2015). U.S. *Smartphone Use in 2015;* Pew Research Center: Washington, DC, USA, 2015. Retrieved 15th June 2022 from https://www.pewinternet.org/2015/04/01/us-smartphone-use-in-2015/.

Smith, R. O., Scherer, M. J., Cooper, R., Bell, D., Hobbs, D. A., Pettersson, C., Seymour, N., Borg, J., Johnson, M. J., Lane, J. P, Sujatha, S., Rao, P., Obiedat, Q. M., MacLachlan, M., & Bauer, S. (2018). Assistive technology products: A position paper from the first global research, innovation, and education on assistive technology (GREAT) summit. *Disability and Rehabilitation: Assistive Technology, 13*(5), 473–485. doi:10.1080/17483107.2018.1473895.

Socio-gerontechnology Network. (2021). Retrieved December 29, 2021, from https://www.socio-gerontechnology.net/.

Song, W., Woon, F. L., Doong, A., Persad, C., Tijerina, L., Pandit, P., Cline, C., & Giordani, B. (2017). Fatigue in younger and older drivers: Effectiveness of an alertness-maintaining task. *Human Factors, 59*(6), 995–1008. doi:10.1177/0018720817706811.

Sorkin, D. H., Janio, E. A., Eikey, E. V., Schneider, M., Davis, K., Schueller, S. M., Stadnick, N.A., Zheng, K., Neary, M., Safani, D., & Mukamel, D.B. (2021). Rise in use of digital mental health tools and technologies in the United States during the COVID-19 pandemic: Survey study. *Journal of Medical Internet Research, 23*(4), e26994. doi:10.2196/26994.

Spence, J. (1998). Women, wives and the campaign against pit closures in county Durham: Understanding the Vane Tempest Vigil. *Feminist Review, 60,* 33–60. http://www.jstor.org/stable/1395546.

Spiller, K., Ball, K., Bandara, A., Meadows, M., Mccormick, C., Nuseibeh, B., & Price, B. A. (2017). Data privacy: Users' thoughts on quantified self personal data. In B. Ajana (Ed.), *Self-tracking: Empirical and philosophical investigations* (pp. 111–124). Palgrave Macmillan. https://doi.org/10.1007/978-3-319-65379-2_8.

SSAFA. (2014–2019). *The map of need project. SSAFA: Main findings (2014–2019).* Retrieved October 20, 2021, https://covenantfund.org.uk/wp-content/uploads/2020/12/Open_Access_SSAFA.pdf.

Starkhammar, S., & Nygård, L. (2008). Using a timer device for the stove: Experiences of older adults with memory impairment or dementia and their families. *Technology and Disability, 20*(3), 179–191.

Statista. (2021, July 21). *Cumulative download of the NHS COVID-19 app in England and Wales as of July 2021.* Retrieved August 23, 2021, from https://www.statista.com/statistics/1190062/covid-19-app-downloads-uk/.

Steen, M. G. D. l. (2008). *The fragility of human-centred design.* IOS Press.

Stowe, S., Hopes, J., & Mulley, G. (2010). Gerotechnology series: 2. Walking aids. *European Geriatric Medicine, 1*(2), 122–127.

Strauss, W., & Howe, N. (1991). *Generations: The history of America's future,* 1584 to 2069. William Morrow.

Stuart, K., & Webber, J. E. (2015, October 26). GoldenEye on N64: Miyamoto wanted to tone down the killing. *The Guardian.* Retrieved August 31, 2020, from https://www. theguardian.com/technology/2015/oct/26/goldeneye-james-bond-n64-nintendo-shigeru-miyamoto-gamecity.

Sung, D. (2011, March 3). Augmented reality in 2011, is it still a long ways off? *Pocketlint.* Retrieved October 27, 2020, from https://www.pocket-lint.com/ar-vr/ news/108949-augmented-reality-interview-steve-feiner.

Tang, A. K. Y. (2019). A systematic literature review and analysis on mobile apps in m-commerce: Implications for future research. *Electronic Commerce Research and Applications, 37,* 100885. https://doi.org/10.1016/j.elerap.2019.100885.

Taylor, T. L. (2003). Multiple pleasures: Women and online gaming. *Convergence, 9*(1), 21–24.

Technopolis (2016). Landscape Review of Interdisciplinary Research in the UK. Report to HEFCE and RCUK by Technopolis and the Science Policy Research Unit (SPRU), University of Sussex. Retrieved 15th June 2022 from https://webarchive.national-archives.gov.uk/20170712122426/http://www.hefce.ac.uk/pubs/rereports/year/2016/ interdis/.

The Map of Need. (2019a). *Evidence based findings about the veteran population in England's North East.* Retrieved October 20, 2021, from https://covenantfund.org.uk/wp-content/uploads/2020/09/Regional_Report_2019_North-East.pdf.

The Map of Need. (2019b). *Evidence based findings about the veteran population in England's Yorkshire and the Humber.* Retrieved October 20, 2021, from https://covenantfund. org.uk/wp-content/uploads/2020/09/Regional_Report_2019_Yorkshire-and-the-Humber.pdf.

The Map of Need. (n.d.). Retrieved October 20, 2021, from https://covenantfund.org.uk/ the-map-of-need/.

The Medical Futurist. (2021, March 21). *What is digital tattoo?* Retrieved October 13, 2021, from https://medicalfuturist.com/wiki/digital-tattoo/.

Topo, P. (2009). Technology studies to meet the needs of people with dementia and their caregivers: A literature review. *Journal of Applied Gerontology, 28*(1), 5–37. doi:10.1177/0733464808324019.

Topo, P., Saarikalle, K., Begley, E., Cahill, S., Holthe, T., & Macijauskiene, J. (2007). I don't know about the past or the future, but today it's Friday – Evaluation of a time aid for people with dementia. *Technology and Disability, 19,* 121–131. doi:10.3233/ TAD-2007-192-309.

Travis, D., & Hodgson, P. (2019). *Think like a UX researcher: How to observe users, influence design, and drive strategy.* ProQuest.

Turkle, S. (1997). *Life on the screen: Identity in the age of the Internet* (1st Touchstone ed.). Simon & Schuster.

Uenuma, F. (2019, December 30). 20 Years later, the Y2K Bug Seems like a joke – Because those behind the scenes took it seriously. *Time Magazine.* Retrieved August 13, 2021, from https://time.com/5752129/y2k-bug-history/.

UK Government. (1980). *Social Security Act 1980. Amendments of Supplementary Benefits Act 1976.* Retrieved August 30, 2020, from https://www.legislation.gov.uk/ ukpga/1980/30/section/6/enacted.

UK Government. (1998, April 10). *The Belfast Agreement.* Northern Ireland Office. Retrieved August 16, 2021, from https://www.gov.uk/government/publications/the-belfast-agreement.

UK Government. (2020, October). *Research and development work relating to assistive technology 2018 to 2019.* Department of Health and Social Care. Retrieved June 23, 2022, from https://www.gov.uk/government/publications/research-and-development-work-relating-to-assistive-technology-2018-to-2019.

UK Government. (2020, November 29). *Guidance for the Christmas period.* UK Government. Retrieved February 19, 2021, from https://www.gov.uk/guidance/guidance-for-the-christmas-period.

UKRI. (n.d.a). *Interdisciplinary research.* Retrieved August 3, 2021, from https://re.ukri.org/research/interdisciplinary-research/.

UKRI. (n.d.b). *Overview.* Retrieved August 3, 2021, from https://www.ukri.org/.

United Nations. (2019). *Growing at a slower pace, world population is expected to reach 9.7 Billion in 2050 and could peak at nearly 11 Billion around 2100.* Retrieved October 23, 2021, from https://www.un.org/development/desa/en/news/population/world-population-prospects-2019.html.

University of Berkley. (n.d.). *The transition from graduated student to assistant professor.* Career Center. Retrieved August 3, 2021, from https://career.berkeley.edu/PhDs/PhDtransition.

UPI.com (1998). Wall goes up in Berlin. Events of 1961 – Year in review. Retrieved August 13, 2021, from https://www.upi.com/Archives/Audio/Events-of-1961/Wall-Goes-Up-in-Berlin.

van Bronswijk, E. M. H., Bouma, H., & Fozard, J. L. (2002). Technology for quality of life: An enriched taxonomy. Editorial. *Gerontechnology, 2*(2).

van Dijk, J. (2020). *The digital divide.* Polity.

van Hoof, J., & Kazak, J. K. (2018). Urban ageing. *Indoor and Built Environment, 27,* 583–586. doi:10.1177/1420326X18768160.

van Hoof, J., Kazak, J. K., Perek-Białas, J. M., & Peek, S. T. M. (2018). The challenges of urban ageing: Making cities age-friendly in Europe. *International Journal of Environmental Research and Public Health, 15,* 2473. doi:10.3390/ijerph15112473.

van Hoof, J., Marston, H. R., Kazak, J. K., & Buffel, T. (2021). Ten questions concerning age-friendly cities and communities and the built environment. *Building and Environment, 199*(15), 107922. doi:10.1016/j.buildenv.2021.107922.

van Schaik, P., Blake, J., Pernet, F., Spears, I., & Fencott C. (2008). Virtual augmented exercise gaming for older adults. *Cyberpsychology & Behavior, 11*(1), 103–106. doi:10.1089/cpb.2007.9925.

van Schaik, P., Fencott, C., & Ling, J. (2005). The effects of direction and movement of attractors on users' behavior in virtual environments. *Cyberpsychology & Behavior, 8*(5), 416–422. https://doi.org/10.1089/cpb.2005.8.416.

van Schaik, P., Turnbull, T., van Wersch, A., & Drummond, S. (2004). Presence within a mixed reality environment. *Cyberpsychology & Behavior, 7*(5), 540–552. https://doi.org/10.1089/cpb.2004.7.540.

Vanden Abeele, V., & de Schutter, B. (2010). Designing intergenerational play via enactive interaction, competition and acceleration. *Pers Ubiquit Comput, 14,* 425–433. https://doi.org/10.1007/s00779-009-0262-3.

Vaziri, D. D., Aal, K., Ogonowski, C., von Rekowski, T., Kroll, M., Marston, H.R., [...] & Wulf, V. (2016). Exploring user experience and technology acceptance for a fall prevention system: results from a randomized clinical trial and a living lab. *Eur Rev Aging Phys Act, 13*(6). https://doi.org/10.1186/s11556-016-0165-z.

Vega, K., Jiang, N., Liu, X., Kan, V., Barry, N., Maes, P., Yetisen, A., & Paradiso, J. (2017). The dermal abyss: Interfacing with the skin by tattooing biosensors. *Proceedings of the 2017 ACM international symposium on wearable computers,* September (pp. 138–145). https://doi.org/10.1145/3123021.3123039.

Vincent, M. (2020, April 4). Thirteen people die in just seven days in just one coronavirus-hit care home. *The Daily Mail.* Retrieved August 10, 2021, from https://www.dailymail.co.uk/news/article-8187463/Thirteen-people-die-just-seven-days-coronavirus-sweeps-care-home.html.

Vogels, E. A. (2019). *Millennials Stand out for their technology use, but older generations also embrace digital life.* Pew Research Center. Washington, DC, USA, 2018. Retrieved March 15, 2021, from https://www.pewresearch.org/fact-tank/2019/09/09/us-generations-technology-use/.

Voida, A., & Greenberg S. (2010). *A gameroom of our own: Exploring the domestic gaming environment.* Alberta. Retrieved March 3, 2021, from https://prism.ucalgary.ca/handle/1880/47934.

Voida, A., & Greenberg, S. (2009). Wii all play: The console game as a computational meeting place. In *Proceedings of the 27th international conference on human factors in computing systems* (pp. 1559–1568). https://doi.org/10.1145/1518701.1518940.

Voida, A., & Greenberg, S. (2012). Console gaming across generations: Exploring intergenerational interactions in collocated console gaming. *Universal Access in the Information Society, 11*(1), 45–56. https://doi.org/10.1007/s10209-011-0232-1.

Wagner, D., & Schmalstieg, D. (2006). Handheld augmented reality displays. In *Proceedings of the IEEE conference on virtual reality.* IEEE Computer Society (p. 321). https://doi.org/10.1109/VR.2006.67.

Wakefield Council. (2021, January). *Wakefield State of the District.*

Wakefield District Housing. (2021). *Digital inclusion.* Retrieved August 28, 2021, from https://www.wdh.co.uk/AboutUs/OurCommitmentTo/DigitalInclusion/.

Wang, C.-H., & Wu, C.-L. (2021). Bridging the digital divide: The smart TV as a platform for digital literacy among the elderly. *Behaviour & Information Technology,* 1–14. https://doi.org/10.1080/0144929X.2021.1934732.

Ward, M. (2006, August 3). How the web went world wide. *BBC News.* Retrieved August 31, 2020, from http://news.bbc.co.uk/1/hi/sci/tech/5242252.stm.

Weisman, S. (1983). Computer games for the frail elderly. *The Gerontologist, 23*(4), 361–363. https://doi.org/10.1093/geront/23.4.361.

Welsh Government. (2021, March). *From inclusion to resilience: An agenda for digital inclusion.* Retrieved August 24, 2021, from https://www.digitalcommunities.gov.wales/from-inclusion-to-resilience-an-agenda-for-digital-inclusion/.

Westin, T., Hamilton, I., & Ellis, B. (2020). *Game accessibility.* Routledge.

White, P. J., Marston, H. R., Shore, L., & Turner R. (2020). Learning from COVID-19: Design, age-friendly technology, hacking and mental models [version 1; peer review: 1 approved]. *Emerald Open Research, 2,* 21. https://doi.org/10.35241/emeraldopenres.13599.1.

Whitlock, L.A., McLaughlin, A.C., & Allaire, J.C. (2011). Video Game Design for Older Adults. *Proceedings of the Human Factors and Ergonomics Society Annual Meeting, 55,* 187–191.

Whitlock, L. A., McLaughlin, A. C., Leidheiser, W., Gandy, M., & Allaire, J. C. (2014). Know before you go: Feelings of flow for older players depends on game and player characteristics. *Proceedings of the first ACM SIGCHI annual symposium on computer–human interaction in play,* October (pp. 277–286). https://doi.org/10.1145/2658537.2658703.

Wilson, G., Gates, J. R., Vijaykumar, S., & Morgan, D. J. (2021). Understanding older adults' use of social technology and the factors influencing use. *Ageing & Society,* 1–24. doi:10.1017/S0144686X21000490.

Wilson, G., McGill, G., Osborne, A., & Kiernan, M. D. (2020). Housing needs of ageing veterans who have experienced limb loss. *International Journal of Environmental Research and Public Health, 17*(5), 1791. https://doi.org/10.3390/ijerph17051791.

Winn, J., & Heeter, C. (2009). Gaming, gender, and time: Who makes time to play. *Sex Roles, 61*(1), 1–13.

Wohlrab, S., Stahl, J., & Kappeler, P. M. (2007). Modifying the body: Motivations for getting tattooed and pierced. *Body Image, 4*(1), 87–95. https://doi.org/10.1016/j.bodyim.2006.12.001.

Women's Institute (WI). (n.d.a). https://www.thewi.org.uk/.

Women's Institute. (n.d.b). *About us*. Retrieved August 27, 2021, from https://www.thewi.org.uk/about-us.

Wong, L. (2016, November 22). REZ retrospective: A look back at Tetsuya Mizuguchi's early days. *Polygon*. Retrieved December 13, 2021, from https://www.polygon.com/2016/11/22/13700394/rez-retrospective-tetsuya-mizuguchi-iam8bit-book-rez-infinite.

Wood, P. (2010, July 16). Transforming Wakefield's digital landscape. *Housing Technology*. Retrieved August 28, 2021, from https://www.housing-technology.com/transforming-wakefields-digital-landscape/.

Woodward, K. (2014). Ageing without children: why is no one talking about it? The Guardian, 25th April, 2014. Retrieved 15th June 2022 from https://www.theguardian.com/social-care-network/social-life-blog/2014/apr/25/ageing-without-children-family-care.

World Health Organization. (2007). *Global age-friendly cities: A guide*. World Health Organization.

World Health Organization. (2011). *World report on disability*. World Health Organization.

World Health Organization (WHO). (2018). The Global Network for Age-Friendly Cities and Communities: Looking Back over the Last Decade, Looking Forward to the Next. World Health Organization, Geneva, Switzerland.

World Health Organization. (2020–2030). *Decade of healthy ageing*. Retrieved March 3, 2022, from https://www.who.int/initiatives/decade-of-healthy-ageing.

World Health Organization (WHO). (2021). Decade of healthy ageing: baseline report. Retrieved 15th June 2022 from https://www.who.int/publications/i/item/9789240017900.

Wu, Y.-h., Damnée, S., Kerhervé, H., Ware, C., & Rigaud, A.-S. (2015). Bridging the digital divide in older adults: A study from an initiative to inform older adults about new technologies. *Clinical Interventions in Aging*, *10*, 193. doi:10.2147/CIA.S72399.

Wu, Y.-h., Wrobel, J., Cornuet, M., Kerhervé, H., Damnée, S., & Rigaud, A.-S. (2014). Acceptance of an assistive robot in older adults: A mixed-method study of human–robot interaction over a 1-month period in the Living Lab setting. *Clinical Interventions in Aging*, *9*(10), 193–200. doi:10.2147/CIA.S72399.

Yablonski, J. (2020). *The laws of UX*. O'Reilly Media.

Yang, H., & Lee, H. (2019). Understanding user behavior of virtual personal assistant devices. *Information Systems E-Business Management*, *17*, 65–87. https://doi.org/10.1007/s10257-018-0375-1.

YEGO. (2021). Retrieved December 29, 2021, from https://www.rideyego.com/.

Zain, S. (2018, August 6). Emojis as news traffic signs. *EZ hire*. Retrieved October 19, 2021, from https://www.ezhire.ae/blogs/2018/08/emojis-new-traffic-signs/.

Zelinski, E. M., & Reyes, R. (2009). Cognitive benefits of computer games for older adults. *Gerontechnology*, *8*(4), 220–235. https://doi.org/10.4017/gt.2009.08.04.004.00

Index